THE
ASTROLOGER

THE
ASTROLOGER

HOW BRITISH
INTELLIGENCE
PLOTTED TO READ
HITLER'S MIND

JAMES PARRIS

The
History
Press

First published 2021

The History Press
97 St George's Place, Cheltenham,
Gloucestershire, GL50 3QB
www.thehistorypress.co.uk

British Library Cataloguing in Publication Data.
A catalogue record for this book is available from the British Library.

ISBN 978 0 7509 9418 7

Typesetting and origination by The History Press
Printed and bound in Great Britain by TJ Books Limited, Padstow, Cornwall.

Trees for Life

For Isabel, who had her doubts

CONTENTS

PROLOGUE

'There's some ill planet reigns:
I must be patient till the heavens look
With an aspect more favourable.'[1]

Baron Harald Keun von Hoogerwoerd, astrologer, to Louis de Wohl, 1930:

Everybody has felt that at some period of his life he was lucky or unlucky. Well, *we* know *when* we are going to be lucky and when unlucky … One is, as it were, in the position of a general who has at his call an excellent secret service. He will be informed in time about the movement of the enemy – and of every movement of the allies too.[2]

Louis de Wohl, *Secret Service of the Sky*, 1938:

I have come to the firm conclusion that a knowledge of astrology is one of the most valuable assets of human life. The use of this knowledge is as ideal as it is practical and I have the feeling of a man who discovered a Bonanza of incalculable value and calls to his friends: 'Come here! Here is Gold! Enough Gold for us all!'[3]

Memorandum, 'Advice tendered to Herr Hitler', 30 September 1940, Rear Admiral John Godfrey, Director of Naval Intelligence:

It has been known for some time that Hitler attaches importance to advice tendered to him by astrologers, and that he studies the horoscopes, not only of himself, but of his own generals and of his more influential opponents ... The significance of Hitler's astrological researches is not therefore whether or not we believe in them or if they represent the truth, but that Hitler believes in them, and to a certain extent bases his acts on the opinions and predictions of his astrological experts.[4]

Louis de Wohl, 'The Orchestra of Hitler's Death', January 1941:

His very love of life will increase his fear of death ... By his astrological advisers he is told this: 'Your death will be Neptunian. This means that it will be mysterious and strange, you will disappear, and the people will not for a long time, if ever, actually know how you have died.'[5]

Dick White, Assistant Director MI5 B Division, to MI5 Deputy Director General Jasper Harker, 19 February 1942:

I have never liked Louis de Wohl – he strikes me as a charlatan and an imposter. He at one time exercised some influence upon highly placed British Intelligence officers through his star gazing profession.[6]

MI5 officer Toby Caulfield's observations on Louis de Wohl, 24 September 1942:

Louis de Wohl ... is widely known as an astrologer and, despite the fact that many people regard him as a charlatan, there are still a great many people eager to take his astrological advice. He has great gifts as a psychologist and excellent insight into the Continental mind.[7]

Lieutenant Colonel Gilbert Lennox, Operations, MI5, 14 January 1943:

The only interest of astrological forecasts to Service Departments, or for that matter to anyone else, should be that it may be interesting and informative to know that the advice given in these reports may be the astrological advice that Hitler is receiving from his astrologers. The danger is that all this sort of pseudo-science is most insidious, and unless you have a complete sceptic or a very strong-minded man dealing with it, quite the wrong point of view may be indulged in.[8]

Ellic Howe, typographer and printer working for Political Warfare Executive, on Louis de Wohl, early 1943:

He asked me to repeat my name and how to spell Ellic. Then, without lowering his persistent gaze, he took a pencil in each hand and simultaneously wrote 'Ellic Howe', normally with his right hand and in mirror or reversed writing with his left one. I felt he was trying to hypnotise me and looked away. That broke the tension and we got down to business.[9]

An Aquarius Born

I

All warfare is a bloody mix of nightmare and farce, but Britain's engagement of an astrologer in the fight against Nazi Germany raised the element of farce to a new level. When Louis de Wohl began his wartime involvement with British Intelligence in 1940, he was a practising astrologer in London with a clientele composed of – in an MI5 officer's words – 'the good and the great'. De Wohl had also been a prolific novelist and writer for the screen in pre-Hitler Germany. He had a network of acquaintances and friends among artists, actors, film directors and diplomats in Britain and among refugees from Nazism in the United States. He was at heart an entertainer who saw the distinction between reality and fantasy as fluid rather than rigidly clear cut. Born with the Sun in Aquarius, de Wohl once described the sign's typical native, knowing he would thereby reveal part of himself to his reader:

> He is everything at one and the same time, conventional and eccentric, conservative and onto anything new like a flash. He has a great sense of the romantic. His strongest asset is his imagination, which stops at nothing. He is gay, lovable, good-natured, but nevertheless keeping an eye open for himself … Sometimes his imagination kicks over the

traces and he builds castles in the air … Everything originates in his mind and imagination. He can make plans like no other can.[1]

De Wohl had become an active informant for MI5, the Security Service, in 1938, three years after his arrival in England from Germany, feeding scraps to his handler about the questions his astrological clients were asking, what concerned them, the advice he was giving. Why, how and who made the initial contact has never been revealed and de Wohl avoids mentioning in books dealing with his life to the role he played informing on others.[2] What evidence there is emerges patchily from the surviving personal file MI5 kept on him.

For a few of his intelligence contacts there were elements of de Wohl's complex character that never quite rang true, the worrying impression he was playing some private and mysterious game, perhaps even a treacherous one. 'Did Louis de Wohl believe in astrology?' a fellow practitioner in the strange concoction of science, art and intuition once asked himself. 'I began to doubt it: he could talk of his practice in the same superficial and often brilliant manner as of any other matter, be it women, card games, a new fashion or the shortage of cigars.'[3] And yet for a time British Military and Naval Intelligence were willing to listen to what he had to say.

Ludwig von Wohl left Nazi Germany in 1935, two years after Hitler took power in Berlin as Chancellor. He became Louis de Wohl on his arrival in London. While not exactly a political refugee or a direct victim of persecution because of his Jewish antecedents, it was a wise decision to leave when he did. In England, at the age of 34, de Wohl had the contacts and self-assurance in 1937 to persuade the respected London publisher George G. Harrap & Co. to take on his autobiography. His narrative talent and facility in dropping names ranging from minor European aristocracy to Hollywood film moguls was undoubtedly an attraction, something for the popular market. In *I Follow My Stars* he presents a confident, carefully constructed and amusing picture of himself as a man with a record of achievement and a story to tell. The de Wohl of the book could easily pass as a character in a 1930s film – one he would script himself – sitting at the bar or a nearby table as Sidney Greenstreet (to whom he bore a resemblance, in bulk at least) and Peter Lorre (another Hungarian who fled Nazi Germany) conspire.

De Wohl claimed he had used astrology to select the luckiest date to publish *I Follow My Stars*, that the first edition sold out in 36 hours, and that in no time at all 1,700 readers wrote asking him to cast their horoscope.[4] A cynical Australian reviewer was unimpressed, identifying a singular ego at work, describing de Wohl as a 'devotee of the first personal pronoun'.[5] Only two chapters of de Wohl's book deal with the stars – 'Astrology Changes my Life' and 'Strange Happenings'. But they are the crucial backbone, essential – though he would hardly have known at the time – to the wartime story to come. These chapters present de Wohl's 'Road to Damascus' conversion. An initial scorn for the belief that the planets exert their influence on human affairs, that the basic features of our lives and characters are mapped out in the sky, is transformed into what he claims is a firmly based conviction.

In Berlin in early 1930, in the wake of the Wall Street Crash, the unsteady Weimar Republic – post-First World War Germany's doomed attempt at democracy – had begun its final collapse as Nazis and Communists wrestled for power in the streets. Despite the crisis, de Wohl was prosperous and successful, a writer in his late twenties with a dozen novels and screenplays behind him. Arriving with his wife at what he anticipated would be a lively and stimulating party thrown by a composer friend, Dengerode, de Wohl was disappointed to discover they had walked into what seemed to be a drawing room class in astrology. The talk of 'malignant Saturn', 'house-cusps', 'trigons' and 'sextiles' first mystified, then irritated him. The tutorial was being conducted by Magnus Jensen, the writer of a widely read primer, *Everybody's Astrology*, first published in 1922. With Germany in chaos, the old certainties gone, many were reaching for astrology and the occult as a comforting prop, a remedy. But de Wohl found himself in sympathy with a psychologist Jensen had criticised for sneering, 'The planets have no more influence over your lives than the creases in your trousers.'[6]

When Jensen told the gathering – in de Wohl's words a dozen or so 'old women of both sexes, soft creamy-dreamy characters' – that the planet Venus was, of course, 'elevated in the sign of the Fishes', de Wohl's wife struggled to stifle her giggles. Taking advantage of a break for refreshments, the couple made their apologies and left the house. As they walked home through the Berlin streets they mocked Jensen's pseudo-scientific jargon and what they both agreed were naïve believers in 'medieval rubbish'. 'If on that evening anyone had told me that I myself would one day study astrology, and seriously too, I should have laughed in his face,' de Wohl wrote later. 'At that time I genuinely put astrology believers on a par with common or garden lunatics.'[7]

Six months later, in November 1930, the experience of one evening transformed de Wohl's entire outlook. True to character, de Wohl is keen in his autobiography to impress readers with the aristocratic provenance of his new faith. He writes that he met an old acquaintance, Henry, Duke of Mecklenburg-Schwerin until 1918, now Prince Consort to Queen Wilhelmina of the Netherlands, at the annual Dutch Ball in the Hotel Esplanade on Potsdamer Platz. The prince introduced de Wohl to Baroness Theresa Keun von Hoogerwoerd, a lady in waiting to Queen Wilhelmina, and the baroness in turn presented de Wohl to her son, Baron Harald, a thick-set man a few years older than de Wohl. 'His profession will interest you as a writer,' she told him. 'He is an astrologer.'[8]

From the outset, de Wohl made it clear to von Hoogerwoerd that he was sceptical about the whole business of astrology, which – describing his recent experience at his friend's house – he regarded as no more than a primitive superstition, a relic of a less enlightened era. The baron agreed the subject did have an unfortunate tendency to attract 'ignoramuses, dilettantes and quacks', probably about as much – he added, to de Wohl's amusement – as the medical profession. When the two men moved to the bar for drinks, the baron surprised de Wohl by saying, 'You are, of course, an Aquarius born. So you will understand quickly.' – 'I am of course a *what*?' – 'An Aquarius born. Is not your birthday between the twentieth of January and the twentieth of February?'[9] De Wohl nodded and said his date of birth, 24 January. The baron produced a small notebook from his pocket, studied it for a few moments, and said the relative position of planets in both their horoscopes promised the two men would enjoy a useful relationship.

Von Hoogerwoerd offered de Wohl an outline character analysis based on what he could glean from his date of birth, but then admitted as he had read three of the writer's novels he did already have in mind a picture of his personality. Perhaps, the baron said, a fairer experiment would be to work from the birth date of a friend, a person he knew nothing about. De Wohl gave that of Dengerode, the composer. Checking the tables in his notebook, the baron delivered what seemed to de Wohl an uncannily accurate description of his friend: his musical talent, his troubled relationships with women, his difficulties with money. Reluctant to be so easily persuaded, de Wohl wondered if he was being tricked by a form of mind-reading and tried setting what he thought would be a harder test. In the ballroom he asked his wife for the date of birth of an old school friend, a person he had never met and knew nothing about. Armed with the information, he returned to the baron. Von Hoogerwoerd studied the date, thought for a moment, took a page from his notebook and wrote a short description of the woman's personality. In the ballroom once more, de Wohl passed the slip of paper to his wife to read. Amazed by the exactness of detail, she said she could hardly have described her friend better herself.

De Wohl's classic conversion story now took the inevitable next step. His initial scepticism began to weaken and he asked von Hoogerwoerd to cast his horoscope, which the baron did, returning a few days later with a chart and an interpretation covering twenty typed pages. It would take very little to draw de Wohl in: two brief but apparently accurate character portraits, followed by a forecast from the baron that de Wohl would shortly suffer pain. This, he said, was signified in de Wohl's horoscope by 'Mars square ascendant' at a particular moment. The movement of the planet Mars would place it 'square' – that is, at 90 degrees – to the astrological sign rising over the horizon at the time of his birth, Cancer. When a day or so later de Wohl cut his cheek shaving with a safety razor not once but twice in succession, drawing blood, he could only be impressed. But doubts remained in his mind. He described in *I Follow My Stars* his conversations with the baron. De Wohl complained that his image of himself was as an entirely self-made man, rising in the world through his own efforts with no help from anyone. 'I should find it unbearable to have to think now that I owe everything I have done, not to my own energy and will-power and my own work,' he told the baron, 'but to some predetermined influence exerted by such and such combination of planets.'[10]

Von Hoogerwoerd's response to de Wohl's objection was that a horoscope was no more than a diagrammatic representation of the position of the planets at the moment of our birth and then of the forces exerted by their movements. 'We are not the puppets of the planets. We are free … We are really free. But we *are* influenced by the tendencies of the planets.' The major part of the course of our life, 60 per cent the baron estimated, depended on our will, our own volition. The baron went on to present arguments de Wohl himself would deploy a few years later to first impress and then to convince British Intelligence that he, armed with astrology, would have a positive role to play in waging war against Nazi Germany:

> Everybody has felt that at some period of his life he was lucky or unlucky. Well, *we* know *when* we are going to be lucky and when unlucky … One is, as it were, in the position of a general who has at his call an excellent secret service. He will be informed in time about the movement of the enemy – and of every movement of the allies too.[11]

The conversation continued, de Wohl raising questions about religion, war, twins, death, the baron answering them at length – obviously having encountered each of them before from other sceptics. The die was cast, de Wohl had been won over. The pieces were being shifted into position for one of the most bizarre episodes in British military history – the employment of an astrologer as a weapon in the armoury of the intelligence services.

How long, de Wohl asked the baron, would it take to learn astrology? To acquire the basic principles, the rudiments, no more than six months. To become a master, a lifetime. 'The study of this science was a permanent succession of revelations,' de Wohl recalled. 'I learned to see into the minds and hearts of people, to understand why they thought and acted as they did.'[12] But a few years later, in 1938, he echoed von Hoogerwoerd when he warned, 'The number of charlatans and rogues, who during the last 150 years have used astrology as a cloak for their swindles, is legion, the number of true, serious astrologers is very, very small.'[13] Was the astrologer playing with his readers, not for the last time, revealing something others would come to suspect for themselves?

2

The one detailed description of de Wohl's early life, the background to the man he became, comes in *I Follow My Stars*, which was published in 1937. By then an accomplished novelist and screenwriter, de Wohl's skill lay in constructing a story, marshalling, manipulating and controlling facts and images for dramatic effect. To that extent, the work could never be taken as actual self-portrait, nor would de Wohl the entertainer have intended it to be. He was working to create a theatrical effect, a memorable performance, rather than attempting to recreate the past accurately. That will always be the question, whether it is the reader asking or British Intelligence: Can he be trusted? Is this man toying with me? A friend, Felix Jay, who first became acquainted with de Wohl in London around the time the book appeared, had no doubt about de Wohl's unreliability. 'I have never been convinced that the autobiographical hints in his writings are entirely trustworthy,' Jay wrote. 'He loved to give the impression of having been in many strange places and at many times.'[14]

In 1945 Lieutenant Colonel Gilbert Lennox, an MI5 officer who had been involved with de Wohl in various ways since the late 1930s, set out his understanding of de Wohl's background in a two-page closely typed minute attached to the astrologer's personal file. 'It clears up one or two points about which we were hitherto somewhat doubtful,' Lennox wrote. 'The information was supplied by himself, but I have no reason to doubt that it is substantially correct.'[15] Lennox sketched what he had pieced together about de Wohl's family circumstances:

De Wohl states that his father was born in Hungary in the area which in 1919 became part of Czechoslovakia. He describes his father as coming from the middle class (probably lower middle class) ... As a young man he joined the Hungarian cavalry and later obtained a commission. On leaving the Army, he studied for Law and became a lawyer … He was also for a time a journalist and a keen politician, but what his brand of politics were de Wohl professes not to know. Later still he became interested in mining propositions and moved to Berlin about the beginning of this century … De Wohl says he was also connected with the Hungarian ambassador, and owing to the work he did for this ambassador, he received some decoration from the Austro-Hungarian government which included the title of Mucsinyi. De Wohl senior married a German woman in Munich (de Wohl himself describes her as half German half Austrian). De Wohl senior died in about May 1914, 3 months before the outbreak of the First World War.

Lennox went on to describe how the family had been comfortably off when de Wohl's father died but, like many, lost much of their money in the war and the inflation that followed in the early 1920s: 'After the father's death the family left the house they had in Berlin and went to live in Bavaria for six months. It then returned to Berlin, where it occupied a flat.'

De Wohl was born in Berlin on 24 January 1903, the 10lb he weighed at birth anticipating his ample grown-up figure. Sefton Delmer, head of the German Section of the Political Warfare Executive during the Second World War, would describe him as a 'vast, spectacled jellyfish'. Another colleague would call him – equally unflatteringly – a 'tall, flabby elephant of a man'.[16] The family was Roman Catholic and both his father and mother had Jewish antecedents. He was to have three names in the course of his life. The first, his Hungarian identity, was Lajos Theodor Gaspar Adolf Wohl. Growing up and educated in Germany, he spoke no Hungarian and – inheriting his father's status as a minor noble – he was known as Ludwig von Wohl. When he left Germany and settled in England in 1935, he became Louis de Wohl, the name by which he was known until his death.

De Wohl's formal education began at the age of 6 and he claimed to have been a precocious reader. In his father's study he found a stock of paperbacks with bright jackets, which he worked his way through enthusiastically: 'They became my friends, and I owe them a lot – my own love of excitement and suspense, my longing for adventure and travel.'[17] He moved on from these to the works of a best-selling author in pre-First World War Germany, Karl May; adventures set in the Orient, the Middle East, Latin America and the Wild West. 'My concern with this building up of my own private world took my attention off what was happening around me.'[18] The young de Wohl shared this taste for May's books with Adolf Hitler, who was still reading them when he ruled Germany as Führer, recommending them to his generals.[19] 'My family might tell me repeatedly, as indeed they did,' de Wohl wrote, 'that he was a liar who had never done one thousandth of the things he claimed, who had, in fact, never left Germany in his life.'

The boy ignored them, determined he would one day emulate May's adventures, or perhaps follow his example by writing as if the exploits he conjured up about his own life were true. Not just a reader, but a writer too. In his late 50s de Wohl would boast: 'I started writing at the age of seven or just a little older, and what really set me off was that some of the stories did not go the way I wanted. I simply decided to change them, and change them I did.'[20] He subsequently showed a tendency to take the same liberties with facts a number of times. He claimed to have written a play at the age of 8, 'Jesus of Nazareth', composing the incidental music, designing the scenery and taking the parts of both Mary Magdalene and the High Priest Caiaphas. A boy living in his mind, a world of imagination, fantasy and make-believe.

A dreamer and a fantasist, perhaps. But status and rank, and acknowledgement by others seemed essential to the adult de Wohl, who was insecure since the evaporation of the family's wealth following his father's death. It was his mother that de Wohl boasted about, rather than the father who had clambered from small town obscurity to minor nobility. His mother, de Wohl wrote, had been noble from birth, an hereditary Baroness of Dreifus. The Emperor Franz-Joseph of Austria-Hungary had been a regular shooting guest at her father's Grueneck estate in the Alps, accompanied by the Empress Elisabeth. Baron Dreifus, a banker, first worked with the Rothschilds and then rose by marrying into the family. Other connections de Wohl claimed on his mother's side were the poet Heinrich Heine, one-time Lord Mayor of London Sir Harry Worms, and the composer and conductor Sir Julius Benedict, little known today but a significant musical figure in mid-Victorian England. One of his wife's aunts – married to an Italian baron and naval officer – had been the first European woman granted an audience with the last Empress of China, Tzu-hsi, before her death in 1908. 'Look where I'm from,' de Wohl was surely saying. 'You must recognise how eminent my background makes me.'

His father's death following a heart attack in 1914, when de Wohl was 11, marked the beginning of a decline in the family's prosperity. 'I loved and admired him tremendously,' de Wohl would write, 'but I think he was disappointed in me: I was too soft, too much of a bookworm.' When de Wohl heard his father say one day he would have been better born as a girl, the boy agreed. 'I came to the conclusion that it would actually be rather nice to have been a girl: they had much prettier clothes … they were treated politely, and no one forced them to learn riding or gymnastics.'[21] Along with this regret there is the traditional passage-to-adulthood story: bullied at school, learning to box and stand up for himself, beating the bullies into fear and then friendship. De Wohl's education continued for a further six years – first in Bavaria, then back in Berlin – through war, defeat, revolution and counter-revolution, latterly on the fringe of vicious and bloody street fighting between rebels and the forces of the state. Lack of money made a university education impossible and in 1920 he went reluctantly to an apprenticeship in finance secured through a family friend, Herbert Gutmann, principal director of the Dresdner Bank.[22]

De Wohl was placed with the Deutsch-Südamerikanische Bank, a subsidiary of the Dresdner. Bored with the plodding routine and – as de Wohl confessed – scarcely competent at what little was expected of him, he survived only a couple of years before his employers dismissed him. He had idled away much of the time at his desk doodling and writing short stories and sketches, becoming unpopular with his colleagues for exposing 'their own system of stretching the minimum of work to the maximum proportion, like a rubber band'.[23] An old school friend, Peter Secklmann, now came to his aid, persuading his own employer – the owner of a dressmaking business – to hire de Wohl as an illustrator in the firm's advertising department. But de Wohl's over-enthusiasm for one of the company models, the daughter of a dispossessed Russian count, led to another sacking when the two were discovered having fun in the factory dressing room.

De Wohl's mother turned once more to the Dresdner director, Gutmann. Showing no hard feelings about his protégé's lack of success or interest in work at the bank, Gutmann introduced the young man to Erich Pommer, the managing director of Ufa Films, the company at the heart of German cinema and in which Gutmann also had a financial interest. De Wohl took up a post in Ufa's publicity department at 300 marks a month – three times what he had been paid at the bank – organising poster displays, composing advertisements and liaising with the press over releases. Enthusiastic about cinema since boyhood, de Wohl felt at first he had arrived at his destination, enjoying the casual and relaxed atmosphere of the entertainment business and the wide range of contacts he was making. But, soon feeling under-occupied and bored, he passed afternoons in his office writing stories, eventually beginning a novel about a prize-fighter. An attack of diphtheria, which kept de Wohl in bed for three weeks, gave him time to complete the book.

The novel was an immediate success and Berlin's main evening paper bought the serial rights for 2,000 marks. As his writing proved increasingly popular, the rights to a second sold for 5,000 marks and the third for 7,000. Seeing he had a winner on his hands, de Wohl's publisher offered a contract for more books, guaranteeing the writer 25,000 marks a year. Close to financial security at last – one pleasure of which was opening a current account at the Deutsch-Südamerikanische, whose bosses had first bored him, then sacked him – de Wohl married. His bride was Alexandra Betzold, nine years older and – de Wohl boasted in his autobiography – the daughter of Princess Iphigenie Soutzo, descendant of Romanian monarchs. He skirted around her background, but his MI5 handler Lennox subsequently persuaded de Wohl to reveal the actual story of his wife's history. 'He states his wife was nominally the daughter of a German Jewish businessman who was married to a "Roumanian princess",' Lennox recorded. 'In fact, de Wohl states, his wife is really illegitimate, being the fruit of a liaison between the "princess" and an Aryan German.'[24] Whatever her family's exact placing in the social hierarchy, the Romanian ambassador in Berlin was a guest at the wedding, beginning a connection with the country's diplomatic corps that would later have an important impact on de Wohl's life.

After a carefree and expensive seven-week Mediterranean honeymoon, including Italy, Malta and North Africa, de Wohl's life took on a pattern it would follow until he fled Germany in the 1930s – intense writing, interrupted by periods of overseas travel. In this he said he was encouraged by his wife, whom he nicknamed Putti, who saw changes of scene and experience as essential nourishment for his creative imagination. De Wohl's depictions of his adventures in *I Follow My Stars* echo those of his childhood literary hero Karl May and, as with May, he leaves the impression that a good story is a more important consideration than the literal truth. De Wohl wrote prolifically, moving easily in the late 1920s and early '30s between novels and scripts for films, sometimes adapting his own or other writers' works, at others producing original screenplays. In 1928 alone he published three novels, three more the following year, as many as twenty before he left Germany in 1935. Not classical literature, as de Wohl admitted, but readable and popular, snapped up by newspapers for serialisation. Parallel with these were adaptations for films, including four in 1928: *My Friend Harry*, *The Criminal of the Century*, *The President*, and *A Girl with Temperament*. His own original screenplays included *Crooks in Tails* and *The Eighteen Year Old* in 1927, *The Last Company* and *Love's Carnival* in 1930, *The Oil Sharks* and *Invisible Opponent* in 1933.

A typical post-marriage journey was to Egypt, accompanied by his old schoolmate and lifelong friend Peter Secklmann, carrying minimal luggage, sailing third class on a Japanese ship from Naples, taking the train from Port Said to Cairo. De Wohl's description of the city is vivid but mechanical, resembling material cobbled together from travel brochures and guide books in the spirit of the revered Karl May:

Five minutes distant from an avenue which can almost compete with the Champs Élysées there are narrow little streets overflowing with natives in multicoloured robes, donkeys, camels, and mules. Even the shops themselves are overflowing with all kinds of vegetables, fruits, carpets, brassware, and their respective swarthy vendors. Seven hundred and seventy-seven different peoples and races pass along those streets.[25]

The two companions – de Wohl wrote – made the usual tourist visit to the Pyramids, moving on to Luxor and the Valley of the Kings, returning north to the port city of Alexandria, where they took ship to Istanbul via Jaffa and Smyrna. De Wohl introduces characters – Japanese, Indians and Malays, a 'villainous' Armenian, a stereotypical Jewish guide 'with a thick white moustache and a bowler hat', an adventuress with 'milk-white skin, vivid red lips ... lovely beyond belief' – each of which seems to have stepped from one of his screenplays rather than real life. In a Smyrna dockside café, de Wohl and Secklmann are supposed to have disarmed a drunken sailor running amok with a pistol, but not before he fired two shots, one into the shoulder of 'a fat Turk', the second into a Venetian candelabra. In Istanbul de Wohl contacted an old friend and minor nobleman, Luca Orsini, the Italian ambassador to Turkey and later to Germany. De Wohl and Secklmann dined at the embassy, discussing Turkish and Italian politics with Orsini.

Once in Biskra, a town on the edge of the Sahara in the then French colony of Algeria, de Wohl claimed he had shared seven full pipes in one evening session of what he described as the best-quality hashish, the only effect being an 11-hour sleep from which he awoke refreshed but disappointed. Not even one vivid dream, he complained. In India he was thwarted in his effort to shoot a crocodile, an easy target, unmissable, because – de Wohl believed – the crocodile had hypnotised him at the very moment he was about to squeeze the trigger. But in Ceylon (now Sri Lanka) he was able to despatch an 8in scorpion with a single blow of his rifle butt. On another of his journeys to India in the early 1930s and in Bombay (now Mumbai), de Wohl was told the date of his death. Two friends, a young Parsee couple, knowing de Wohl's interest in Eastern religions and mysticism, persuaded him to visit a yogi living near what was then the city's Victoria Station. Expecting a straggly bearded ancient with matted hair, de Wohl was surprised when he was introduced to a youthful, clean-shaven Doctor of Philosophy called Sarmananda. De Wohl was further taken aback to find him smoking a cigarette.

Dr Sarmananda offered to answer any question his visitor wished to ask. 'I only want to know two dates – the day of my birth and the day of my death.' De Wohl reasoned that if the yogi could correctly tell the first date, then there was every chance he would also be accurate when it came to the second date. But to avert the danger he would be a victim of mind reading, de Wohl concentrated his thoughts on the wrong birthdate, 12 May 1904. Sarmananda closed his eyes for a few moments and then spoke: 24 January 1903. 'Do you still wish to know on what day you will die?' De Wohl thought the matter over, unsure now whether this was something he really did wish to know. He answered, 'Yes.' Sarmananda closed his eyes again and remained silent for a full minute. 'According to your calendar, the sixteenth of February 1964 – the date of your death.' De Wohl wrote in *I Follow My Stars*, 'I felt a certain wave of relief: I had a good many years ahead of me, and that spelled life and love, adventures and experiences. I was satisfied.' But he could not help wondering how he would feel as the date Sarmananda had foretold came closer.[26]

3

De Wohl said in *I Follow My Stars* that a year or so after his first meeting with Baron von Hoogerwoerd he had absorbed the basics of astrology – largely self-taught – and was giving advice and pointers to friends and acquaintances based on their horoscopes, working his way towards a greater understanding of what he believed to be a science. He claimed in his autobiography to have persuaded a friend not to take a particular flight to Munich. The aircraft crashed and all on board died. He warned Herr Leborius, the owner of a film company to which de Wohl was hoping to sell rights to a novel, that he appeared from his horoscope to be sailing close to the wind in his financial affairs and risked entanglement with the law. The man laughed, dismissing de Wohl's 'science' as not as exact as he imagined. 'I was feeling absolutely sick,' de Wohl wrote, 'for I saw with horrifying clearness that this man was doomed without knowing it … He did not see the heavy clouds gathered above his head.'

Three days later German newspapers splashed the news that Leborius had been arrested for evading currency controls by moving money to London without official authorisation. At his subsequent trial he was sentenced to thirteen years with hard labour. De Wohl explained his method in *I Follow My Stars*, one that went beyond merely an understanding of the movement of the planets:

> All this I could not tell by knowing only the date of his birth, but then I have had that appalling sensation of sudden and terrific clairvoyance many times in my life and long before I ever came across astrology. One can call it psychic, telepathic, or just uncanny, but I know to which aspect I owe it. It is not at all a pleasant gift to have, and yet I would not wish to lose it.[27]

De Wohl also claimed to have become closely acquainted with senior police officers in a number of cities while collecting materials for his novels – London, Paris, Marseilles, Port Said, Bombay, Calcutta, as well as Berlin. In *Secret Service of the Sky*, published in 1938, he claimed he had been able to use astrology to assist Inspector Giuseppe Calvi of the Naples police in a case involving the theft of two paintings from the home of a wealthy merchant, Giacomo Alberti. There were four, possibly five, suspects but Calvi had come up against a blank in his investigation. De Wohl asked Calvi to provide the birth dates of those he considered might be responsible. Casting horoscopes for not only these five, which included servants in the house, but also Alberti himself, de Wohl was able after a few days to identify the 'victim' as the thief. The merchant had been attempting an insurance scam. 'It was child's play. It is easy to see dishonest tendencies from a horoscope. Whether the man gives way to them or not, is quite another matter,' de Wohl wrote in his description of the case. Not only did Alberti's chart reveal a character inclined to dishonesty, but on the day of the theft transits of planets showed bad luck lying in wait for him. 'The Sun and Jupiter were in bad aspect to the

Cusp of his twelfth House (enmity, misfortune). It was no wonder that the attempt failed.'[28]

In the case of Leborius, the Berlin businessman, de Wohl had brought up his own gift as a clairvoyant, something going beyond the simple interpretation of a horoscope. But at other times he emphatically rejected the idea of prediction or clairvoyance, insisting astrology was a science that examined ever-shifting planetary influences on the lives of individuals, businesses and nations. A horoscope was an illustration of possible tendencies in a person's life, not a description of determining factors. There was absolutely no fortune telling involved, he declared in *Secret Service of the Sky*:

> An astrologer can never say: 'At six o'clock in the afternoon on the 17th of September, you will have an accident and will be taken to hospital, where two hours later you will die!' Such a prediction is either clairvoyance or a swindle – and in 999 cases out of 1,000, the latter! What the astrologer *can* say is: 'On the 17th of September between 5 and 7 in the afternoon, you have a bad Mars aspect, which owing to the unfavourable position of Mars in your Natal Horoscope, brings with it the danger of an accident.'[29]

De Wohl published *Secret Service of the Sky* a year before the outbreak of war in Europe in 1939. Imagine, he said, astrology at the service of the state, not as a destructive weapon to be wielded in battle but as a guarantor of peace. 'If each country had its astrological secret service, then it would be *au fait* with the general development of *all* countries.' The result would be, he was confident, that 'Surprise and sudden attacks are impossible, since no-one will be found unprepared and the result is an exceptionally sound balance of power ...'[30] Were these the seeds in de Wohl's mind of his wartime involvement with British Intelligence?

De Wohl tempted fate in *Secret Service of the Sky* when he made a forecast about British politics that turned out to be spectacularly mistaken, one on the future of the Secretary of State for War, Leslie Hore-Belisha. A National Liberal – Liberals who had allied with the Conservatives in the ruling National Government – Hore-Belisha had been a rising star and was proving an effective reforming political head of the army as war approached. 'In any walk of life this man would rise to the top,' de Wohl wrote after constructing and interpreting his horoscope. 'The moon in Leo, wonderfully aspected, and Uranus in Scorpio, equally well aspected, predestine him for leadership.' He was destined to rise, the astrologer said, to take the supreme office of state, prime minister. Dismissed by Chamberlain in January 1940 after he had fallen out with the army high command, Hore-Belisha never reached high office again.

Was the Secretary for War one of de Wohl's clients among the 'good and the great' MI5 had identified and had the astrologer decided to give him a public boost? Or was the astrologer being over-generous to what he saw as a kindred spirit? One writer describes Hore-Belisha's 'flamboyance, his 'chutzpah', his love of publicity, his habitual unpunctuality, his perceived effeminacy, his 'foreign' air'.[31] These were characteristics – flaws in their eyes – that MI5 officers and others subsequently said they found in de Wohl. But if the astrologer could be so wide of the mark in his prophecy of Hore-Belisha's destiny, where else would he be mistaken? Had anyone in British Intelligence ever taken the elementary step of reading de Wohl's books, if only to check his form when it came to astrological interpretation? It seemed not.

4

Secret Service of the Sky was not only a basic guide for the general reader on the construction and interpretation of horoscopes. The book also sketched the outline of de Wohl's wider thinking on the subject of astrology, its possibilities and limitations. There was, he was anxious to show, far more involved than merely the twelve signs – Aries, Taurus, Gemini, Cancer, Leo, Virgo, Libra, Scorpio, Sagittarius, Capricorn, Aquarius and Pisces – readers were increasingly amusing themselves with in popular newspaper predictions. Most people going no further into the subject understood their 'horoscope' to be their Sun sign, the astrological sign in which the Sun was notionally found on the day they were born. Entertaining as this might be – and de Wohl's first attraction to the subject had arisen through Baron von Hoogerwoerd's description of his 'Aquarius-born' character – astrology's practitioners believed it contained significantly greater depth and complexity.

De Wohl was hardly unique in his adoption of astrology in post-war Germany. The writer Theodore Zeldin has remarked on the stubborn survival over centuries of this form of soothsaying, its persistence 'despite all its mistaken predictions, and even though it has been condemned repeatedly by religion, science and governments'.[32] First curiosity and then faith had taken hold in the minds of many Germans as their country passed through an era of disorientation and anxiety following the country's defeat in 1918, revolution and the hyper-inflation of the early 1920s. 'The belief that one could glean knowledge from reading the stars or uncovering hidden forces operating in everyday life was remarkably widespread in interwar Germany,' the historian Eric Kurlander writes:

> By the mid-1920s astrology in particular had experienced an expansion in popularity, followed by a mainstreaming of astrological periodicals, institutes, and organisations. More than two dozen astrological journals and manuals alone competed for readers during a period of expanding interest in the occult. Academic institutions followed suit. In 1930 one local university offered a course given by the astrologer Heinz Artur Strauss.[33]

One argument followers of astrology used in its defence was the everyday acceptance of the role the Sun and Moon played in life on Earth: heat from the Sun as the pre-condition for existence and the observable effect of the Moon on the ebb and flow of the tides. The argument goes back at least as far as the second-century Greek scholar Claudius Ptolemy, reputedly the 'father' of Western astrology. In his astrological study *Tetrabiblos*, Ptolemy set out in detail what he saw as the influence of the Sun, Moon and the planets in human lives and the ways in which it was possible to make predictions of future events. Von Hoogerwoerd made a similar case when de Wohl questioned the idea that a planet could possibly be involved when he cut his cheek shaving, a weak analogy the baron's listener was prepared to accept. 'I wonder if it would seem absurd and ridiculous to you if you got sunstroke or prickly heat,' the baron asked. 'And moon madness, what about that? Everyone admits that that is the result of a star's influence, nobody dares to doubt it.'[34]

Western astrology views the heavens as divided into twelve constellations, spanning Aries to Pisces. These are denoted in the horoscope as astrological signs, along with twelve houses in a chart, each of which represents an aspect of human life: the first house, for example, is the individual's personality and look, the fourth matters connected with home and family, the seventh relationships and partnerships, the eighth birth, death and transformation, the tenth career and reputation. According to the French-born American astrologer Dane Rudhyar: 'The birth-chart has to be understood as the archetype or seed-pattern of one's individual being – as the symbolic "form" of one's individuality, and therefore also of one's identity, for the two are identical.'[35]

At the moment of birth, the Sun, Moon and the other planets will each stand in a specific sign and house and this will be represented diagrammatically in a person's horoscope. For example, the Sun may be in Aries in the fifth house and this position will have its own significance for the astrologer. Each planet is said to exercise an influence on the individual character and on events: Mars, for example, governs courage and drive, Venus love and artistic undertakings. Just as important in the individual horoscope as the position of the Sun is the ascendant or rising sign. This is the astrological sign appearing over the eastern horizon at the moment of birth. A person may, for example, be said to have 'Libra rising', as Hitler did, or 'Cancer rising' as in the case of de Wohl. The ascendant represents an individual's appearance and ways of behaving in the eyes of the world, the outward physical manifestation of personality.

Astrologers provide a basic analysis of a person's character, habits, and areas of strength and weakness by interpreting complex interrelationships in the horoscope. One important element they consider is the dynamic between the different planets, the angles they have to one another in the chart. Two planets in close proximity are described as being in 'conjunction', while planets at 180 degrees are said to be in 'opposition'. Among other relations are 'square' (approximately

90 degrees apart) and 'trine' (roughly 120) degrees. These are known as 'aspects' and astrologers make assessments of individual personalities and the course of their lives from these.

When astrologers attempt to describe what may or may not happen in the future, they look to what they call 'transits'. These are the movements of planets over time in relation to their original position at the moment of a person's birth. As the planets transit they make and remake angles – aspects – to each other. Astrologers believe they can draw valuable conclusions from these ever-changing relationships. They claim, for example, to be able to suggest when a certain action is favoured and likely to succeed or – as in the case of de Wohl and his shaving cuts, frivolous though the example was – moments when a course of action is risky and inadvisable. De Wohl's first instructor in astrology, Baron von Hoogerwoerd, told his pupil the accident in the bathroom had been in the air because during that period the movement of the planet Mars had placed it 'square' to the ascendant in his horoscope at birth. De Wohl gave his own broad description of astrology, what it could and could not do:

> Astrology is a science, for it is a matter of knowledge and its object is the study and application of certain laws of Nature. Let us get this straight from the start: it is not prophecy. It is not dealing with certainties, but with tendencies. It has a fairly wide margin for error – but it works.[36]

In *Religion and the Decline of Magic*, the historian Keith Thomas describes the complex problems an astrologer encounters in trying to interpret what a horoscope is signifying. Although Thomas is writing in the context of the sixteenth and seventeenth centuries, the difficulties remained the same in the twentieth and were those de Wohl was likely to face in his work for British Intelligence:

> The planets … were only one variable in a densely crowded mosaic of fluctuating constituents – elements, humours, qualities, houses and signs of the zodiac. The client's own horoscope might also need to be compared with that of the country in which he lived, or those of the

other persons with whom he had dealings. The astrologer thus found himself involved in a welter of combinations and permutations which greatly complicated the task of interpretation ... Any interpretation was in the last resort bound to be subjective.[37]

A horoscope can be constructed for a nation, a city, a business, an institution or an organisation in exactly the same way as for an individual. The 'birth' of the United Kingdom, for example, is said to be 1 May 1707, when the Act of Union between England and Scotland came into effect. But there is an argument that it is more accurate to say the nation was born on 25 December 1066, the day William 'the Conqueror' was crowned, or 1 January 1801, when Ireland was incorporated into the United Kingdom. Similarly, was the Germany de Wohl was dealing with based on the proclamation of 18 January 1871, the birth of the republic on 9 November 1918, or the arrival in power of the Nazis on 30 January 1933? There is less dispute about when the United States was 'born': 4 July 1776, the date of the Declaration of Independence. Some states – for example, Sri Lanka (formerly Ceylon), Thailand, and Myanmar (formerly Burma) – were even established when astrologers calculated what would be propitious times. As with an individual, astrologers go on to claim that it is possible to describe the character of a nation and to make predictions about events in its life and destiny.

The claims for successful astrological prediction on a scale larger than the individual are scarce and rarely convincing. Hitler and Germany would be for de Wohl and British Intelligence a complex and fascinating intermingling of possibilities. De Wohl's tendency was to take the fate of the leading personalities as the destiny of the nation: Hitler, Churchill, Roosevelt, Mussolini. Elizabeth I of England reportedly turned to the court astrologer John Dee to select an auspicious date for her coronation – 15 January 1559. Her reign was long and saw the early flowering of England as a nation state. Was there any connection? Astrologers would say the choice of a propitious date played a positive part in the country's fortunes. The seventeenth-century astrologer William Lilly – a supporter of Parliament in the English Civil War – is said to have predicted the beheading of King Charles I a year before it took place in 1649. He went on to foretell both the bubonic plague that swept London in 1665 and the devastating Great Fire the following year in his book *Monarchy, or No Monarchy in England*, published in 1651. Lilly's forecasts described first 'a great sickness and mortality … people in their winding-sheets, persons digging graves …', followed by 'a great city all in flames of fire'.[38]

Raphael's Almanac, which had appeared annually in Britain since 1827, suggested in the 1913 edition that there were strongly marked 'indications of war and disaster' for the following year in the horoscope of the German Kaiser, Wilhelm II, connecting his individual fate with that of his country and of the European continent. The First World War broke out in 1914. The aspect of Mars square to Saturn in the Kaiser's chart, another publication said, signified Wilhelm's inevitable defeat and humiliation, and with these of Germany. In de Wohl's own time, the often-consulted clairvoyant Cheiro (an Irishman, born William Warner) forecast in 1931 in the magazine *World Predictions* that the Prince of Wales, Edward, would abandon the throne rather than lose the object of his affection.[39] This Edward went on to do five years later. In 1930 the astrologer R.H. Naylor warned in the 5 October edition of the *Sunday Express* of the imminent danger of an accident involving a British aircraft. As the newspaper was coming off the presses, the airship R101 – bound for India via Egypt on its maiden flight – crashed in flames on a hillside in France with the death of forty-six of the fifty-four crew and passengers.

De Wohl may have claimed astrology was a science, but it was paradoxically a science he believed to be incompatible with rationalism, the harmful roots of which he believed could be found in the French Revolution:

> The age of rationalism will soon be called by history the second dark age of mankind. For rationalism has very, very little to do with reason. By their fruits shall ye know them – and these fruits have been materialism, anarchism, nihilism, and the concept of the ant state as the progressive ideal, with everybody working for progress and no one asking in what direction.[40]

5

By the early 1930s de Wohl's career as a novelist and screenwriter was thriving and he had become a significant and respected figure in the German film industry. Six of his novels had been adapted for silent films and he found no difficulty in adjusting to the new approaches and techniques the introduction of talkies demanded. His first script involving dialogue was *The Last Company* for the Ufa company, a film set during Prussia's war against Napoleon, starring Conrad Veidt, a well-known actor of the period. Veidt fled the Nazis in 1933 with his Jewish wife, moving first to Britain and then to the United States. Among other prominent people in the business de Wohl worked with were the directors Curtis Bernhardt and Henry Koster (born Hermann Kosterlitz), and the screenwriter Carl Mayer, all of whom would be forced to flee Nazi Germany in 1933. His closest colleague – who would become a lifelong friend – was the director and producer Joe May, born Joseph Mandel in Vienna in 1880. May left for Hollywood in 1933, establishing himself at Universal Pictures. In each case, Germany's loss proved to be Hollywood's gain.

De Wohl was flattered, as he showed in his autobiography, to receive a letter via his publisher from Hermine, wife of ex-Kaiser Wilhelm (living in exile in Holland since Germany's defeat in the First World War), saying her husband had particularly enjoyed one of his novels. The former Kaiser, she added, read selected excerpts to his entourage every night. Whatever de Wohl produced was now so popular that, as the editor of a Berlin newspaper that serialised his fiction told the not entirely happy writer, 'You know … we don't read your novels anymore … We just print them, that's all.'[41] De Wohl responded by producing a book in three months under an assumed name – Edith Alice Gordon, purportedly an English woman living in Berlin – dressing in female clothes and presenting the completed manuscript in person to the editor. The disguise was convincing. The man who shaved three times a day and was rarely without an 8in cigar in his hand passed as a woman. De Wohl revealed himself only after the editor had praised the novel, accepted the work for serialisation and the paper's accounts department had handed

'Miss Gordon' a cheque. He went on to write a series of articles on his experiences living dressed as a woman for ten days, but Hitler's arrival as Chancellor first delayed and then prevented their publication.[42]

De Wohl's interest in astrology continued, running parallel with his career as a writer and his growing involvement in the film industry. Occasionally the two became intertwined, as in an incident early in 1933 involving Alfred Zeisler, the producer and director of the film *Gold*, the story of a scientist who has discovered the secret of transforming lead into the precious metal, the dream of alchemists. Having already invested over a million marks in the production, but facing obstacle after obstacle, Zeisler began to doubt that *Gold* would be completed, and if it was whether it would make a profit. De Wohl asked Zeisler his birthdate and, establishing that the Sun was in conjunction with Jupiter in his horoscope ('a marvellous aspect'), told the producer he need have no fears, success was certain. Zeisler was unconvinced, but work proceeded smoothly until one evening the director, Karl Hartl, complained of a headache. He then went down with a high temperature and a red rash on his face and body. Zeisler was certain financial and artistic disaster loomed and prepared to abandon the project.

De Wohl remained convinced that the astrological advice he had given Zeisler still stood but contacted his mentor Baron von Hoogerwoerd for guidance, giving him Hartl's birthdate. Hoogerwoerd reported that on the evening Hartl had been struck by the mysterious illness, the planet Neptune was square his ascendant, which suggested the director had suffered food poisoning. All was now well, the baron reported, and the danger had passed. Relieved, Zeisler secured a further injection of 500,000 marks to complete the film. On its release in 1934 the *New York Times* described *Gold* as long but 'thrilling … excellent'.[43] But like many others in the industry, the American-born Zeisler felt impelled to leave Germany for Britain in 1935. De Wohl was later to work with him in England on the film *Crime over London*.

Another of de Wohl's friends who shared his interest in astrology was the Austrian-born actor and director Fritz Lang, like de Wohl a Roman Catholic of Jewish heritage. Lang had made the ground-breaking science fiction film *Metropolis* in 1927. His wife, the screenwriter Thea von Harbou, was an ardent Nazi sympathiser and the couple divorced when she took the step of becoming a full party member. Hitler, ironically, had admired two of Lang's early films, reading them as attacks on the Jews. As the Nazis tightened their grip on power, Lang left Germany for good following a tense meeting in which Propaganda Minister Joseph Goebbels lavishly praised his work as a film maker but then made pointed remarks about his Jewish ancestry. Goebbels' ministry had effectively taken control of the cinema industry through the establishment in 1933 of the Reich Film Chamber, which everyone working in the industry was obliged to join. 'In 1935 and 1936 the Party encouraged cinemagoers to send in enquiries about the racial and political affiliations of leading screen actors.'[44] Lang could see the shape of the future under the Nazis, going first to Paris, then to Hollywood where he built a career that spanned two decades.

De Wohl would be the next to leave. He moved to Britain in September 1935 where, beyond a few acquaintances in the film world, he was largely unknown. He gave a number of reasons for his decision to abandon Germany permanently. In *I Follow My Stars* he described a darkness that descended on the country after the Nazi accession to power in January 1933. The regime, he wrote, 'towered over everything, even over the most intimate friendships and the private work of every person living in Germany'. Politics became irrelevant because only the Nazis were in a position to influence events in any way. De Wohl said that as far as writers and artists like him and his colleagues were concerned 'nobody in Germany knew what it was permissible to write: every day new books, plays, and films were banned, and newspapers had to close down for weeks, sometimes even for months, if they had fallen into disfavour with the authorities'.[45]

There were clearly pressures, both personal and professional. Though de Wohl was not a German citizen – born in Berlin, he held and retained Hungarian citizenship through his father – his Jewish heritage marked him out once the Nazis seized the opportunity to put their anti-Semitic policies into practice. Had he remained in Germany he would, in all likelihood, have eventually been murdered by the Nazi regime. It was surely no coincidence that he abandoned Germany in September 1935, the month Hitler summoned Reichstag deputies to the annual party rally to rubber stamp the racist Nuremberg Laws. The Reich Citizenship Law withheld rights from all but individuals with 'German or related blood'. The Law for the Protection of German Blood and German Honour banned marriages and sexual relations between Germans and Jews (who were deemed no longer Germans). Jews were disenfranchised and denied all political rights as part of the dehumanisation that would culminate in the Holocaust. The regime determined who and who was not Jewish and de Wohl, though a Catholic, would certainly have been categorised as a Jew because of his antecedents. Hitler had announced the Nazi party's swastika emblem was now Germany's national flag and there were sporadic attacks on Jews in the streets. De Wohl could hardly feel other than personally vulnerable, though in his autobiography he was at pains to say: 'All I do wish to record is that I left Germany in September 1935 entirely voluntarily and unmolested.'[46]

De Wohl's description was more vivid and emotional in an interview with an American newspaper a few years later. 'Neither I nor members of my family were ever molested, but I saw and heard stories that sickened me. Friends disappeared.'[47] Personally unmolested he may have been, but De Wohl said he had found it increasingly difficult to work in Berlin once the Nazis were in power. This was in part because the film industry was altering its complexion as Jewish producers, directors and writers recognised their vulnerability under the regime and fled. With his ability to speak both English and French and his international contacts, de Wohl believed he too could succeed abroad. 'I had travelled much and had friends in every part of the world,' he wrote. 'And last, but not least – in my horoscope foreign countries were favoured.'[48] In Vienna for the opening night of a play he had recently completed, he received the news that further work in Germany would now be entirely out of the question. De Wohl does not say from whom or by what means he heard this, but the promulgation of the anti-Semitic Nuremberg Laws must surely have played some part. Had he heard the sale of his books was about to be banned, as proved to be the case? With – de Wohl said – many regrets, he did not return to Berlin, travelling directly to England, leaving his wife Putti behind.

That was de Wohl's version of events in 1938. When he set out his wartime experiences in *The Stars of War and Peace* in 1952 there was a significant change to the story, one involving astrology. To open, de Wohl repeated what had become a familiar narrative: Hitler had been taking astrological advice since the failure of his attempted seizure of power in Munich in November 1923. An astrologer had cautioned against taking this action but Hitler ignored the warning; the coup failed, he was tried for high treason and sentenced to five years confinement in the fortress of Landsberg, of which he served only nine months but where he dictated his autobiographical testament *Mein Kampf*. De Wohl claimed he had no doubt that from then onwards Hitler invariably took astrological advice before any important move. It was in this context that in 1935, de Wohl said, 'I had been approached by a party member who hinted that I might be able to do "very important work for Germany" in connection with astrology and suggested that I should see "the people concerned". I answered evasively, and took the next opportunity to leave Germany for good.'[49]

Who exactly had approached him? De Wohl does not say. How could he be sure that he was being asked to work for Hitler himself? Once again, de Wohl does not say. But he insisted it was the Führer seeking his services. 'I did not care particularly to become the astrologer of a tyrant with one of the most dangerous horoscopes I had ever seen.' Ellic Howe, who made de Wohl's acquaintance when they were both engaged in Second World War Political Warfare Executive 'black propaganda' – and who had a deep interest of his own in astrology and the occult – doubted any of this was true. 'This story about the smartly-uniformed party official does not hang together.'[50] In 1940 de Wohl published a novel, *Introducing Doctor Zodiac*, in which Hitler attempts to employ a Hungarian astrologer and psychologist as his personal astrologer – an example of fiction drawing from real life, or more likely fiction building on fiction. As de Wohl had shown with his early autobiography *I Follow my Stars*, he was a master in overlapping fact and fiction in the interests of a good tale.

2

An Air of Baroque Opulence

1

Whatever de Wohl's actual reason for his decision to flee to England, there was clearly some urgency. As he left Vienna rather than his home he could not have carried much with him. Clothes, a few books perhaps. He even left his wife, Putti, behind in Berlin. His later explanation was that he was short of money and could not afford to take her with him, but at some point she joined her husband in England before moving to Chile early in 1939. Why she left London and why South America, de Wohl never explained.[1] An MI5 officer who had met her – presumably during her brief stay with her husband – found her 'a very pleasant person', but added the observation, 'She is fond of de Wohl, but I should describe her attitude as more motherly than wifely.'[2] De Wohl had been unhappy in her absence, writing that his first weeks in London were 'terrible … I felt utterly, utterly lonely.'[3] However, the same MI5 officer later commented on de Wohl's subsequent 'amatory adventures and habits' once his wife had been packed off to South America.[4]

De Wohl was a well-known enough figure in the industry for the American entertainment magazine *Variety* to report in its 'Chatter' column in November 1935 that Ludwig von Wohl (the name by which he had always been known in Germany) was now 'to make London his permanent home'.[5] The tip would presumably have come from de

Wohl himself. The *Variety* piece gave no reason for his change of country, though many in the business would have understood the cause for the move without need for further explanation. In his autobiography *I Follow My Stars*, published only two years after his arrival in London, de Wohl describes how fond he was of the English, finding them much friendlier than their European reputation had led him to believe. Indeed, the book's final chapter – paragraph after paragraph of praise for English people's sense of humour and their romanticism – reads like the preliminary to an application for British citizenship (which he would go on to make in 1940 and which the authorities would have their reasons to deny him until after the Second World War). De Wohl knew how to play with words, but the emotion nonetheless seems genuinely felt.

Given his gregarious character, social ease and well-developed eye for the main chance, de Wohl took no time at all to establish himself in London, despite his complaints of loneliness. He lived for a number of years at the Esplanade Hotel, Warrington Crescent, in the Maida Vale area, a place popular with central European refugees from the Nazis, including briefly Sigmund Freud and his daughter Anna in the summer of 1938.[6] A friend, an astrologer like de Wohl, described his room in the Esplanade as 'littered with books, papers in complete confusion, a large desk covered with all sorts of mementoes and frames and signed photographs and the inevitable leather cases of big cigars. Most objects of daily use were engraved with a baronial coat of arms.' De Wohl, the friend went on, loved luxury, cultivating 'an air of baroque opulence', whatever his financial state, receiving visitors to the Esplanade in 'a flowing robe or silken dressing gown'.[7]

At the turn of the year, only a few months after arriving in London, de Wohl made the acquaintance of a man who was to play a central role in his wartime life. The British theatrical trade paper *The Era* reported in February 1936 that the playwright Gilbert Lennox had completed an English version of de Wohl's drama *Tropenluft*, to be performed in London under the title *Storm Centre*.[8] It was while de Wohl was in Vienna in September 1935 to view the production of *Tropenluft* at the Raimund Theatre that he had made his decision to abandon Germany for good. Lennox – for a while de Wohl's theatrical colleague – had been an officer in the Indian Army, retiring with the rank of major in 1932. Lennox moved remarkably quickly from military life to a successful career as a dramatist. His adaptation of the play *Close Quarters* – the original was by the German writer W.O. Somin – had opened at the Embassy Theatre in London in June 1935 and was to show on Broadway in New York four years later. The significance of the involvement of the two men in the translation and production of *Storm Centre* was that in 1939 Major Lennox would be recruited to MI5, becoming responsible for liaison with the Directorate of Military Intelligence at the War Office. In this role he was de Wohl's handler and his go-between with British Intelligence.

De Wohl, meanwhile, showed himself to be an effective self-promoter. His story reached across the world to Australia, and in July 1936 the Sydney *World's News* described him as a 'walking thrill-factory', a crime writer whose stature in Germany was equal to that of Edgar Wallace in Britain. He could reportedly produce a book in fourteen days and to date had published thirty-three. However, the story went on, he had been 'expelled' from Germany when 'it was found that his maternal grandmother's grandmother had some of the Hated Blood in her veins'.[9] De Wohl understood precisely what anti-Nazi buttons to push to ensure good coverage. In June the same year Harrap – the firm that had published *I Follow My Stars* – brought out *Plunge into Life*, a translation from the German of a de Wohl comic romance set in a Swiss sanatorium run by a fraudulent doctor. One reviewer praised the novel for its 'brightness and vivacity', while another described de Wohl as 'a prolific young writer, whose books are selling like hot cakes on the Continent (except in Germany, where they are banned)'.[10]

According to Felix Jay, the fellow astrologer who first came into contact with him about this time, de Wohl had another source of income, one that cast a light on a different aspect to his character. 'I also discovered that he played cards for money,' Jay wrote. 'Though the stakes were comparatively low, I came to the conclusion that he supplemented his uncertain income by gambling.'[11] A gambler, a chancer, just as one senior MI5 officer would subsequently come to see him.

De Wohl renewed his friendship in London with Alfred Zeisler, the cinema producer and director who had fled Germany in 1933.

Persuasive as an astrologer, de Wohl had shored up Zeisler's faltering confidence when he was struggling to complete the film *Gold*. The two now worked together at Isleworth Studios on *Crime over London*, based on de Wohl's novel *The House of a Thousand Windows*. The film, the plot of which involved a New York gang's thwarted effort to rob a London department store, culminating in a shoot-out with police, was first screened in October 1936. De Wohl's growing professional success in his new homeland was confirmed when *The Era* reported that a film company was negotiating the purchase of adaptation rights to his recently published novel *Plunge into Life*. A second of his books, *Satan in Disguise*, a story of smuggling and gun-running set in Egypt, appeared in translation early in 1937. The *Yorkshire Post* reviewer described the work as 'light reading and no more, but very decidedly good of its kind'.[12]

Most remarkable was the publication by Harrap in October 1937 of de Wohl's autobiography *I Follow My Stars*. Though he acknowledged 'with gratitude' the assistance he had received with editing and revising the manuscript from Margaret McDonell (who had also translated *Satan in Disguise*), the book was nevertheless a significant achievement by a man for whom English was a second language. He had the advantage, of course, of having honed the skills of structure and pace producing a long run of novels and screenplays. *I Follow My Stars* charted the course of his life through a series of adventures and travels, some of which gave the impression they derived more from his imagination than lived reality. One reviewer commented, 'Mr de Wohl has had an abundance of unusual experiences and he tells them unusually well', but doubted the sections on astrology would appeal to many. Another, however, recognised de Wohl had identified a market to be tapped. These chapters, the reviewer said, would be welcomed by 'everyone interested in astrology, the oldest of sciences, the popularity of which is increasing by leaps and bounds'.[13]

De Wohl knew and understood his market's dreams: men and women of noble background, exotic travel, adventure, horoscopes, humour and fate. Though only two chapters dealt with astrology, de Wohl claimed that after *I Follow My Stars* appeared in the bookshops:

I received bagfuls of letters from every class of people and from all corners of the globe. Peers and peeresses, bank clerks, hairdressers, chemists, artists, salesmen, scientists, solders and an army of women wrote to me wishing to learn more, wanting advice. I helped where I could. But I met with such an incredible lack of knowledge of the subject that I got the idea of writing a book telling what I know of astrology ...[14]

It was an astute publisher – The Cresset Press this time, rather than Harrap – who persuaded the always eager de Wohl to follow up the success of his autobiography with that book, *Secret Service of the Sky*. He now devoted his full attention to the subject of astrology, setting out his intention in the first chapter: 'What I wish to do is to give the reading public a grasp of what astrology actually is, what it can do, and whither it leads.'[15] *Secret Service of the Sky* was partly a basic astrological manual, describing the significance of the planets and the underlying personal attributes and attitudes of individuals born in each of the twelve Sun signs. 'According to astrological experience a special star of our Solar System rules each sign, which receives from it, as in a lover's embrace, the seed of its nature,' a lyrical de Wohl wrote.

What de Wohl was saying about astrology was elementary, an introduction to what he claimed was a science, which was to be the usual pattern in books that followed. More interesting were the horoscopes he included in the book of nine contemporaries, ranging from King George VI to the Italian dictator Mussolini, the United States President Roosevelt and the German Führer Hitler, with his interpretations of their characters and prospects. He also offered a horoscope reading of the fate of the liner *Titanic*, which sank in 1912 after striking an iceberg in the North Atlantic. This was a dramatic disaster still in living memory. Here he gave an example of how an astrologer could take an incident from the past and find the evidence to fit the event – a reverse 'I could have told you' prophecy – which de Wohl and others of his profession often indulged in. 'This is why that happened' was far easier to argue than 'This is what will happen', though ultimately a less impressive demonstration of astrology's supposed predictive power.

The *Titanic* sank in the early hours of 15 April 1912 with the death of over 1,500 passengers and crew. According to de Wohl, the ship's fate had been cast from the moment of its launch in Belfast, at 12.42 p.m. on 31 May 1911. As far as he was concerned, there could have been no less auspicious time astrologically and disaster was all but inevitable. 'The Cusp of the House of Death (eighth) lies in the Mars sign – Aries – and Mars itself stood in opposition to the Ascendant. Further, the Cusp of this house forms an evil square with Neptune (sea journeys).' Even worse was the time the *Titanic* set forth from Southampton on her maiden voyage, noon on 10 April 1912. 'To an astrologer the picture is staggering … The Cusp of the House of Death was 28 degrees in Aquarius, and thus ruled by Uranus, by catastrophe.' Finally, there was the ship's captain, Edward Smith, who was among those who died in the disaster. Smith's horoscope showed 'Neptune in the House of Death (eighth). In the ninth House (long journeys) there is Saturn (hindrances) and Uranus (catastrophes).' De Wohl concluded, 'This man should *never* have become a ship's officer.'[16] If Baron von Hoogerwoerd was correct when he said the planets were responsible for only 40 per cent of what occurs, presumably had those in charge at each stage not launched the *Titanic* at the time they did, not sent the ship on its voyage at the time they did, and had appointed a different individual as captain, the iceberg would not have taken the toll it had.

2

Given the tense international political situation when de Wohl was composing *Secret Service of the Sky* – the dictators Mussolini and Hitler were convincing the world their authoritarian methods worked and were impossible to resist, Italy had seized Ethiopia, civil war was raging in Spain, France was in political chaos – readers and reviewers would be concerned to read de Wohl's forecasts for the future, for Europe in particular. Completing the book in June 1938, de Wohl gave many hostages to fortune. The heading of one provincial English newspaper review a fortnight after British Prime Minister Chamberlain's appeasement of the

German Führer at Munich summed up de Wohl's message: 'Why Hitler Has Succeeded'.[17]

What had Hitler succeeded in doing? His declared purpose on becoming Chancellor in 1933 had been to reverse what most Germans saw as the humiliating burden forced on the country by the 1919 Treaty of Versailles. Germany had been pressed at Versailles under the 'war guilt clause' into taking responsibility for the outbreak in 1914 of the First World War, to give up territory and population in Europe and cede her colonies in Africa and the Pacific, to drastically reduce the strength of her armed forces, and to pay reparations to the victors for war damage. Hitler's ultimate aims, as he had set out unmistakably in *Mein Kampf*, were racial and territorial: to assert what he saw as the superiority of the Aryan 'race' over the Jewish and to seize *lebensraum* – living space – in the east from the Russians, whom he also saw as racially inferior and infected with Bolshevism.

From 1935 on, Hitler grasped opportunities as they came to undo the Versailles treaty, violating its terms one by one. In March 1935 Germany embarked on a major rearmament programme and restored military conscription. In June Britain agreed to allow expansion of the German navy, including the construction of submarines, until then banned. In March 1936, Nazi troops reoccupied the Rhineland, which had been demilitarised in 1919 to secure France's eastern frontier against the possibility of a renewed German threat. In March 1938 Germany incorporated Austria into the Reich, an act the treaty had specifically forbidden. In September 1938 came seizure of the Sudetenland, the German-speaking border territory merged into the new state of Czechoslovakia after the First World War.

Under their policy of appeasement, Britain and France – the leading European powers – had allowed Hitler to proceed unhindered, hoping to avert or at least delay war by placating his demands. British Prime Minister Chamberlain's Munich Agreement with Hitler in September 1938 over the Sudetenland, detaching the German-speaking region from Czechoslovakia, was the final desperate move in the strategy. One writer describes what happened with painful bluntness: 'On 29 September 1938 the appeasers brought off the criminal government of Germany by "giving" it Czechoslovakia, a country … with an ancient history and a modern reputation for having made a success of democracy.'[18] A joke current in England at the time ran: 'What's the difference between Chamberlain and Hitler?' – 'Chamberlain takes his weekends in the country. Hitler takes countries at the weekends.'[19]

Was some occult power involved as Hitler went apparently unstoppably from success to success, or was it his astute reading – he called it an 'intuition' – of his opponent's political motivations, above all their reluctance to resort to arms to make Germany abide by the terms of the Versailles Treaty? 'I am walking with the confidence of a sleepwalker the path Providence tells me to walk,' he told a cheering Munich audience following the Rhineland triumph in 1936. A year later he told a rally in Regensburg, 'If I look back at the past five years, I believe I can say: That was no mere human accomplishment, If Providence hadn't guided us, I often wouldn't have found those dizzying paths.'[20]

The truth of the situation was that Hitler had found himself pushing at an open door when he confronted Britain and France. Neither celestial aid nor intuition were required. But de Wohl's explanation in *Secret Service of the Sky* for Hitler's triumphant progress was less the Great Powers' acquiescence through their policy of appeasement, more a case that he was acting on the basis of astrological advice, moving only when his horoscope forecast success. Each of his actions 'had been done just as the right time, "under very good aspects".'[21] The editor of Britain's leading astrological magazine *Astrology*, Charles Carter, took the same line as de Wohl, writing of Hitler in the September 1939 edition, 'We have long known that he made use of our art. Presumably non-believers will continue to expatiate on the wonderful power Hitler possesses of acting at the right moment …'[22]

Would Britain and Germany go to war? Writing a year before the outbreak of the Second World War, de Wohl forecast they would not. 'One of the reasons why in spite of many disquieting signs *I do not believe in a war in the near future* is that the horoscopes of the Italian as well as the German dictator indicate that a war would be their end – and at least Hitler is astrologically advised.' He went on to suggest the possibility of dramatic upheaval in Germany in September 1938 and January 1939.

'A world-known personality will be wounded, if not killed.'[23] Hitler narrowly escaped an assassination attempt in Munich in November 1939 – see page 65. De Wohl was not alone in his view that a European war was unlikely. The editor of *Astrology*, Charles Carter, giving his opinion at the beginning of August 1939 on what Britain and Europe might face, was circumspect, placing his money carefully on two horses but coming down on the same side. Carter said that among astrologers there was 'a widespread belief that things will move rapidly and dangerously at or about the end of the month'. But, pointing to what he said was 'the very favourable direction' of the aspect Venus trine Moon, he concluded, 'Hence I remain very hopeful of peace.'[24]

De Wohl suggests in places, but does not go into any detail, that in the years immediately before the Second World War he was also working as an astrologer in London, charging fees for casting and interpreting horoscopes. As he published only one novel, *The Last Thug* in early 1939, and wrote a single screenplay – *Make-up*, directed in 1937 by Alfred Zeisler – he needed another source of income to supplement whatever royalties may have been coming in. The novel, set against the background of the Indian *thuggee* cult, did receive a favourable review in the *Daily Mirror*, the readers of which would have been among his target audience, so presumably sales were buoyant. 'If you want something to make cold shivers trickle gently up and down your spine,' the *Mirror* reviewer wrote, 'go to and read this!'[25]

There were rumours, picked up later by MI5 and fed into his file, that de Wohl had been in touch with the Bata Shoe Company (a business first established in the former Austro-Hungarian empire), offering to act as the firm's agent in the United States. But given his background, astrology would have been the more obvious and easy way of making money. 'There are many who are secretly interested: university professors, lawyers, doctors, etc.,' he wrote in *Secret Service of the Sky* in 1938. 'How often have I heard: "Please, Mr de Wohl, make me a horoscope for next year again, but, of course, this must be kept between us two!"'[26] This was what he did and his activity in this area, and his range of clients – some from overseas – attracted the attention of the Security Service, MI5, as war approached.[27] One in particular of de Wohl's clients – Viorel Tilea, the Romanian ambassador in London from 1938 to 1940 – would play a key part in facilitating the astrologer's contact with British Intelligence. MI5 already had a file on Tilea, PF53105.

3

In one sense astrology had been built into the foundations of the Reich in 1871. The Prussian Chancellor, the architect of German unification, Otto von Bismarck, together with his army chief of staff, Helmuth von Moltke, reportedly consulted an astrologer before triggering the war against France in 1870 that was to prove decisive. 'Its subsequent course went so well for them that when they reached Versailles, they sent the man a handsome reward.'[28] In January 1871 Bismarck humiliated a defeated France by proclaiming the establishment of the German Empire in the palace of Versailles. De Wohl would insist that Hitler's astounding political rise in Germany and his diplomatic triumphs in Europe could be ascribed to his belief in astrology and the advice he received. But Hitler's public words gave a different impression. His attitude towards the occult, mysticism, and everything connected, was dismissive and condemnatory.

If de Wohl asserted astrology was not fortune telling, that it was scientific and had no relationship with the occult, others disagreed, placing it in the category of mystical mumbo-jumbo. At the Nazi party's annual Nuremberg rally in September 1936 Hitler attacked what he called 'those elements who only understood National Socialism in terms of hearsay and sagas, and who therefore confuse it too easily with vague Nordic phrases … based on motifs from some mythical Atlantean culture'.[29] This went only so far. He was more explicit two years later, in September 1938, again at Nuremberg:

> National Socialism is a cool, reality-based doctrine, based upon the sharpest scientific knowledge and its mental expression … We have no desire to instil in the people a mysticism that lies outside the purpose and goals of our doctrine … For the National Socialist movement is not a cult movement … Its meaning is not that of a mystic cult … In

the National Socialist movement subversion by occult searchers for the Beyond must not be tolerated … The only cult we know is that of a cultivation of the natural and hence of that which God has willed.[30]

Reich Minister of Public Enlightenment and Propaganda Joseph Goebbels had spoken similarly in 1935 when he warned the media against publishing anything that implied there was a connection between cults and the regime's ruling party: 'Unclear mythical concepts must disappear from the German press where they are used in conjunction with the essence and idea of National Socialism.'[31] And before this, in 1934, the regime had tightened laws already on the statute book against clairvoyants and tarot card readers on the grounds that they claimed access to information that was 'not possible to know through natural means', an attitude remarkably close to that of the Roman Catholic church.

However, the situation was not as clear cut as Hitler and Goebbels tried to suggest, as they would have realised but found it convenient to ignore. It was no surprise that a party blatantly opportunistic enough to campaign in one election on the slogan 'We are the opposite of everything there is today' could be capable of incorporating apparently contradictory elements. The Nazi leaders combined an enthusiasm for adopting the most modern technology while sinking to the crudest racial pseudo-theories. Beyond its fundamental race obsession and lust for power, Nazi ideology is never easy to pin down. Connections between the occult and the Nazi party – or at least some of its leading members – have been well documented, if sometimes exaggerated, but historians continue to dispute their extent. George L. Mosse, in *The Crisis of German Ideology: Intellectual Origins of the Third Reich*, argues that while Nazism absorbed a range of late nineteenth-century anti-Enlightenment beliefs and practices, leading party figures – with a few significant exceptions, notably Heinrich Himmler – recognised their absurdity, but found it acceptable to use elements for purely propaganda purposes. Nicholas Goodrick-Clarke, in *The Occult Roots of Nazism*, agrees. In his view, while the occult may have played a part in the rise of Nazism among the movement's earliest supporters, it had no real influence once the party had achieved its overriding objective: power. Peter

Staudenmaier, however, suggests in *Between Occultism and Nazism* that some mystical elements were more deeply rooted and that the regime's criticism of occultism was often inconsistent.[32]

One obvious forerunner of the Nazi party had been the Thule Society, a *völkisch* (nationalist, folkish) group established under the leadership of Rudolph Freiherr von Sebottendorff (the assumed aristocratic identity of train driver's son Adam Alfred Rudolf Glauer) in Bavaria in the final stages of the First World War. The Society adopted a variant of the swastika as its emblem and combined anti-Marxism and vehement anti-Semitism with an assortment of occult notions and practices (sometimes referred to as 'border sciences'): the role in the world of unseen mystic forces and the use and value of chiromancy, phrenology, graphology and astrology.[33] The movement's founder was a prolific and widely read writer on astrology. Members held to a myth of a lost northern continent, the original home of 'the Aryan race'. Though Hitler himself never joined the society, his biographer Ian Kershaw describes the Thule membership list as reading 'like a *Who's Who* of early Nazi sympathisers and leading figures in Munich'.[34]

Among Thule members were Rudolf Hess (Nazi deputy leader from 1933, an enthusiast for astrology, parapsychology and homeopathy), Alfred Rosenberg (the party's leading 'theoretician', drawing up what passed for an ideology with strands of racism, paganism and supernatural imagery), and the journalist and mystical poet Dietrich Eckart, who acted for a time as tutor to Hitler in oratory and dramatic self-presentation. In January 1919 three Thule zealots – Anton Drexler, Karl Harrer and Eckart – formed the nationalist and anti-Semitic DAP (Deutsche Arbeiterpartei, German Workers' Party). Hitler was recruited in September. 'Goodness, he's got a gob,' Drexler had said on first hearing him address a meeting. 'We could use him.'[35] The DAP was renamed the NSDAP (Nationalsozialistische Deutsche Arbeiterpartie, National Socialist German Workers' Party) in February 1920 and Hitler – his oratorical talent marking him out as the party's dominant personality – took control a year later.

Hitler retained an interest in some aspects of the pseudo-science he had first encountered in his rootless drifting life in pre-First World

War Vienna. He embraced, for example, the 'World Ice Theory', which argued that Aryan man's origins were in 'divine sperma' brought to Earth by meteors, unlike lower races – Jews, Slavs, black people – who were descended from apes. The universe and solar system had been created, the theory said, by blocks of ice falling into the Sun, triggering an explosion. Followers claimed the theory represented a total explanation and evidence of the superiority of German (and later Nazi-oriented) science over mainstream natural science, which was condemned as 'Jewish' in its fundamentals. The editor of the virulently anti-Semitic Nazi tabloid weekly *Der Stürmer*, Julius Streicher, and Walther Darré, the party's prominent 'blood and soil' enthusiast, shared Hitler's belief in radiesthesia, the ability to detect the presence of animate and inanimate objects by use of pendulums and rods. Immediately after President Hindenburg appointed him Chancellor in January 1933, Hitler summoned a dowser equipped with a divining rod to use his skills to deal with potentially life-threatening cancerous 'death rays' at the Reich Chancellery in Berlin.

Astrology was the aspect of the occult with which de Wohl was most involved, though he would always want to argue there was no connection between the two. He insisted there was nothing magical about the link between the stars and human existence. By the end of the 1930s many practitioners and adherents of what they insisted was a 'science' had no doubt that Hitler not only believed in astrology but that he was guided in his actions by advice from astrologers, so much so he had a professional team working for him. This was despite the lack of any solid evidence and the fact that Hitler had only once at this point openly expressed an opinion on this particular subject. Elsbeth Ebertin, an astrology writer in her early thirties, published a warning and a prophecy about the Nazi party leader in the 1924 edition of her annual almanac, *Ein Blick in die Zukunft* ('A Look into the Future'), published in July 1923. A Nazi supporter had sent Ebertin, Hitler's birthdate and asked for her opinion as an astrologer of his prospects. Without naming Hitler, Ebertin responded in an article in the almanac:

A man of action born on 20 April 1889, with Sun in 29 degrees Aries at the time of his birth, can expose himself to personal danger by excessively incautious action and could very likely trigger off an uncontrollable crisis. His constellations show that this man is to be taken very seriously indeed; he is destined to play a 'Führer-role' in future battles. It seems that the man I have in mind … is destined to sacrifice himself for the German nation … and to give an impulse, which will burst forth quite suddenly, to a German Freedom Movement.[36]

A few months later, on the night of 8–9 November Hitler launched the 'Beer hall putsch', a hastily prepared and half-hearted attempt to seize power in Bavaria. Sixteen Nazis and four police officers were killed in a clash in the Munich streets. Hitler sensibly dropped to the ground when the shooting began, was arrested two days later and put on trial for treason. Told of Ebertin's forecast of 'incautious action' and 'personal danger' by a number of his followers, Hitler reportedly laughed and asked, 'What on earth have women and the stars to do with me?'[37] When Ebertin's prophecy became known she was pestered by politicians from both right and left of the spectrum eager for whatever clues she had to pass on about 'the future'.

What was the astrological explanation for Hitler lurching so clumsily into the November putsch? De Wohl himself gave a detailed analysis in *Secret Service of the Sky*, with all the intricate jargon of his profession:

> Saturn, the father of hindrances, stood in opposition to his seventh House (party!). Jupiter stood in the inimical Scorpio and the Moon (also in Scorpio). Venus stood in opposition to Hitler's Neptune (in the House of Death). *The putsch could not be successful.* Hitler had practically the entire solar system against him … But Hitler himself got away with a short term of imprisonment, thanks to his good Jupiter in his natal horoscope …[38]

This was de Wohl's mental world as an astrologer. After the Second World War, he had a story in *The Stars of War and Peace* on how the Munich coup had been predicted, writing Ebertin and her prophecy out of events, tailored to fit his assertion that Hitler was an enthusiastic follower of astrology. He said that in 1923 the Thule Society founder

Rudolph Freiherr von Sebottendorff, who was also an astrologer, had studied Hitler's horoscope and advised him against attempting a seizure of power or any dramatic political move in the near future. Hitler ignored the warning and ended up in Landsberg prison with Rudolf Hess. Here, according to de Wohl, Hess reminded Hitler of Sebottendorff's prediction that action in Munich would end in failure:

> He had become interested in astrology as far back as 1923 ... Hitler's interest flared up. He had astrological books sent to him and started studying. Soon he realized that the subject matter demanded years of study and experience, and from then on he had experts working for him. Astrology was to provide him with the correct timing of his actions. That, to him, was its main value. Thus started that 'mysterious' and 'uncanny' thing, which was to keep so many people guessing in all the countries of the globe – *Hitler's time-table.*[39]

The Stars of War and Peace was not published until 1952, well after the events concerned, and de Wohl gives no evidence for his story of Hitler's turn to astrology in the wake of the Munich debacle. Nor did Hitler ever mention any sudden realisation of the truth of astrology in *Mein Kampf*, the autobiography he dictated to Hess during their spell together in Landsberg. This was an odd lapse of memory had he undergone such a dramatic realisation of the power the horoscope possessed. If de Wohl's story was true, perhaps Hitler had been reluctant to reveal a dependence on others for guidance. What Hitler did actually say about his state of mind during his imprisonment in 1924 was recorded in his wartime table talk. On the night of 3/4 February 1942 he told his companions, 'It was during this incarceration ... that I acquired that fearless faith, that optimism, that confidence in our destiny, which nothing could shake thereafter.'[40] Was this a hidden reference to astrology?

Two senior Nazi figures who were undoubtedly devoted to astrology were Rudolf Hess and Heinrich Himmler. A dedicated disciple of Hitler from the party's birth, Hess became Deputy Führer when the Nazis took power in 1933. Hess's faith in the reliability of astrology's predictive power had a dramatic effect in 1941 when he made a solitary flight to Britain under what appeared to be the misapprehension he could bring about peace talks and end war with Britain to enable the attack on Russia. Himmler, leader of Hitler's personal bodyguard, the Schutzstaffel (SS), which he skilfully expanded into Germany's most powerful tool for repression, held on to a range of interlinked mystical and racist dogmas. As far as astrology was concerned, in January 1939 – following Hitler's speech distancing the Nazi party from any taint of occultism – he wrote to the head of counter-intelligence, Reinhard Heydrich: 'As you know, I do not consider astrology to be pure humbug, but believe that there is something behind it.'[41]

Heydrich was heard to have mocked Himmler behind his back, comparing him with a notably ambitious German general, saying, 'One is worried about the stars on his epaulette and the other about the stars in his horoscope.'[42] Himmler believed in the power of astrology, but was concerned its benefits should not be too widely shared. He told his personal astrologer, Wilhelm Wulff, 'We cannot permit any astrologers to follow their calling except those who are working for us. In the National Socialist State astrology must remain a *privilegium singulorum*. It is not for the masses.'[43] Wulff later commented in a book he wrote about the influence of astrology in Nazi Germany, *Zodiac & Swastika*, 'One of the strangest features of the National Socialist state was that while it persecuted astrologers and murdered some of them in concentration camps, it saw no harm in employing them for its own purposes at the same time.'[44]

But what about Hitler himself? His recorded utterance on the subject in 1924 – his response when he was told about Ebertin's prophecy – had been a mix of humour and contempt. Yet in the build-up to the Second World War it was asserted with total confidence in Britain and the United States that he believed astrology had a rational basis and that he saw it as a valuable, if not essential, guide to action. The editorial in the September 1939 edition of the British magazine *Astrology* reported:

Recently an eminent American, quoted by the Observer, remarked that Herr Hitler is guided by a board of five astrologers. We have long known that he made use of our art. Presumably non-believers will continue to expatiate on the wonderful power Hitler possesses of acting at the right moment, and will then speak of the strange weakness which led him to employ astrologers, not seeing that the two facts may be related![45]

Writing at the same time, Grant Lewi – described as 'the father of modern astrology in America' – declared in a tone of absolute certainty:

In the fall of 1939, Nicholas Murray Butler came back from Germany with the story, which he said was well authenticated, that Hitler has five astrologers, each of whom reports to Der Führer independently. Hitler takes a cross-section of their opinions and findings and decides what to do, being thus assured that no individual or collective astrologer can betray him.[46]

Lewi was referring to a person of significance. Butler, an American philosopher and diplomat, president of New York's Columbia University for more than four decades, had been awarded the Nobel Peace Prize in 1931 for his work towards improving relations between the European powers. What Butler had not done, for all his eminence, was to explain why he was so certain Hitler believed in astrology to the extent that he employed a dedicated team of men to interpret his horoscope and guide his actions. Was he simply spreading a rumour, one that an intelligence service of one country or another might find useful?

A later story, which had all the hallmarks of having been planted in the press as a mischievous piece of 'black propaganda' by British Intelligence, was a report following the sudden descent of Hitler's deputy Rudolf Hess from the sky in Scotland in May 1941. A special correspondent allegedly reporting from the 'German Frontier' wrote in *The Times*: 'Certain of Hess's closest friends … say that Hess has always been Hitler's astrologer in secret. Up to last March he had consistently predicted good fortune and had always been right. Since then … he had declared that the stars showed that Hitler's meteoric career was approaching its climax.'[47]

4

On 1 September 1939 German troops entered western Poland, armoured columns pushing across the frontier as the Luftwaffe bombed civilian and military targets. Two days later Britain and France – both having abandoned appeasement in March 1939 with their pledge to uphold Polish independence against any external threat – declared war on Germany. De Wohl had confidently predicted in *Secret Service of the Sky* a year previously that a European war was (astrologically) inconceivable, a view his peers shared. How could they have been so mistaken, their readings so out of line with what was taking place in the real world? Now an astrologer by profession, de Wohl could not simply ignore this and offered two explanations. The first, in March 1940, was that in fact they were not essentially wrong. In the midst of the 'Phoney War' (also called 'the Bore War'), the period between September 1939 and May 1940 when there were no significant clashes between troops on the Western Front, de Wohl explained to a reporter at the British astrologers' annual convention in Harrogate, 'What we have had has not been a real war, although hostilities were actually declared.'[48] Thinking along the same lines as de Wohl, Prime Minister Chamberlain naively said in April 1940 that Hitler had 'missed the bus'.

Later, in 1952, de Wohl had worked out a different reason for his failure to foresee the outbreak of war in 1939. As the planet Saturn in transit made a conjunction with Hitler's natal Sun, the portents had not been in his favour, the aspects were bad. In these circumstances, no astrologer could imagine Hitler would be so foolish as to start a war that, given what the planets were saying, would ultimately lead to disaster for him and for Germany. The invasion of Poland in September 1939 had therefore been 'incomprehensible' as far as de Wohl was concerned and Hitler must either have ceased taking astrological advice or ignored what he was being told. 'I certainly do not blame any astrologer who did not predict war for that time. They could not very well expect that Hitler would start a major war under "Saturn conjunction Sun" …'[49] Astrology: correct when it was correct, and correct in another way when it was wrong.

De Wohl had retained his Hungarian citizenship and Hungary was as yet neutral in the conflict. But the fact that he was born in Berlin and had lived prosperously and apparently contentedly in that city from 1903 until his flight to Britain in his early thirties suggested to the authorities he was not entirely above suspicion. His application in 1940 for British citizenship – five years after he had first arrived in London, the earliest possible opportunity – was turned down on grounds that were never explained, despite MI5 raising no objection. Although in no immediate danger of internment as an enemy alien, he was rejected for service in the army and air force and in civilian Air Raid Precautions. He later complained:

> I was not even allowed to dig a trench in Hyde Park. I was angry. I was so angry that I decided that they would have to take me. And as they would not have me as a simple soldier, they would have me as an officer. For this I needed an idea. I looked for it, found it, and went into action.[50]

While developing 'the idea', de Wohl passed the early months of the war writing and continuing his private practice as an astrologer. His clientele had been of interest to MI5, the Security Service, for some time. He was said by an MI5 informant to be charging 'as much as 25–30 guineas' to draw up horoscopes and provide an interpretation of their meaning, a substantial amount at the time and a reflection on the wealth and status of his clients.[51] The first of two personal files opened on de Wohl by MI5 was 'destroyed by fire' when the Luftwaffe bombed Wormwood Scrubs Prison, where the Security Service had moved a few days before the outbreak of war. This makes it difficult to determine what degree of interest MI5 had originally taken in de Wohl and his clients and the nature of the concern the authorities felt about where his true loyalties lay. There are two clues about de Wohl's early relationship with MI5. This first was a passing comment in December 1939 by Guy Liddell, head of MI5's counter-espionage B Division, in his diary: 'This man is one de Wohl. We have considerable records of him as he is already suspect.'[52] Suspected, the context made clear, of being a German agent.

The second clue about de Wohl's pre-1940 involvement with MI5 is in a minute written as the Second World War was coming to a close by the astrologer's handler Gilbert Lennox, then a lieutenant colonel. Lennox wrote:

> It is a fact that he has continually offered his services to the British Government since 1938 and it is also a fact that he has also been employed by the British Government directly and indirectly in various capacities and has undoubtedly done a lot of good work … He has certainly done more for the Allied cause than a great many of his foreign brethren.[53]

From Lennox's statement it is seems that de Wohl was, as early as 1938 – just three years after he had arrived in Britain – offering MI5 information about the clients he was serving as an astrologer. Possibly he was also informing on the activities of some of his fellow refugees from Germany and Austria, a few of whom the Security Service may have suspected were Nazi agents. If the information he had provided since 1938 had already filled a complete file, it would surely have been extensive and detailed. What this amounts to is that before de Wohl began work as an astrologer for British Intelligence, he was a notably active informant for MI5.

The initial steps in de Wohl's wartime involvement with British Intelligence were now about to be taken. The first entry in the surviving volume of de Wohl's personal file is an enquiry to MI5 dated 31 August 1940 from a secret Foreign Office propaganda section known as Department E.H. based in the Cable & Wireless headquarters at Electra House on the Embankment in London. The department had been formed in 1938 following Germany's annexation of Austria. The reason for the enquiry was given as 'For possible employment in Department E.H'. The department subsequently merged with other organisations to form the Special Operations Executive, SOE. MI5 replied that de Wohl had 'a widespread trade in horoscopes amongst highly placed individuals in this country'. He had lately come to MI5's notice, the reply went on (misleadingly given their connection since 1938), over a woman named Margaret Titford. She was suspected of carrying out espionage in Britain for Germany and had been interned early in the war. An informant had identified de Wohl as one of her contacts but when the matter was investigated nothing had been found to implicate him directly. MI5 added that de Wohl's wife was living in Santiago, Chile, though gave no hint as to whether or not this was significant.[54]

Department E.H.'s interest in engaging de Wohl – in what capacity they did not disclose to MI5, but presumably the intention was that he would be using his astrological knowledge in propaganda work – suggested his attendance at a dinner at the Spanish ambassador's residence at which Foreign Secretary Lord Halifax was present had been influential. Ellic Howe, who was acquainted with de Wohl in the Political Warfare Executive, remarked that he 'did his best to frequent Establishment circles'.[55] Once hostilities began he was keen to play a part in, and perhaps benefit from, Britain's war effort against Germany – 'For this I needed an idea' – though in what role was not as yet clear.

If de Wohl was considering offering his talents as an astrologer, another person appeared to have had the idea before him. On 6 March 1940, the minutes of the Services Consultative Committee of Department E.H. noted that the belief in astrology was widespread in Germany. 'There was a rumour that Hitler himself believes in astrology and had employed the services of an astrologer. We suggest obtaining from a well-known astrologer a horoscope of Hitler predicting disaster to him and his country and putting it into Germany by secret channels.' A few weeks later there was a report to the committee on progress, the sardonic tone showing the reluctance there was to take astrology seriously. 'I expect the most carefully worked-out horoscope shortly, but owing no doubt to the hideous nature of the sidereal revelation it has not yet been completed. It is interesting to note that the publication of horoscopes has now been forbidden in Germany. This should increase interest in documents of this kind.'[56] De Wohl made no reference in *The Stars of War and Peace* to a Department E.H. operation, so presumably he was not involved and may have had no knowledge of it. It is interesting, however, that an element of British Intelligence had already been in touch with an astrologer, unnamed, before de Wohl came on the scene.

Electra House had described de Wohl on their request for information to MI5 as 'Writer (on Astrology)'. His latest book, *Commonsense Astrology*, appeared in the spring of 1940, combining a basic primer in astrological methods with forecasts of the likely progress of the war. He believed 'the final peace, the absolute settlement' would come in 1942, though Hitler's 'ferocious, raucous voice will be silenced long before then'.[57] Was he repeating the forecast in *Secret Service of the Sky* that a leading Nazi would be assassinated in September 1938 or 1939? That particular prediction had come to nothing and it would have suited de Wohl for it to have been forgotten. *Commonsense Astrology* was well received by the quarterly magazine *Astrology*, where the reviewer said de Wohl should 'be congratulated for the signal service he has rendered to astrology by the production of this fascinating work'. There was a criticism, though, of the impression he gave that Hitler was his *bête noire*: 'I recommend this book in spite of its political bias.' The reviewer had examined the structure of de Wohl's horoscope for clues about his personality and had discovered there an explanation for his astrological method:

> Mercury in Aquarius, conjunction Venus, conjunction Jupiter, close sextile Moon and Uranus. The Moon and Uranus are in close conjunction in Sagittarius. It is evident, therefore, he is a gifted astrologer, and a very attractive writer. There seems however, in his system, a far too great dependence on transits and transit aspects, a form of quick improvisation …[58]

De Wohl had been busy, also producing a novel, *Introducing Dr Zodiac*, which went on sale early in 1940. Astrology was the central theme. The main character, a Hungarian called Dr Zodiac, meets Hitler at his 'Eagle's Nest' retreat, near the town of Berchtesgaden. Zodiac has been invited on the strength of his international reputation as an astrologer. He rejects the Führer's offer of the post of personal astrologer and goes on through a rigmarole of adventures to expose a Nazi spy ring in London. Fast-paced but superficial, it was typical of de Wohl's output. The book was generally well received, though one reviewer objected, 'There is too much talk in it about the technicalities of astrology for our taste.'[59] One element of the novel's plot, the call to work for Hitler, would later make an appearance in de Wohl's *The Stars of War and Peace*, published in 1952, this time as a real event in his life.

De Wohl had also given his views in March 1940 on the progress of the war at the annual convention of Britain's astrologers in the Yorkshire town of Harrogate over the Easter weekend. He addressed the gathering on what was to become his main theme (and a source of income), 'Hitler and his Stars'. Described as a 'Hungarian astrologer and novelist', de Wohl said in an interview in the local *Yorkshire Post* that Hitler's horoscope showed he was facing imminent danger. Any 'new enterprise' he attempted would fail. 'It is an amazing fact that from his natal horoscope it was clearly visible that the man would come to power in the second half of his life, and also that he would get into real difficulties by overstepping his ambition.'[60] The convention organiser, H. Hosking Burnell, echoed what de Wohl had told the audience. Astrologers, he said, had not the slightest doubt the Allies would win the war. He was certain that Hitler had now passed the peak of his power. 'His end should come violently, but whether by "friends" or enemies we do not know.'[61] Three months later Nazi forces had swept through Denmark and Norway, followed by the Netherlands, Belgium and France, countries Germany would occupy for four years. Hitler's end would come, but not as soon as de Wohl and Burnell had forecast.

De Wohl had confidently declared at Harrogate that any action Hitler took in the near future was destined to fail. Later his story changed and he claimed he had known all along that Germany would launch an offensive in the west 'when Jupiter was in conjunction with his Sun, in May 1940'. He went on, 'I tried to warn; but all I met was embarrassment and suspicion. Then the attack came and succeeded even beyond Hitler's own expectations.' To reconcile the two, de Wohl had to engage in paradox: in Hitler's success in 1940 lay the roots of ultimate failure because he threw away the opportunity to invade and subdue England at once. With British troops withdrawn across the Channel through Dunkirk in Operation Dynamo, heavy equipment and transport abandoned on the beaches, England was 'offered to him on a silver platter'. Instead, Hitler concentrated his armies on crushing France and capturing Paris. 'And for these emotional triumphs he had lost the war. For he who gives England time, loses the war against England.'[62] In fact, the decision to halt German troops outside Dunkirk was taken by army commanders locally who thought it prudent to consolidate in case of a British break out. Hitler had endorsed the decision.

The astrologer recalled that he realised at that moment there was one service he had to offer his adopted country: his knowledge of Hitler's horoscope. But for de Wohl to convince the authorities of his usefulness, he had to manoeuvre himself into position. This was no easy task for an alien novelist, a man seen by the authorities as an individual who – as he put it – went in for 'tea-leaf reading and crystal-gazing'. Astrology had proved useful during the first five years of de Wohl's life in England, a source of income and valuable contacts. A friend, a fellow astrologer, recorded: 'He mentioned quite early on that he had an extensive astro-logical practice, occasionally dropping some titled name or that of a rich refugee tycoon, indicating that he had begun to move in London society.'[63] What de Wohl needed to find now was an influential ally to endorse and promote him, one with a sympathy for and experience of astrology and possessing the necessary political contacts. He found that person in the 44-year-old Romanian ambassador to Britain, Viorel Virgil Tilea.

De Wohl does not say in his recollection of his wartime activities how he came into contact with Tilea, simply that he 'did a great deal of astrological work for him' and that he became a close friend.[64] But Ellic Howe, who knew both men, believed de Wohl was introduced to Tilea by a Romanian banker, Oscar Kaufmann, in the early months of 1940.[65] Through this introduction Kaufmann brought into existence an unexpected chain of individuals: de Wohl, the Hungarian astrologer and refugee from Germany; Tilea, the Romanian diplomat, who went on to live in exile in England; Karl-Ernst Krafft, a Swiss-German astrologer who worked for the Nazis. When de Wohl told Tilea about his interest in astrology, Tilea described experiences he had had with Krafft and how impressed he had been by his contact with astrology.

In the spring of 1937 Tilea, who had not yet been appointed Romanian ambassador to Britain, was in Zurich with his wife, who was undergoing treatment at a clinic. The head of the clinic asked Tilea if he would like to meet an astrologer of his acquaintance, Karl-Ernst Krafft. Tilea said he really had no real interest in the subject but he saw no reason to decline the invitation. He found Krafft – a strong admirer of Germany and of the Nazi racial policies – both personally and politically disagreeable but he accepted the astrologer's proposal to cast his horoscope. When Krafft presented the result a few days later, Tilea was impressed with the revelation of details about his earlier life of which there was no possibility the astrologer could have been aware.

A year later, in 1938, the Tileas were once more in Zurich and renewed contact with Krafft. Now intrigued by astrology following his previous experience, Tilea asked Krafft to co-operate in an experiment. He gave the astrologer two specimens of handwriting, together with the details of the dates, times and places of birth of two individuals. He did not reveal who they were. Krafft returned shortly with horoscopes for both and his written interpretation of their meaning. The first person, he said, suffered from a schizoid personality and was unlikely to survive beyond November 1938. The second, Krafft reported, was in a position of authority but would suffer a reversal of fortune around September 1940. Krafft did not know that the first man was Corneliu Codreanu, founder and leader of the Romanian fascist and anti-Semitic Iron Guard. On 30 November 1938 Codreanu was shot 'attempting to escape' while in prison after being found guilty of sedition. The other person was King Carol II of Romania. On 6 September 1940 he was forced to abdicate by the right-wing government in favour of his more pliable son Michael, who became a figurehead for Ion Antonescu's fascist regime. A month later German troops occupied the country.

On his appointment as Romanian ambassador to London in January 1939 Tilea had embarked on a round of diplomatic manoeuvring to stiffen the British Government's resolve against Hitler's expansion into central and eastern European. Germany had begun making economic demands on Romania, attempting to dominate and then control the market in oil, gas and grain supplies. A pessimistic Tilea claimed he believed a German invasion would be the next step. On 13 March Nazi forces occupied the remainder of Czechoslovakia, violating the

September 1938 Munich Agreement under which Germany had been allowed to absorb the Sudetenland. A few days later, on 17 March, Tilea unofficially disclosed to Lord Halifax, the British Foreign Secretary, the extent of German pressure on Romania. This, combined with the seizure of Czechoslovakia, prompted Britain – joined by France – to end the policy of appeasing Hitler and to guarantee military assistance to Poland, Romania and Greece in the event any of these countries came under attack. This pledge made war inevitable when German troops crossed into Poland in September 1939 and Hitler rejected an Anglo-French ultimatum calling for withdrawal.

German intelligence were well aware of Tilea's hostile attitude to the Nazi regime, his activities in London and of his earlier, and now potentially useful, contacts with the astrologer Krafft. Krafft had left Switzerland for Germany in 1939, moving to a village in the Black Forest. He was taken on by a friend, Heinrich Fesel, an official at the headquarters of the Reichssicherheitshauptamt – Head Office for State Security – which came under Himmler's SS. Krafft was given a job providing commentary on economic and political matters based on his astrological observations. He was paid 500 marks a month. On 2 November he reported in writing to Fesel that he had been studying Hitler's horoscope and feared there was to be an assassination attempt using explosives between 7 and 10 November 1939. Fesel did nothing with the information, simply filing the paper in a cabinet. But the significance of the dates Krafft had given was that on 8 November every year Hitler travelled to Munich to attend a reunion of surviving participants in the 1923 Munich putsch, speaking at the Bürgerbräu beer hall.

Hitler entered the beer hall at 8.10 p.m., mounted the stage, made his speech, and left earlier than had been on the programme, a little after 9.10 p.m.. Ten minutes later a bomb, hidden behind a wooden panel by an anti-Nazi cabinet maker, exploded, killing seven people on the stage. When he heard the news, Krafft sent a telegram to Hitler's deputy Rudolf Hess at the Reich Chancery boasting how he had warned Fesel such an attack was imminent, adding that Hitler remained in danger. Fesel was ordered to retrieve the information, which eventually made its way into the hands of Propaganda Minister Goebbels, who then showed it to Hitler. Though Hitler put his escape down to the working of Providence, both he and Goebbels were impressed by what appeared to be the accuracy of the astrologer's prediction.[66] But rather than being summoned for praise, Krafft was arrested by Gestapo officers and accused of involvement in the assassination plot against the Führer. He was able to persuade them he was not and gave what must have been a convincing demonstration of how he had used astrology to make the prediction.

Having survived the Gestapo's attentions, the part Krafft was ordered to play in the German war effort changed. Goebbels had become interested in the propaganda potential of the prophetic quatrains of the sixteenth-century seer Nostradamus, which were obscure and open to a range of suitable interpretations.[67] Krafft had been studying the work of Nostradamus since the 1920s and believed some verses could be read as genuine forecasts of Germany's rise from ruin in 1918 to triumph under Hitler. Goebbels, more cynically, saw them as another useful weapon to be deployed in psychological warfare and 'black propaganda'. Goebbels recorded in his diary, 'The whole world is full of mystical superstition. Why shouldn't we exploit that in order to undermine the enemy front?'[68]

Early in 1940 Krafft was called to a meeting of prominent Nazi officials, including the Governor General of occupied Poland, Hans Frank, who introduced him flatteringly with the words, 'This is the man who accurately predicted the attempt on the Führer's life.'[69] Krafft produced interpretations of Nostradamus's quatrains predicting Allied collapse in the face of German attack. These were circulated as pamphlets in Germany to boost military and civilian morale. Translated into French, Dutch, English and other languages, they were used to provoke a sense of inevitable British and French defeat.[70]

Krafft's other value to the German regime was his relationship with Tilea, with whom he had remained in contact since their pre-war meetings in Switzerland. Sensitive to the Romanian ambassador's anti-Nazi views and his influential position as a diplomat in London, Himmler's intelligence service encouraged Krafft to write a series of letters to Tilea in the latter months of 1939 and early 1940. These included, as well as reflections on Tilea's own horoscope, opinions on the positive astrological portents of German victory, clearly intended to undermine the ambassador's confidence in the Allies. When Krafft sent a long letter from Berlin in March 1940, Tilea – who had become convinced of Krafft's astrological skill in 1938 – felt sure from its content and tone he held an important position in the regime's highest circles. There was no doubt in his mind what that position was. Tilea's autobiography noted that during this period he received what he described as 'a twelve-page typed letter from Karl E. Krafft, Hitler's astrologer'.[71] The letter according to de Wohl – but not to Tilea, to whom the letter had actually been sent – included a reference by Krafft to 'bad aspects' in Hitler's horoscope suggesting the Führer would die in 1941. 'It is worth wondering,' de Wohl would ask, 'whether he has been courageous enough to tell Hitler about it.'[72]

Ellic Howe – who was acquainted with de Wohl through their joint work in the Political Warfare Executive, and who interviewed Tilea after the war – suggests that what happened next came at the ambassador's instigation. Tilea had convinced himself that Krafft was Hitler's astrologer. Howe writes, 'Since Krafft must be working for Hitler, it only remained to persuade the British to take the necessary counter measures.'[73] According to de Wohl in *The Stars of War and Peace*, Krafft's letters praised Hitler, vilified the Jews, and asserted that Germany's horoscope forecast the country's inevitable victory. Tilea and de Wohl considered whether there was a way to use what they both now believed was Hitler's dependence on astrology. De Wohl's recollection of how their conversation proceeded, while not necessarily entirely reliable, is worth quoting in full for an insight into the sequence of events leading to his wartime connection with British Intelligence:

> Tilea had had enough astrological experience to know that astrology 'worked', but that, he said, did not mean that he could persuade the British War Cabinet to believe in astrology.
>
> And then I suddenly found the formula.
>
> 'Never mind what they believe. What matters is that Hitler believes in astrology; and if I make the same calculations as Hitler's astrologer, I shall know what Hitler is advised by a man in whom he believes. And that should be of advantage to the British.'

Tilea beamed. 'It is an appeal to their common sense. You've got it. It will work, and I shall get you the connections you need.'

He was as good as his word.[74]

The scene was set. Tilea believed Hitler was being advised by the German-Swiss astrologer Karl-Ernst Krafft; de Wohl accepted, or thought it worthwhile to accept, that this was the case. Most astrologers were convinced (and perhaps even flattered) that the Führer took what they had no doubt was a reputable science seriously and was being advised by at least one of their profession. The American academic Nicholas Murray Butler had even confidently informed the world after a visit to Germany in 1939 that Hitler had not just one astrologer, Krafft, but a team of five reporting to him. What view would British Intelligence take? There was one thing of which Tilea, de Wohl, and the astrologers were unaware. Wilhelm Wulff, SS leader Himmler's personal astrologer throughout the Second World War, would write when the dust had settled: 'Early in 1940 the British learned that Krafft was in Berlin and immediately jumped to the completely false conclusion that he *must* be working for Hitler. Krafft never met Hitler – though he would have liked nothing better …'[75] And Ellic Howe – who knew not only de Wohl and Tilea but also met Wulff after the war – had no doubt that 'the Krafft legend … had no foundation'.[76]

5

One writer on intelligence has total confidence that de Wohl did 'so much to make the British Secret Service take astrology seriously'.[77] Was that really the case and, if it was, how did the astrologer achieve this extraordinary feat? It is difficult to reconstruct completely the progression of events over the summer of 1940 that brought de Wohl into his close relationship with British Intelligence. The only information available comes from de Wohl and Howe, who himself goes largely – with some qualification – by what de Wohl says in *The Stars of War and Peace*. De Wohl's version is that Tilea arranged the first of a series of contacts with influential people 'a few days' after their conversation about Krafft's work in Berlin for Hitler. Howe believes developments were distinctly more intricate and that Tilea had already been involved in discussions with the Foreign Office. His version seems the more plausible of the two.

According to Howe – and de Wohl knew nothing of this – the Romanian ambassador had first discussed 'the Krafft business' with Sir Orme Sergeant, deputy undersecretary of state at the Foreign Office. Tilea made three main points: first, that he had been impressed with Krafft's ability to predict events, particularly his forecast of the Romanian fascist Codreanu's death; second, that Krafft was now in Berlin and, he believed, working directly for Hitler; third, that astrology could be usefully deployed in psychological warfare. Sergeant gave the impression he was impressed by the third point, which implied he had been prepared to accept the first two. When Tilea and Sergeant met again, the latter said he had arranged for enquiries to be made, discreetly, of astrologers but none had seemed optimistic that anything positive could come of Tilea's proposal. For that reason, Sergeant regretted, he was reluctant to proceed any further. Tilea, again according to Howe, replied, 'I know an astrologer who is not pessimistic. His name is Louis de Wohl.'[78]

Meanwhile, Tilea's clear sympathy with the Allies had brought him into conflict with Romania's right-wing government in Bucharest, which he ostensibly represented in London. On 23 July 1940 Bucharest Radio announced his recall over the air. A telegram from the Romanian Foreign Minister confirmed the following day that he was to leave the embassy at once and return home. Tilea was given no explanation but told he would learn the reason when he arrived in Bucharest. Tilea met the British Foreign Secretary Lord Halifax on 25 July, showed him the telegram, and said he would be relieved at no longer having to represent a government that had 'cast their lot 100% with the Axis' and with which he disagreed.[79] What Tilea did not tell Halifax was that he had discussed his recall with de Wohl and had asked what advice the astrologer could give him on the basis of his horoscope: whether he should go or stay in Britain.

De Wohl was now in touch with MI5 and his handler was none other than Gilbert Lennox, the army officer turned playwright with whom de Wohl had worked on the play *Storm Centre* in 1936. Lennox was recruited to MI5 on the outbreak of war with the rank of major – his rank when he retired from the Indian Army in 1932 – and was primarily conducting liaison work with the Directorate of Military Intelligence. A fellow MI5 officer involved in Lennox's recruitment described him as a 'hearty soul … a man of the world, shrewd and of sound judgement with a taking manner'.[80] Lennox reported to Dick White, assistant director of MI5's B Division, on de Wohl's dealings with Tilea: 'On Louis' advice he [Tilea] did not return, for which advice he is now said to be devoutly thankful, as he is sure that his return would have cost him his life.' De Wohl had added in conversation, Lennox wrote, that Tilea was 'trustworthy' and if handled properly could prove useful to the Allied cause, particularly in the United States where the ambassadorial title 'His Excellency' would open doors.[81] Tilea sought political asylum in Britain, moved to Oxfordshire with his wife, and was soon engaged in setting up a 'Romanian National Committee'.

Tilea now held good on his promise to de Wohl that he would arrange introductions to influential people who could help with their joint plan. The first meeting was with a small group at Tilea's house, including Earl Winterton – Member of Parliament for Horsham, and until 1939 a minister in the Chamberlain government – and Viscount Horne, who had briefly served as Chancellor of the Exchequer in the early 1920s. They seemed impressed by what the astrologer had to say. A third participant at the meeting, Lord Dundonald – a Scottish peer and former army officer – went on to introduce de Wohl to Mrs Ronald 'Maggie' Greville, a well-connected society hostess. She in turn presented him to Lord and Lady Londonderry, Lady Chamberlain – widow of Austen, Prime Minister Neville Chamberlain's half-brother – and, in the event most significant of all, the Duke of Alba, ambassador to Britain of the newly installed Spanish dictator Franco.

The Duke, who also bore the title Duke of Berwick and had been educated at Eton, was officially recognised as Spain's representative in Britain in March 1939. MI5 were aware he was passing a combination of political gossip and hard intelligence to Madrid, highlights of which were then sent on to Franco's Nazi backers in Berlin. The Duke invited de Wohl to dinner at the Spanish Embassy on 28 August 1940. Among the other guests was Lord Halifax, the Foreign Secretary, and as the evening developed it appeared de Wohl had been invited precisely to meet him. Had Sergeant, the Foreign Office deputy undersecretary, to whom Tilea had mentioned de Wohl, set this up as a way of introducing the two men, as if by coincidence?[82] Dinner finished, the ambassador called on the astrologer to 'tell Lord Halifax about Hitler's horoscope'. De Wohl later recalled:

> At that moment I realised that this was a kind of climax of the chain of seemingly purely social events of the last two weeks; that the evening had as its purpose to give the Foreign Secretary an unofficial opportunity to hear a story too unorthodox to go through ordinary channels … I had not been prepared for this. I had no notes. It didn't matter. By now I knew Hitler's horoscope by heart.[83]

De Wohl addressed his small but influential audience for an hour, in the midst – he later claimed, colourfully and in his customary self-dramatising way – of a German air raid. He gave Halifax an outline of what Hitler's horoscope revealed about his character, noting the times at which he had chosen to act and the connected planetary configurations, outlining the impact future aspects and transits in his chart were likely to have. The foreign secretary occasionally interrupted to question de Wohl on points of detail in what he was saying.[84] It could hardly, then, have been a coincidence that three days after the dinner, on 31 August 1940, the Foreign Office propaganda section based at Electra House contacted MI5 to ask what, if anything, was known about de Wohl as they were considering employing him. MI5 replied the same day: 'Arrived in U.K. 1935. Author and "astrologer". Said to have a widespread trade in horoscopes amongst highly placed individuals in this country.'[85] The reply was confirmation in itself that MI5 had been taking a close interest in de Wohl.

3

A Perfectly Splendid Chap

I

De Wohl flattered himself a few months later with the thought that he had enlightened Halifax at the Spanish Embassy dinner by explaining why Hitler was destined to lead the Nazi regime to destruction in the war. When German tanks and troops had swept their way into France in May and June 1940 they had, inexplicably it seemed, allowed British forces to escape from the Dunkirk beaches and failed to follow up their clear advantage by crossing the Channel to invade England. With Britain still fighting on and so in a position to build alliances, possibly with the Soviet Union and most prized of all with the United States, Germany faced certain defeat. Why had Hitler made what would prove to be such a critical strategic error? Because, de Wohl said, he had been driven by his emotions to seize Paris, something the German Army had failed to do in the First World War, in which he had fought 'as one of William II's simple soldiers'. De Wohl wrote in a report passed by his MI5 handler Lennox to the Directorate of Military Intelligence in March 1941:

> I explained all this to Lord Halifax … and since then I am happy to see that he agreed with me. For in his first interview with the American Press as Ambassador to the United States, he made a statement which

according to the London papers was 'the revelation of a well-kept secret': namely, that Hitler had lost the war in June by going to Paris, instead of going to London.[1]

De Wohl was not sure what part Halifax played directly in developments following the meeting at the Spanish Embassy. He was inclined to believe that Viscount Horne – the former Chancellor of the Exchequer whom he had met at Tilea's house – was responsible for pressing matters forward. Horne had written to de Wohl on 22 August, six days before the Spanish Embassy dinner, thanking the astrologer for sending him an illustrated interpretation outlining what appeared to be a clear-cut relationship between planetary aspects and Hitler's political and diplomatic moves over the past few years. De Wohl highlighted the Führer's successes in particular. According to de Wohl, Horne was impressed and promised he would be discussing what he agreed was the document's importance with 'some of those who controlled the actions of Great Britain'.[2]

After his meetings in the summer with the Foreign Secretary, Lord Halifax, and with Viscount Horne, the former Tory minister, de Wohl was introduced to what he loosely described as the heads of 'various Service departments'. Initially, little seemed to be coming of this and he was not sure whether he would eventually be found what he called a 'niche' where he could carry out astrological work as his contribution to the war effort. He understood why the War Office and the Admiralty might be reluctant to engage him directly. 'The very idea that one fine day a member of the House of Commons might get up and ask whether it was true that His Majesty's Government was employing a star-gazer, made many of my new friends shudder,' de Wohl wrote. He nevertheless set to work on his own account in September 1940, just as the German Blitz on London was about to commence in earnest. 'We were bombed day and night,' he later wrote. 'It was a peculiar thrill to work against Hitler in such circumstances.'[3]

The 'niche' de Wohl had been waiting for took the form of the Special Operations Executive, SOE. In August Department E.H., the Foreign Office's propaganda arm based at Electra House, had sent the form to

MI5 asking what they knew about de Wohl as they were considering employing him, though they did not say in what capacity. In July the process had begun of absorbing the department with two other secret organisations into the SOE under the political leadership of Hugh Dalton, the Minister of Economic Warfare.[4] Formed with Prime Minister Churchill's enthusiastic backing, SOE's role was to organise and conduct sabotage and subversion and to disseminate anti-Nazi propaganda in German occupied Europe. Dalton wrote in his diary, 'The War Cabinet agreed this morning to my new duties. "And now," said the P.M., "go and set Europe ablaze."'[5]

Precisely how de Wohl was recruited into SOE is unclear, but the Director of Military Intelligence, Major General Frederick Beaumont-Nesbitt, certainly believed that was the right place for him. His main sponsor in the organisation was Charles Hambro, a merchant banker, awarded the Military Cross in the First World War, a Bank of England director since 1928, deputy head of SOE's SO2 (operations) section from its formation. He was knighted in 1941 and became head of SO2 in May 1942. Hambro not only gave de Wohl permission to run a one-man self-styled 'Psychological Research Bureau' on SOE's payroll, but provided the money for the astrologer to move in late 1940 from the Maida Vale hotel room where he had been living since his arrival in London to suite 99 on the fifth floor of Grosvenor House Hotel in Park Lane. Ellic Howe, who subsequently worked with the astrologer in the Political Warfare Executive – while not a friend, certainly a close acquaintance – commented, 'The hotel itself is one of London's most luxurious establishments and it struck me that it was typical of de Wohl that he should locate his Psychological Research Bureau at a "good' address".'[6] How de Wohl achieved this vast improvement in his style of life, with the services of a secretary in Hambro's office to select furniture for the suite, he never explained. Did Hambro perhaps feel some affinity with a man who had once toiled in banking, however reluctantly? Hambro was said by one not entirely happy MI5 officer to be convinced de Wohl was 'a perfectly splendid chap and won't hear a word against him'.[7] The money, of which there seemed no shortage, came like all SOE's finance from secret funds, over which there was no parliamentary control.[8]

De Wohl described his Grosvenor House research bureau's officially sanctioned activity as producing what he called 'essays on the psychology of leading men of the Third Reich and a good many other things'. But his real interest, he said, and what he devoted much of his time to, was 'the unofficial side of my work: to check on what Hitler was likely to be told by his astrological adviser'.[9] It was this parallel – and to him the most important and potentially fruitful – activity that he had originally used to present himself to the Directorate of Naval Intelligence and the Directorate of Military Intelligence. These connections came about in what appears a typically ad hoc and casual way. The picture that emerges is of sets of men (with the occasional woman) forming affinity groups to pursue their own pet interests, sometimes regardless of any actual value they had to the war effort. The atmosphere is something like Evelyn Waugh's classic Second World War *Men at Arms* trilogy of novels, in which 'chums' recruit 'chums' over drinks into units for what they intend to be a jolly good war.

2

De Wohl had other irons in the fire and as well as the Special Operations Executive he was in touch with Rear Admiral John Godfrey, Director of Naval Intelligence since 1939. There can be few images more surreal than the combination of a portly and vaguely sinister Hungarian astrologer and a senior naval officer in all his gold-braided glory at the Admiralty. But, as an obituary noted, Godfrey saw earlier than many the need for 'elaborate deception of enemy intelligence; for psychological warfare …'.[10] The meeting's immediate result was little short of sensational. The Director gave the impression that de Wohl had not just convinced him, he had overwhelmed him. He eagerly accepted the astrologer's proposition and took immediate steps to persuade his naval superiors to share his interest. Godfrey's enthusiasm led to what must be one of the most remarkable documents ever circulated by a senior naval officer. On 30 September 1940, the Director (known to his subordinates as 'Uncle John', but also described as 'formidable'), despatched a note to the First

Lord of the Admiralty (the navy's political master, A.V. Alexander), the First Sea Lord (Admiral of the Fleet Sir Dudley Pound), and the Vice Chief of the Naval Staff (Vice Admiral Tom Phillips) headed 'Advice tendered to Herr Hitler' and marked 'By Hand'." Godfrey declared in a tone of absolute confidence:

> It has been known for some time that Hitler attaches importance to advice tendered to him by astrologers, and that he studies the horoscopes, not only of himself, but of his own Generals and his more influential opponents.
>
> It should be observed that astrology is claimed to be an exact science and that given the hour, date and place of birth (without the name) all reputable astrologers will arrive at roughly the same conclusion. This being so, it is not a science which lends itself to deception as in astrological circles the deception would soon be bowled out.

The text read as if de Wohl had stood at Godfrey's shoulder personally dictating it word for word, as he may very well have done. The Director described de Wohl in the memorandum as an 'expert astrologer, whom I have met'. Godfrey went on:

> The significance of Hitler's astrological researches is not therefore whether or not we believe in them or if they represent the truth, but that Hitler believes in them, and to a certain extent bases his acts on the opinions and predictions of his astrological experts.
>
> It therefore follows that this approach is one that should not be ignored, and might well be turned to practical use. The names of the astrologers who work for Hitler are known, and he has recently also acquired the services of a Swiss. In astrological circles they are names of repute.

The Director of Naval Intelligence had clearly been impressed when they met with the way de Wohl presented his proposal and the astrological – as opposed, perhaps, to the factual – background he delivered. De Wohl's skill in pitching a plausible story, honed writing fiction and in his pre-war meetings with publishers and film producers, was undoubtedly in play. What was strange, even alarming, was that Godfrey left the impression he accepted entirely and unquestioningly what de Wohl was saying. This was despite the fact that in his role as Director, Godfrey insisted his subordinate officers worked to a scheme of grading intelligence rigorously in terms of reliability on a scale from A to E before passing information on. He had persuaded the War Office and MI6, the Secret Intelligence Service, to adopt similarly stringent procedures.[12] He was even said to have warned his officers against indulging in any kind of 'crystal-ball gazing' when making their assessments. Godfrey was described as 'exacting, inquisitive, energetic and at times a ruthless and impatient master ... with his own quick and penetrating mind'. He was also seen by some as 'highly strung'.[13]

Now, when it came to what de Wohl had told him about Hitler's reliance on interpretations of his horoscope by a team of astrologers, the Director gave every sign of having swallowed the story with no hesitation. Godfrey was certainly no tyro. Fifty-two years old, he had held commands at sea and staff posts at the Admiralty before his appointment as Director a year previously. Ian Fleming, the writer of the James Bond books, served in Naval Intelligence during the Second World War and partly based Bond's MI6 boss 'M' on Godfrey, with whom he had worked closely.[14] In their discussions, did Godfrey ask de Wohl the source of his information about the names and numbers of astrologers reputedly in Hitler's service? 'It has been known for some time' hardly seemed adequate. Without firm confirmation, the plan Godfrey was proposing to put into action would be constructed on the flimsiest of foundations.

The belief that Hitler relied on astrology when making crucial decisions was, of course, widespread. Similar rumours had spread through Britain about the German Kaiser in the First World War. The implication was that both were suffering from a shameful weakness, an aberration, while paradoxically acknowledging the Führer's success and ascribing this to astrological advice. In December 1939 one British newspaper reported that Hitler had despatched his favourite astrologer, 'Dr Huber', to a concentration camp. There were any number of suggestions about the German leader's superstitious beliefs. He was said, for example, to be a follower of numerology. One paper said he had been told his lucky number was seven and that explained why he took his most dramatic actions on Sundays. In October 1939 another newspaper reported that Friday was his lucky day and it was then he could be expected to make his move. Hitler did once bring numerology up in conversation. 'I myself would never launch an attack on the thirteenth, not because I myself am superstitious, but because others are.'

Did the British public find it easier to accept the stories that Hitler was influenced by astrology because they themselves were seeking guidance in their lives from horoscopes? The first newspaper astrology column had appeared in the *Sunday Express* in 1930. The feature proved so immediately popular that other newspapers and magazines soon followed suit. A survey in London shortly before war broke out found two-thirds of women believed or partly believed newspaper horoscopes, though the proportion of men was a fifth. A government investigation a year or so later estimated four in ten British people had some interest in astrology, but – apart from among what the report called a few 'neurotics' – this was at a superficial level.[15]

Godfrey concluded his 30 September 1940 memorandum by presenting what he obviously saw as a useful example of the possibilities astrology promised. De Wohl had told Godfrey the names of two astrologers he said were advising Hitler – Fritz Brunnhuebuer and Karl-Ernst Krafft.[16] Godfrey set out what the astrologers were 'probably' advising Hitler on the basis of their reading of his horoscope:

The most favourable period for Hitler's enterprises will be from 28th October 1940 until 9th March 1941, particularly from 6th to 28th December. In addition there is a short favourable period on 12th and 13th October.

Between September 15th and October 19th, and especially October 1st to 14th, conditions are generally unfavourable to Hitler. Such conditions recur from March 8th 1941 to April 10th, and again between April 18th and May 5th 1941.

It is not suggested that Hitler will only act when Brunnhuebuer tells him his luck is in, but it seems probable that Hitler would not take personal charge of an enterprise unless the stars favour him.

When Godfrey continued with the theme in a further memorandum on 1 October 1940, there were signs of wariness in the Admiralty's higher reaches about the Director of Naval Intelligence's new-found fascination – it could almost be described as infatuation – with astrology. He proposed carrying out an 'historical analysis' to determine how far Hitler's actions might be related to properties in his horoscope. De Wohl had already been working on this and had provided Lord Horne with examples in the summer. Horne had said he was impressed. The wording of the Director's 1 October memorandum showed how thoroughly he had even begun to absorb astrological terminology:

This would involve a close study, not only of the extent to which Hitler's astrological 'aspects' have been borne out by subsequent events, but an analysis of the horoscopes of his principle advisers, Generals and Admirals, and of the Statesman, such as Mussolini, with whom he has had dealings.

The formation of a group of sincere astrologers prepared to work on these subjects is by no means a fantastic idea and is one which could certainly be organised.

At this point came the revelation of how persuasive the Director's astrologer had been: 'My belief is that Mr de Wohl, with whom I am in close touch, could organise such a group.' If Hitler had a team of astrologers advising him, then Naval Intelligence would take the same path. The First Sea Lord, Sir Dudley Pound, commented dismissively at the foot of the minute the same day: 'Interesting but I should like to work on something more solid than horoscopes.' Pound did not say, but must surely have thought, while Naval Intelligence was delving into the occult why not try a ouija board or a séance? On 2 October the Admiralty's political head, A.V. Alexander, wrote briefly, 'I agree with the 1st Sea Lord.' Another officer contributed drily, 'We might have a new department of NID.'[17]

Despite the doubts expressed by both Pound and Alexander, Godfrey maintained his interest and despatched two Naval Intelligence officers to set about recruiting a team of astrologers. Their understanding according to one of the officers, Ewen Montagu, was that having a group of astrologers working would overcome the problem of individuals using different working methods, with possibly conflicting results. An astrologer in Berlin might be operating with one predictive approach, an astrologer in London with another and the results – because astrology was not as scientifically reliable as de Wohl and others liked to claim – could be, if not contradictory, then at least inconsistent. Montagu thought the problem was not insurmountable. 'One *might* get round that if one tried a lot of astrologers and if experience showed, as time went on, that the lucky periods in one horoscope did in fact coincide with times when Hitler took a plunge, one would at least have something to work on.' He concluded laconically: 'So Ted Merrett and I were sent round to a vast number of astrologers. The results were very entertaining but useless. However, it *might* have worked and, surely, was well worth trying.'[18]

As far as Naval Intelligence were concerned, an initial enthusiasm for de Wohl's scheme had begun to wane as quickly as it had arisen. De Wohl did not mention his involvement with Rear Admiral Godfrey in his post-war memoir *The Stars of War and Peace*, apart from a general reference to 'the heads of various Service Departments'. There could be two reasons for this. The first may have been de Wohl's disappointment that, after an eager reception from Godfrey had raised his hopes Naval Intelligence would take astrology seriously, the project had come to nothing. As important, or probably more so, was the reaction of MI5 officers when de Wohl first presented a manuscript of his memoir for inspection in 1945. The astrologer revealed in his draft what could only be viewed as a worrying lapse in security, a scene in which de Wohl sat in the Director's office while Godfrey read out to him the names and birth dates of admirals in the Royal Navy to enable de Wohl to cast their horoscopes.[19] To allow that to become public knowledge would be embarrassing in the extreme, raising awkward questions about what exactly had been going through the minds of senior naval officers at one of the most perilous moments in British history.

One interesting question is what had de Wohl told the Director for him to find the proposal so persuasive? Was it simply de Wohl's ability to make a compelling case? Or was the Director so short of sources of intelligence at this stage of the war that, as Montague said, it 'was well worth trying' – anything was worth trying? There seems no substance to the suggestion from Ellic Howe – who worked in the Political Warfare Executive and is often a useful source of information about what was happening behind the scenes – that Godfrey was 'speedily posted a few thousand miles away from London when it was discovered that he was actually beginning to believe in astrology'.[20] De Wohl and Godfrey were in contact in late 1940. The Rear Admiral remained Director of Naval Intelligence in London for a further two years and was not moved east by promotion to a new role commanding the Royal Indian Navy until 1943, hardly a hurried transfer.

Persuading the Director of Naval Intelligence, briefly at least, to take astrology seriously was one thing, but for de Wohl to have convinced the Chiefs of Staff of the three armed services there was something in the stars can be seen as truly astounding. It was a sign of their desperation for intelligence of any kind from any source. De Wohl's revelations to Godfrey about how a study of Hitler's horoscope gave a clue to the timing of a German invasion made their way in October 1940 from the Admiralty, via the Joint Intelligence Sub-Committee to the War Cabinet Chiefs of Staff committee. This resulted in a minuted record of a discussion this vitally important group of men held as remarkable as Godfrey's notes to his Admiralty colleagues of 30 September and 1 October.

The committee was made up of the armed forces' most senior figures: Marshal of the Royal Air Force Sir Cyril Newall, Chief of the Air Staff, chairing the meeting; General Sir John Dill, Chief of the Imperial General Staff; and Vice Admiral Thomas Phillips, Vice Chief of Naval Staff. Also present was Major General Hastings Ismay, War Cabinet deputy secretary, Prime Minister Churchill's personal link between government and the armed forces chiefs. The first item on the agenda was preparation for what seemed a likely German invasion of Britain. A major input into one outstanding paragraph in the minutes of the 18 October 1940 meeting would have come from the Admiralty's representative, Vice Admiral Phillips, and it is so remarkable it is worth quoting in full:

> The Committee discussed the likelihood of an invasion being attempted in the immediate future. It was pointed out that information received from the Joint Intelligence Sub-Committee suggested that a period starting on the 19th October appeared to be favourable. During this period the moon and tides were suitable, the incidence of fog likely, and Hitler's horoscope, a sign to which he was reported to pay considerable attention, was favourable during this period. Invasion was not, of course, to be regarded as inevitable; nevertheless, the situation demanded increased vigilance and a higher degree of readiness.[21]

So seriously did the joint chiefs view the possibility of a German attack in the period beginning 19 October – a prediction de Wohl came up with through his reading of Hitler's horoscope – they agreed that 'Service Ministries should be instructed that, from the 19th October, all forces prepared to resist an invasion should be held at an increased state of readiness.'[22]

De Wohl would not have known at this crucial point in British history – if he ever did – that his influence as an astrologer had extended as far as the War Cabinet, albeit without his name being mentioned. Had Prime Minister Churchill known about the advice de Wohl was giving British Intelligence, he was asked a few years later. 'I am not at all sure about that. I have never enquired.'[23] But there was one thing of which neither the astrologer nor the combined chiefs of staff were aware, something Hitler's horoscope had failed to reveal to the astrologer. By the time of the 18 October meeting Hitler had already abandoned any intention of invading Britain.

On 16 July he had issued a war directive ordering preparations to begin for mounting 'Operation Sealion' if Britain had refused to accept a negotiated peace settlement by the middle of August. On 19 July he made what he called an 'appeal to reason' to Britain 'to avert the destruction of a great world empire', while simultaneously building up a flotilla of barges in Channel ports to ferry 500,000 men across to England. But for the attack to have certainty of success, German forces needed air superiority over southern England. The Royal Air Force's frustration of the Luftwaffe's efforts in the Battle of Britain denied them this, Germany's first major setback of the war.[24] In September 1940 Hitler assembled his senior military commanders to inform them he would postpone any invasion until at least the spring of 1941, but that they should maintain the impression an attack on England was still in active preparation. In reality, troops in France originally earmarked for the mission were to be released for deployment against the Soviet Union.

3

While awaiting an official response to the suggestions he had made at that summer's round of meetings, de Wohl had produced a nine-page report dated 14 September 1940 with the title 'The Astrological Tendencies of Herr Hitler's Horoscope September 1940–April 1941'.[25] What he claimed he was able to do was to reproduce exactly the advice Hitler was being given by what he insisted was the team of astrologers working directly for the Führer.

> This is not the place for a long dissertation about the elements of astrological knowledge. It may suffice to say that Hitler regards the good and bad aspects of his horoscope as the <u>factors of good and bad luck</u>. He will hardly hesitate to undertake action under bad aspects, if this action does not necessarily need the support of 'luck'. When, however, he is up against heavier odds, he will wait 'until the aspects are good', id est, until he has luck on his side.

This, de Wohl told his prospective readers, was why Hitler had failed to make any move from October 1939 to April 1940, the period of 'Phoney War' between the German subjugation of Poland and the invasion of Denmark and Norway. 'He likes to start action under New Moon ('Lunation'), as this is fortunate for an enterprise according to astrological teaching.' The purpose of his paper was, de Wohl went on:

(1) To find out when Hitler is likely to undertake major action. This is, of course, in agreement with his 'good aspects'.

(2) To find out at what time or period of time Hitler is 'badly aspected' and therefore believes to be unlucky.

He will in such case either do nothing at all, or else leave action to others.

If British forces were to undertake a major action *against* Hitler when he was 'badly aspected', the astrologer said, that would have a discouraging effect on him. 'He knows he is not lucky then, which affects his self-confidence.' He went on to list the periods in which Hitler would be advised by his own astrologer his luck was bad: 16 September to 19 October 1940, 8 March to 10 April 1941, 18 April to 5 May 1941. The 'periods of luck were from late October 1940 to the first week of March 1941, which suggested this – for Hitler – would be the most favourable time to mount an invasion of Britain.

De Wohl then went into greater detail, laying out his full report in two columns. The first gave what he called an 'astrological interpretation', with comprehensive descriptions of aspects and transits that only an experienced astrologer could possibly understand. The second column was the 'meaning', a relatively simple explanation for the layman. As the British Government's overriding fear after the fall of France in June 1940 was of a German invasion, and the area in which the intelligence available was at its most meagre, de Wohl focussed on the likelihood of this. What exactly was in Hitler's mind? During September 1940, he said, the advice the Führer's astrologers would be giving him ruled out any action in which luck would play a part. From 15 September onwards the outlook for Hitler was 'decidedly unlucky'. De Wohl concluded for the month as a whole, 'The idea of invading Gt. Britain before the gales of the Equinox under bad planetary tendencies must be strongly opposed by astrological advice.' Hitler would use the time to prepare his forces for the offensive.

Hitler's bad luck would continue into October and his astrologers would be advising him to avoid committing his forces to any major action. On the contrary, de Wohl said, 'If we should be in the position of dealing a military blow to him between Sept.15th and Oct.19th, and especially between Oct.1st and 14th he knows that luck is against him.' The position would change in November, when the movements of the planets would create a revival in Hitler's fortunes:

From Oct. 30th on we must expect Hitler to move as from now on his aspects become better and even good, although not as good as in May/June 1940. We have here the beginning of a good period for him, lasting up to the middle of February 1941.

As he knows that after this his aspects will become bad again, his interest must be to finish us off until February latest if there is any hope from a military point of view of doing so. The Neptune position may make him believe in FOG being an ally for an invasion.

De Wohl's predictions of likely events in December 1940 were bizarre in the extreme, moving into strange waters. What he was saying would have perplexed any military or political observer, leading them to wonder if he was allowing his creative imagination to run too freely. December would certainly be favourable for Hitler, the astrologer said, but would be unfavourable for Mussolini, the fascist leader of Italy, Germany's ally. Hitler, de Wohl declared – shifting from straight astrological forecast into what he described as 'astro-diplomacy' – faced two possibilities: 'Either he must conclude the war by victory over England and use Mussolini's bad aspects by forcing him into a bad peace or he will lure him into major action so as to see him humiliated through a defeat of the Italian Army or Navy.' Why? Because, de Wohl said, as far as Hitler was concerned there must not be two giants in Europe. Any victory in war must be entirely German, not German-Italian:

> He is clever enough to calculate that Gt. Britain can afford to make peace if she has 'saved her face' by at least defeating the Italians ... He needs a purely German hegemony at the end of the war. Hitler knows that if peace is not achieved by the end of February he is due for very bad aspects.

In a 'Supplement' to the report, de Wohl said his comparison of the horoscopes of Hitler and Mussolini showed as personalities they were 'natural enemies' and were bound to dislike each other intensely.[26] Hitler, according to de Wohl, even arranged conferences with Mussolini when the latter's chart was badly aspected. The astrologer claimed that Hitler had forced Mussolini to declare war in June 1940, 'when the Italian is badly aspected'. Mussolini, he said, 'does not know that Hitler is using his astrological knowledge against him'.

De Wohl forecast that January 1941 was 'good' for Hitler but February would be the last such fortunate month. 'All that has not been done yet will have to be done more quickly and it may include another peaceful arrangement which, however, has little chance of success. We must not give up now – very soon he will be under most discouraging influences.' March promised to be even worse. From the ninth of the month 'the aspects become very bad, and the factor of luck is not any more on his side.' The worst days for him would be 12 and 13 March, 'but all the surrounding days are bad too.'

What in this, apart from the astrologer's tone of absolute conviction, had so impressed the Director of Naval Intelligence? Had Godfrey been so short of the intelligence he needed to understand Hitler's motivation and intentions that he was grateful for what de Wohl had to offer? For lack of anything else, the access to enemy thinking the astrologer offered must surely have been tempting. Two writers on British Intelligence believe this was the case and that the feeling of desperation went wider than Naval Intelligence.[27] As Peter Fleming, an officer in British Intelligence, later wrote of the 'story-book atmosphere of those exciting months. Almost anything might happen, almost anything was worth trying.'[28] At the height of the invasion scare in the summer of 1940, the Directorate of Military Intelligence briefly employed a water diviner called 'Smokey Joe' – he was in the Royal Engineers – who claimed he could reveal from afar when German troop-carrier barges were concentrating and their future movements. He was able to operate for a time – based in Yorkshire, with pay and expenses – before being exposed as a charlatan. Even then he turned up again in April 1945 in some obscure official role, crossing into Germany with Field Marshal Montgomery's 21st Army Group.[29]

Why would senior intelligence officers be prepared to turn to water diviners and astrologers for a clue to Hitler's intentions when his overall aims had been set out in *Mein Kampf*, the book he dictated to Hess in prison in 1924? Neville Chamberlain had read the book, even going so far as to annotate his copy. Though Hitler was an opportunist, seizing chances as they came, the broad thrust of his ambition could be found there.[30] But the problem with *Mein Kampf* was that the English mentality found it difficult to take its author seriously: the text was the literary equivalent of the goosestep, menacing but at the same time laughable. The assumption the senior British figures who were aware of *Mein Kampf* made was that as he did not share their ways of thought, his unpredictability must be driven by something else. That something, the opinion had become, was the irrational, the occult, the movement of the planets across the sky. If the answer to the urgent question they were asking – 'When will they invade?' – was not to be found through any of the classic sources of intelligence then, as Fleming put it, 'Almost anything was worth trying', even turning to an astrologer for guidance.

4

De Wohl's dealings with Naval Intelligence's army counterpart, the Directorate of Military Intelligence, were arranged through his theatrical acquaintance, Major Gilbert Lennox – MI5's liaison officer with the Directorate – and MI14. The latter had been set up in August 1939 to devote specific attention to Germany (including, subsequently, German-occupied Europe) and Nazi forces' order of battle. According to a former member of this small section, one of MI14's tasks was 'to advise the Chief of the Imperial General Staff what Hitler would do next … the most pressing problem was to gauge how likely Hitler was to invade England.'[31] MI14's head was Lieutenant Colonel Kenneth Strong, a former British military attaché in Berlin. According to one historian, because there was a lack of 'precise and reliable intelligence on the enemy' Strong was persuaded by the War Office to entertain the services of unusual individuals like 'Smokey Joe' and de Wohl.[32] Strong, however, had his own view of de Wohl and had been particularly impressed by one piece of the astrologer's work. De Wohl was never less than persistent in pressing what he believed was the valuable combination of astrological interpretation and psychological insight at his command. Strong did complain in his memoirs that in the summer of 1940, when the prospects for Britain were at their bleakest, MI14 was 'plagued by all sorts of people – some of them cranks – who felt they had a definite contribution to make to winning the war'.[33] Strong did not put de Wohl into the 'crank' category, at least not yet.

On 17 September 1940 Lennox reported to Dick White, assistant director of MI5's B Division, on a discussion he had had with the astrologer over lunch:

> He handed to me an essay, which I had requested him to write, on German psychology and counter Nazi propaganda. I have shewn the essay to Lt.-Col. Kenneth Strong of the German Section, and in his opinion, it is absolutely correct in every detail, and he considers the writer a very clever man. Strong thinks that if ever a proper propaganda section is founded, then Louis' place would be with that section, and he considers that a man with Louis' knowledge and experience would be extremely useful. I am passing this suggestion on to D.M.I.[34]

On 21 September Lennox himself went even further in praising de Wohl, writing to White that de Wohl's essay was 'most excellent', that it was not only Strong who had been impressed but also Major

General Frederick Beaumont-Nesbitt, the Director of Military Intelligence. De Wohl's paper, Lennox added, was now being read by the Vice Chief of the Imperial General Staff, Lieutenant General Sir Robert Haining.

All appeared to agree that de Wohl was reputable and reliable, though there was the sign of a possible sting in the tail. Beaumont-Nesbitt had suggested to Lennox, MI5's liaison officer with Military Intelligence, that de Wohl would be useful at Electra House, the propaganda section Department E.H., which was in the process of being absorbed into the new Special Operations Executive. Was the general trying to have de Wohl deployed where he would be most useful to the war effort, or was he trying, politely, to wash the Directorate of Military Intelligence's hands of him? If the latter, de Wohl would not be so easily brushed off. Lennox's view was slightly different. He thought it urgent to get de Wohl involved in work of this type 'to keep Louis' idle hands occupied, or rather brain'. What was it about the astrologer's mind that worried Lennox? What was it feared he would do if left to his own devices? This was never spelt out, at least in the pages of de Wohl's MI5 file.

There were two other matters in Lennox's letter to White that had clearly been nagging at de Wohl and which he must obviously have brought up with his MI5 contact. The first was his hope of securing British nationality. He often, when he mentioned British prospects in the war, wrote 'we' to underline where he wanted to be seen as standing. As a Hungarian citizen de Wohl was an alien, though not as yet an enemy alien. But the way in which the situation was developing in Hungary, it was only a matter of time before the country entered the war on Germany's side.[35] In that case, de Wohl could face internment. Lennox told his MI5 colleague it was 'essential' that de Wohl be given British citizenship, 'by way of payment to Louis for what he has done, and also to have a very definite hold on him, at least this is D.M.I.'s opinion ...'. He added that the Directorate of Military Intelligence had asked whether MI5 could do anything to expedite de Wohl's naturalisation.[36]

What other services had de Wohl been providing British Intelligence? It could not just be his essay on Nazi psychology, however informative and insightful some seemed to have found it. Nor could it be his offer of astrological insights into Hitler's strategic and tactical intentions. Little of significance in this line had yet emerged. Was it his role in persuading the Romanian ambassador Tilea to remain in London, where he might prove useful in holding together anti-Nazis exiles from that country? Had de Wohl been supplying information to British Intelligence on what MI5 had described as 'highly placed individuals' among his astrological clientele? None of this was immediately spelt out, though it would be shortly, but Lennox was adamant that de Wohl should be rewarded 'for what he had done'. The need 'to have a hold on him' ran parallel, with MI5 often showing signs of concern about both de Wohl's allegiance and his potential for causing embarrassment.

The second issue involved something that had been bothering de Wohl since he was rejected for military service of any kind on the outbreak of war in September 1939 even, as he had put it, from helping to 'dig trenches in Hyde Park'. He wanted an appointment, a uniform, and a rank. There is a tone of friendly mockery in the way Lennox put this, a laughing reference to the astrologer's flamboyant personality and natural exhibitionism. 'I am only sorry,' he wrote, 'that Louis' own heart's desire of giving him a commission and appointing him to a Highland Regiment cannot be granted. The sight of Louis in full Highland dress would have been the most cheering spectacle.'[37] Lennox, ex-Indian Army but a theatrical like de Wohl, was anxious to see his friend's vanity satisfied.[38]

White's reply to Lennox on 27 September 1940 showed how seriously de Wohl was being taken by MI5 and by Military Intelligence, how convinced both organisations were that he had worthwhile services to offer to the national war effort. White was as keen as Lennox that the astrologer should become a British subject. He arranged for de Wohl's Home Office file to be sent across so he could see for himself how the application was proceeding. He suggested Lennox should ask Military Intelligence to play their part by contacting the Home Office naturalisation branch. The Directorate should say they would appreciate a speedy resolution as they intended to employ de Wohl 'in an advisory capacity on German matters'. White added they should emphasise the fact that

MI5 would not oppose de Wohl's naturalisation and 'in view of a considerable amount of further knowledge regarding this man … they were no longer prepared to raise objections to his naturalisation'.[39]

What this 'further knowledge' was and what MI5's previous doubts were White felt he did not need to spell out. But a few weeks later Lennox revealed a particular service de Wohl had provided in the past, and was continuing to provide. Writing to a fellow MI5 officer, Major Kenneth Younger, Lennox said de Wohl – whom he described as one of 'the funny people who report to me' – was working with British Intelligence while at the same time carrying on his private practice as an astrologer:

> He numbers among his clients a great many interesting people, including some of the good and the great. As it is often of considerable interest to know who is consulting an astrologer and for what reason, and it is sometimes even more interesting to hear the advice which the Stars give, I have made a private arrangement by which I get reported to me the names and details of Louis's clients.[40]

'Reported' by the astrologer himself Lennox was presumably saying. Was this genuine anti-Nazi activity on de Wohl's part, or had he been trying to ingratiate himself with British Intelligence as a step towards obtaining citizenship? Perhaps both. As an astrologer, he was not bound by anything resembling the sanctity of the confessional, though a client might expect discretion. There seemed something dubious about de Wohl passing private information, trivial though much of it might be, to MI5. He was carrying out the role of informer, one for which he was paid twice – first by his clients (at as much as 30 guineas a session), secondly by the intelligence services through his Psychological Research Bureau.

Despite the support MI5 were prepared to give de Wohl over his citizenship application, there was suspicion about his position as not only an alien, but one who had lived in Germany from birth until he fled the country at the age of 32. He had said himself in *I Follow My Stars* in 1937 that he had not suffered any direct persecution by the Nazis. Was it possible he was playing a double game with British Intelligence? Was he a potential fifth columnist? This was a natural anxiety when Britain faced the prospect of German invasion any day. On 2 October 1940, not long after White's letter supporting the astrologer's naturalisation, Lennox of MI5 met de Wohl for what seems to have been their regular lunch. The MI5 officer asked what he knew about two people: Titford (who had been placed in internment as a possible threat to national security) and another suspect called Boyle. Both had been marked down by MI5 as German agents. Lennox told White the next day he had 'jumped' de Wohl, 'put him through it', and used 'a certain amount of common or garden blackmail' about his hopes of obtaining British citizenship to get him to talk. The astrologer said he knew nothing about either Titford or Boyle and Lennox came away convinced he was telling the truth. 'He was desperately anxious to give any information he could.'[41]

The Titford case involved a Czech-born woman originally named Margaret Otto, now living in London. She had entered into what was clearly a marriage of convenience before the war to obtain a British passport. Leaving her husband not long after they were married, she became a prostitute and had been arrested and convicted three times. When one of Titford's clients, a petty criminal and police informant now working as a War Office driver, told her where he was working her interest was aroused and she offered him 'big money' for any information he picked up. The head of MI5's counter-espionage B Division, Guy Liddell, recorded in his diary that Titford told the driver she had 'numerous other contacts and that she required him to act as courier between this country, Basle, Lausanne and Zurich'. A few days later Liddell noted, 'Our informant in the Titford case has extracted from the lady the name of one of her principals. This man is one de Wohl. We have considerable records of him as he is already suspect.' Liddell added that a meeting had been arranged in Bath involving the informant, though it was unclear who else would be involved.[42]

Lennox's 3 October 1940 letter to White skimmed the surface of what both would both understand was the astrologer's possible involvement in the Titford case. Lennox questioned de Wohl at lunch about Zurich, where, incidentally, the former Romanian ambassador Tilea had first come into contact with Karl-Ernst Krafft, still thought by many to be Hitler's personal astrologer. De Wohl told Lennox he had never stayed in the city, had merely passed through, and his only contact there was 'a woman who is an agent for some astrology paper'. Were MI5 concerned de Wohl might be in touch with the Swiss-German Krafft and indirectly through him with Hitler, or at least with German Intelligence? Or was de Wohl suspected of working directly as a German agent, that he had come to Britain in 1935 for that purpose? Liddell's note in his diary suggested that might very well be the case. Lennox's letter to White continued, 'I asked him for the names of any German harlots whom he had ever met in this country.' De Wohl thought and then recalled a Mrs Self, a German with dyed red hair married to an Englishman. Lennox believed she was the now the interned Margaret Titford. No more seems to have come of this, though doubts about de Wohl remained.

An officer of MI6, the Secret Intelligence Service, also raised questions with MI5 about de Wohl, specifically about his wife, who had been living in Chile since the beginning of 1939. The MI6 officer – apparently unaware of de Wohl's relationship with MI5, the Directorate of Military Intelligence and the Special Operations Executive – told Dick White their 'representative in Montevideo' had reported on 28 November 1940 concerns about the activities of Alexandra Wohl – 'known locally as La Baronesa' – in Santiago. She had been seen regularly with Germans known to be Nazis and had received batches of airmail letters, many originating in Germany. The MI6 officer enclosed copies of two intercepted telegrams between de Wohl and his wife. 'It may of course he that she is hard up for money as her telegrams appear to indicate, but there may be something more in it.'[43] The question from MI6 suggested they too feared de Wohl was a Nazi plant, communicating with Berlin through her, or at least that he was vulnerable to pressure from German intelligence through his wife. Lennox replied, confirming he knew de Wohl and that there had been an above-board arrangement through the Westminster Bank since March 1939 for him to transmit money to his wife, which he occasionally neglected to do when he was low on funds.

De Wohl's hope of gaining British citizenship was to be disappointed for the time being. A notice appeared in the personal column of *The Times* on 5 November 1940, an announcement by the Aliens

Department at the Home Office that Louis de Wohl-Mucsiny had applied for naturalisation. Anyone with reason to believe this should not be granted was asked to let the department have a written statement setting out all relevant facts. One letter arriving at the Home Office showed every sign of professional jealousy. R.H. Naylor, resident astrologer at the *Sunday Express* since 1930, protested against even considering allowing de Wohl the privilege of British citizenship. He complained that de Wohl had 'under an atmosphere of great secrecy been publicising a claim that he has been appointed official astrologer to the War Office'.[44] Despite de Wohl having the backing of both MI5 and the Directorate of Military Intelligence, the Home Office rejected his application and he retained his unwanted and uncomfortable alien status for the remainder of the war.

5

In November 1940 de Wohl gave his MI5 contact Lennox a series of pen portraits of leading German Army personalities – based on a combination of astrological interpretation (but based only on Sun signs) and psychological analysis – to pass to Military Intelligence. At the outbreak of war, Military Intelligence had discovered they had little information on the qualities and figures of senior German Army personnel. Astrology, the consideration seemed to be, was probably better than nothing. De Wohl later explained why he considered information of this kind was a valuable weapon in the hands of British military commanders and political leaders:

> The main reason for working out Solar equations for my long list of German high-ranking officers, from *Generalmajor* to *General feldmarschall*, was not of a purely psychological nature. It was clear that Hitler chose his generals not only according to their character traits, but also from the point of view whether they were 'lucky'. In this he was following Frederick the Great's maxim 'I demand of my generals that they are lucky'.

But Hitler went a step further, motivated – according to de Wohl – by the German leader's long-running belief in the essential part astrology played when he came to make strategic decisions. 'He did not simply demand that they had good fortune, he preferred to make sure of it, by appointing them, whenever possible, at a time when they had good aspects ahead of them.'[45]

Two of the astrologer's pen portraits are available in released War Office files, those of generals Wilhelm Keitel and Walter von Brauchitsch. There is an interesting scribbled comment by an unidentified MI14 officer on a paper attached to the file, which reveals the ambivalent feelings about de Wohl's contributions in some parts of British Intelligence. The officer quotes the view of the classical scholar W. W. Tarn on 'Greek-Babylonian horoscope writings' – 'Rubbish!'. The officer then adds, 'But Hitler is believed to fall for it!' As well as providing a sketchy character analysis based on his construction and interpretation of their horoscopes, de Wohl outlined briefly what he called the 'chances' for each of the generals from November 1940 through to December 1941. Keitel had been General Field Marshal and Chief of Staff of the High Command of the Armed Forces since 1938. His submissiveness and constant flattery of Hitler as a political and military virtuoso earned him the nickname *Lakeitel* (lackey) among fellow officers.[46] De Wohl's badly typed and idiosyncratically worded portrait of Keitel gives a taste of what British Intelligence might expect from his astrological readings:

> Strong critical faculties, much method and precision. Rather irascible. Sharp intellect, but fondness of tricks. Vane [sic] about his own clever-ness. Ambitious. Can be extremely disagreeable to inferiors, humble to superiors. What they call in Germany a 'Radfahrernatur', a 'cyclists' nature': bending his back to all that is above, trodding [sic] on what is below. Capable of self-deception. Presumption can cause setbacks. Well capable of wrong decisions in the decisive moment. Should be decidedly unpopular. Looks like an upstart's Horoscope to me.[47]

De Wohl's analysis of Keitel's 'chances', or luck, found late 1940 and early 1941 to be 'neutral', after which the situation promised to become more active. March 1941 was 'not too good', April 'better, but not without dangers', May 'the same, except for May 17–25, which are good'. June was 'not bad', July 'not without danger, but good'. August 'good', September 'not so good'. October was 'good and bad mixed, dangerous', November 'the same', and December, ominously, 'very dangerous'. What a military intelligence analyst was meant to make of this is difficult to imagine. De Wohl concluded that Keitel's horoscope 'fits well with Hitler's Horoscope', which suggested he would remain in his post for some time to come. Keitel did indeed retain his position until the end of the Second World War, when – after his leader's suicide – he signed the unconditional capitulation of German armed forces in Berlin on 8 May 1945. Tried at Nuremberg for war crimes and crimes against humanity, he was executed in October 1946.

The astrologer's second character analysis was of von Brauchitsch, whom de Wohl seemed to find personally appealing and gave at first reading a more flattering description than that of Keitel. Descended from a long-established Prussian military family, von Brauchitsch had been appointed commander-in-chief of the German Army in 1938. De Wohl was almost certainly unaware that von Brauchitsch was personally indebted to Hitler, who had persuaded the general's wife to accept a divorce and paid the costs of proceedings, enabling him to marry staunch Nazi Charlotte Rueffer, under whose strong influence he then came. Von Brauchitsch was seen by his military peers as weak and compliant, incapable of summoning the nerve to confront Hitler, even when he disagreed with his military judgement. Only a hint of this appeared in de Wohl's analysis, and that came in a roundabout way. But he concluded with one notable prediction:

> Doubtlessly a Gentleman. Should be good looking and elegant, type of cavalry-officer of the ancient regime. Generous, intelligent, patient, diplomatic. Sound views. Conservative and yet progressive. I can not find anything bad to say about that man. I rather like him. Should be exceedingly popular with his men. Judgment very good, generally, but 'the wrong sort of inspiration' under bad Transit-aspects can spoil a lot. A man who … can survive a score of different regimes without losing

his position. Reason: clever diplomacy in the mask of polite frankness. Although this man can hardly be a Nazi at heart, his Horoscope fits well with that of Hitler, except for the Neptune-position: which makes it certain that there is not absolute frankness between the two. I am not going so far as to say that B. may betray Hitler – but it is not quite out of the question.[48]

De Wohl forecast that von Brauchitsch's 'chances' for late 1940 and early 1941 were 'fairly good'. April was 'good, but not without dangers', May would see 'dangers, and yet not bad', June 'not too good', July 'very good, in spite of dangers', but August was 'dangerous throughout', as were September and October. November was 'very dangerous' and December 'neutral'.

Von Brauchitsch's star had shone brightly during the triumphant advance through the Low Countries and France in 1940, as they were to continue to do through the campaigns in the Balkans, and the early stages of the attack on the Soviet Union in the summer of 1941. But his lustre began to fade with the failure to seize Moscow and inflict a rapid defeat on the Red Army, though the blame for the setback could be ascribed as much to Hitler's interference as to his commander in the field. De Wohl's later unusually combined astrological and meteorological explanation for the general's failure was that 'when Saturn became conjunct, his Jupiter position was first slowed up (Saturn – duration and limitation) and then brought to a complete standstill by the Russian winter'.[49] In November 1941 (a 'very dangerous' month, as de Wohl had prophesied) von Brauchitsch suffered a heart attack. Hitler dismissed him from army command in December and he was relegated to the reserve. He was aware of the plot to assassinate Hitler in July 1944, but not actively involved. Arrested at the end of the Second World War by the British, von Brauchitsch died from pneumonia on the eve of trial before a military court on a charge of crimes against humanity.

One question was left hanging in the air. Interesting as these astrological depictions of senior German military commanders were, despite their impressionistic and almost gossipy form, was there any likelihood that British generals would soon be facing them in the field? Unless

Britain intended to mount an invasion of Western Europe in the course of the coming year (or if Germany were to invade England), the answer was 'No'. In which case, what use was this information, what purpose did it serve? Did it contribute anything to discovering the secret of German military strategic thinking, what the Wehrmacht's next moves were likely to be? Or was de Wohl simply clearing his throat, preparing the ground for his real intention, which was to act as British Intelligence's commentator on the workings of Hitler's mind?

In what he told Lennox was his 'first long report about Hitler's Horoscope', de Wohl forecast that the Führer would not order any major land action between August and the end of October 1940, but that he could be expected to provoke some form of clash between the last days of that month and March 1941 at the latest. The beginning of any action would most likely coincide with the New Moon.[50] During what the astrologer forecast would be a quiet period, Hitler ordered preparations for Operation Sealion, then postponed and effectively abandoned the invasion of Britain when the Luftwaffe failed to wrest air supremacy from the Royal Air Force in the skies over the Channel and southern England. Germany's military effort against the British Isles was then confined to bombing raids on the cities.

At the end of September 1940 Germany signed the Tripartite Pact with Italy and Japan, a pledge of mutual assistance between what became known as the Axis powers. In February 1941 a German army was deployed in North Africa to stiffen Italian troops falling back under British pressure. By the end of March, the position was reversed. The Afrika Korps under Rommel had driven the British from Libya and back into Egypt, threatening the Suez Canal and, beyond that, the Middle East oil fields. At the beginning of April, Germany invaded and quickly overwhelmed Yugoslavia and Greece. How far had de Wohl forewarned British Intelligence of any of these reverses on the basis of his reading of Hitler's horoscope?

4

WHEN HITLER KNOWS HE IS LUCKY ...

I

What was extraordinary as the year 1941 opened was what de Wohl – a refugee living a comparatively impoverished existence in 1939, a novelist, a part-time astrologer, occasional gambler, still not entirely trusted by MI5 – had accumulated. Rejected by every branch of the armed forces for service, he had persuaded the British authorities to place him on the public payroll under the guise of the 'Psychological Research Bureau' – a one-man band it was true, but impressive-sounding nonetheless – and to furnish him with a suite of rooms in one of London's grandest hotels. The scrappiness of his typed reports suggested one thing he lacked so far was regular secretarial help. But what he still desperately longed for was the official acknowledgement of his status signified by an army commission and a uniform. His father had, after all, been a cavalry officer in the Austro-Hungarian Empire. A fellow astrologer, Felix Jay, visiting his friend at Grosvenor House after his dream had been realised, described coming 'face to face with Captain de Wohl, dressed in a splendid officer's uniform, complete with a Sam Browne, an expensive, leather-covered cane lying in a chair and an enormous beautifully tailored greatcoat hanging near the entrance door ... Louis was like a boy who had just received his Christmas presents.'[1] How had this finally come about?

There is, as with most aspects of de Wohl's life, a mystery about when and how he became a British Army officer, even whether the commission he held was genuine. An air of masquerade always hung about him, a sense of things not being quite what they seemed. De Wohl's story in *The Stars of War and Peace* says simply that he became a captain 'later', at some indeterminate time after he had set up the Psychological Research Bureau. His friend Jay dates his sighting of de Wohl in uniform as 'late 1940', though as he was writing some years later he could easily have been mistaken about the date. What sounds like the definitive – and ludicrous – version comes from de Wohl's MI5 handler, Lennox, the man who said he wanted more than anything to see his friend kitted out in full Highland regalia. In 1942 Lennox explained to an MI5 colleague in a file note how de Wohl had come to acquire the rank and pay of captain. He said de Wohl had been taken up personally by Charles Hambro for attachment to the Special Operations Executive and that it was he who arranged things for the astrologer. He was to be given the three pips and pay of a British Army captain:

> On de Wohl enquiring when he would be sworn in I gathered that a ceremony was staged at the Horse Guards in which Brigadier Gubbins [later head of SOE] swore him in, following the wording of an ordinary recruit's Attestation Form. Even apart from this farce de Wohl had every reason to believe and still believes that he is a Captain in the British Army. Indeed, as he has never been told he is not, I presume technically he is still, in fact.[2]

De Wohl it therefore seemed both was and was not a commissioned officer, though he had every reason to believe he was entitled to the uniform, pay, allowances and status that went with it. He was attached to no military unit and commanded no men. A colleague of de Wohl's in the Political Warfare Executive, Ellic Howe, adds to the uncertainty by providing three different versions in *Astrology and Psychological Warfare* as to the way in which the astrologer might have acquired his rank, only the third of which bears much resemblance to Lennox's account. He goes on to paint the picture of a 'tall and running to fat' de Wohl in officer's uniform 'walking down Piccadilly looking just like an unmade bed'. But when Howe contacted the Ministry of Defence in the 1960s to ask about the astrologer's commission, a Directorate of Manning official told him they had no record of an army officer called de Wohl.[3] There is also no announcement in the wartime *London Gazette* – where all military and naval commissions and promotions were posted – of de Wohl ever having been officially appointed captain. His uniform when it came to it was no more than fancy dress.

2

It is worth looking in detail at what exactly de Wohl was offering British Intelligence in his astrological evaluation of Hitler's strategy. Was the information relevant? Was it accurate? Was it useful? He passed three reports to the Directorate of Military Intelligence through his MI5 handler Major Lennox in early 1941: on 6 January, 21 January and 21 February. These provided a test not only of his competence as an astrologer (which would naturally be hard if not impossible for an intelligence officer to judge, unless he was an astrologer himself), but also what practical use his interpretations of Hitler's horoscope might be. As background, an astrologer of de Wohl's acquaintance wrote after his death: 'Retrospectively it is clear to me that Louis' astrological wisdom was entirely second-hand and that like the film script writer he had been, he served up the evergreen ingredients garnered from others in an attractive, amusing and often sensational manner.'[4]

De Wohl's claim was not that he was acting as a shadow military strategist but was simply providing British Intelligence with insight into what advice a German astrologer would be giving Hitler. In this way, as it was commonly believed that the Führer relied on astrological guidance when making decisions, it would be possible to gain a valuable insight into his thought processes. De Wohl described his role clearly: 'To check up on advice likely to be given to Hitler by his astrological advisers (including German Astrologer Fritz Brunnhuebuer and the Swiss Astrologer K.E. Krafft, whose collaboration with Hitler I have been able to prove) …'[5] This sounds like a purely technical process – draw up the horoscope, read off the transits and aspects. What strategic or tactical value could this have? Did de Wohl have any military experience to determine this or did he see himself simply as passing on raw information for those who did have that experience to interpret and put to practical use? When de Wohl's reports are examined, what becomes clear is how many imaginative leaps he takes, perhaps a necessary part of the astrologer's art. Is it then just a version of his fiction? As de Wohl had put it in *Secret Service of the Sky* in 1938, 'The astrologer's work of deduction has to be aided by exceptional intuition, a very precisely working brain and that little touch of genius …'[6]

On 6 January 1941 de Wohl compiled what he called a 'Report about the astro-political situation in the Balkans', issued on Psychological Research Bureau headed paper.[7] He began by apologising for the fact that the report was necessarily 'rather incomplete' because he did not know the birth hour of King Boris of Bulgaria and he had no birth data on a number of major figures in the Balkans story, including the Bulgarian prime minister, King Peter of Yugoslavia, and Prince Paul, the country's Regent.[8] This suggested that – given how crucial accurate and precise details of place, date and time were in constructing a horoscope – any conclusions de Wohl drew would be sketchy at best.

De Wohl dressed up his report with astrological jargon, as if to satisfy the officers of the Directorate of Military Intelligence he was not simply making things up. King Boris of Bulgaria's horoscope was, he said, a 'peace horoscope', with Jupiter remaining in trine with Venus, as it had been a month earlier. He went on: 'In February the situation changes decidedly for the worse, and the famous conjunction of Jupiter falls in square to the King's Sun and Mercury.' He forecast that the king would be 'unlucky' in February and March and prospects for the rest of the year hardly seemed better. De Wohl reported that he did not see how Boris could 'remain out of trouble' and that even abandoning his throne was not out of the question. 'Comparison between Hitler's and the King's horoscopes shows many hostile aspects. On the other hand, no action against Bulgaria need be expected before 30 January.' He had gleaned this latter point from his study of Hitler's horoscope:

That Bulgaria is at the moment very much in Hitler's mind is certain. Hitler's good aspects at present and up to the end of February are Jupiter trine Moon, Jupiter trine Jupiter and Saturn trine Jupiter. Both Moon and Jupiter are in Capricorn in Hitler's map, and Capricorn rules Bulgaria. (It also rules India, by the way).

He then turned to the prospects of Greece, Bulgaria's southern neighbour. Italy had invaded Greece on 26 October 1940, troops crossing the border from occupied Albania and encountering unexpectedly determined resistance. The Greek Army had driven the Italians back in a counter-attack – the first Axis setback on land of the war – but there were continuing clashes between the two armies. De Wohl reported that King George of Greece had a 'very strong' horoscope and that the conflict would run on through 1941. He doubted Germany would intervene in support of a stumbling Italy before – 'at the earliest' – February. 'Hitler knows that Mussolini's bad aspects extend up to the end of this month, and he is hardly likely to risk "good money for bad business", to use commercial language … The King's aspects in February are not so good, but they will be better in March, still better in April and splendid in May …'

Hitler, de Wohl continued, had no confidence in Italian military commanders and would have been told by astrologers that Mussolini's aspects were 'still bad, and those of the King of Greece still good' for the rest of January. But there was something of interest he wanted to offer:

The horoscopes of Hitler and King George [of Greece] compared with each other do not make it likely that one will suffer through the other – except for one point: Hitler's Neptune is in 'square' with the King's Saturn in the Death sector. This might mean the possibility of a treacherous attempt against the King's life, but it is not at all a certainty.

What were harassed officers in Military Intelligence to make of all this, desperate as they were to get solid information on events? Once the astrological jargon – aspects, trines, sectors, Jupiter, Neptune, Saturn – was stripped out, was de Wohl telling them anything definite, anything useful for those with the task of determining British strategy? More of a similar nature was to come.

De Wohl issued a further report under the Psychological Research Bureau brand on 21 January 1941 in the form of a typed note to his MI5 handler, Major Lennox.[9] He claimed that to build the most complete picture possible, he had analysed the horoscopes of Hitler, Britain's King George VI, the British Prime Minister Churchill, the Foreign Secretary Eden, the Irish Prime Minister de Valera, the head of the Luftwaffe Goering, and the German generals Keitel and Brauchitsch. What he had to reveal was forceful in expression but remarkably thin on detail. The Royal Navy, despite the initial enthusiasm of the Director of Naval Intelligence, Rear Admiral Godfrey, had lost interest in astrology early on. Naval intelligence had been more highly developed over a longer period than that of the army and officers preferred their own sources and interpretive methods. But Military Intelligence still seemed prepared to listen to de Wohl. 'This is from our friend L. de W. You may care to read,' MI14's head, Lieutenant Colonel Kenneth Strong wrote on a covering slip to de Wohl's 21 January report a few days after it arrived. It was Strong who had been so impressed by de Wohl's analysis of German psychology in September 1940. However, an unidentified officer noted on the slip after reading the astrologer's forecasts, 'If we get more like this someone else's "aspects will deteriorate" in my eyes.'

In his 21 January report, de Wohl reiterated his recent conviction that Hitler only commenced a major action at the New Moon. The fact that he had made no dramatic move since October 1940 should be taken seriously as it signified that he had been engaged in preparation. 'It happens very rarely that Hitler wastes time,' the astrologer declared.

I believe that he is going to strike very soon now, as he knows that he has only got about six weeks left. After the first week of March his aspects deteriorate and are becoming bad already in the second week of March, to remain bad for quite a while. If I would be his Astrologer, I should certainly advise him to strike with all his might by New Moon, Jan. 27th.

As always, de Wohl set out the astrological reasoning he had used to reach this conclusion. Hitler's aspects, he said, were almost as favourable as they had been at the time of the sweep through the Netherlands, Belgium and France in the summer of 1940. 'These aspects are decidedly good (Jupiter trine Moon, appl. trine Jupiter, Saturn trine Jupiter exact) and he simply must use them.' If he failed to seize this opportunity it would signify there was something at fault with 'the entire German war mechanism'. In addition, both King George's and Churchill's horoscopes would be badly aspected on 27 January, while Goering's aspects were good and Brauchitsch's 'not bad'. De Wohl forecast heavier Luftwaffe bombing attacks on Britain, London in particular, where the numbers of deaths would soar. Hitler would also attempt to relieve pressure on Mussolini, though he did not specify where. 'Thus,' de Wohl wrote, 'the astrological stage seems definitely set for the big blow.' There was, however, some hope, an optimistic prospect: 'We must, in all circumstances, resist the attack at least until Febr. 22nd (about), from which date on Hitler's aspects have not anymore got full strength. If we can do that, all is well. But the lives of our main personalities should be well guarded!' What did this latter cryptic remark mean? Assassination attempts? He did not say.

De Wohl's 21 February 1941 report, under the heading 'Hitler's Present Military Policy', was richer in detail, running to three pages of single-spaced typing and dealing in depth not only with Western Europe, but ranging widely across the international scene.[10] He said Hitler's greatest disappointment had been that Britain had refused to recognise her vulnerability and to accept his peace initiative following the swift collapse of France in 1940. But he was unlikely to attempt an invasion before the end of May at the earliest. 'Up to then he will only try things for which he does not need exceptional good luck.' There would be increased U-boat activity against shipping and intensified bombing raids, particularly from late April onwards. The astrologer continued:

Both these matters are not of a decisive nature, although they are the necessary preparation for the decisive stroke in summer. He has done his best to construct something like a United Europe under his more or less benevolent rulership. There is however still a number of independent or semi-independent countries left. From East to West: Turkey, Bulgaria, Greece, Yugoslavia.

One essential fact had always to be borne in mind: 'When Hitler knows that he is lucky, he risks anything.' From March to May 1941 he would be out of luck. This, de Wohl said, explained the renewed peace efforts Hitler appeared to be making through Emperor Hirohito of Japan. Hirohito's present aspects – 'Jupiter conjunction Sun, Saturn conjunction Sun' – fitted him perfectly for the role of mediator. De Wohl suggested the best policy would be to play up to Hitler's hopes that he could reach an agreement with Britain:

> It could be an astro-diplomatic masterstroke on our part if we could <u>pretend</u> to take the mediation seriously into consideration, thereby seemingly fulfilling Hitler's last phase of good aspects for some time (up to the first week of March inclusive) – and to cause an incident of some sort at the beginning of March so that Hitler's hopes are spoiled. We need not, of course, publish anything about that in the papers – it would have to be an underground diplomatic step of some sort.

The overriding British strategic purpose, de Wohl said, was to prevent Hitler from seizing the military initiative in the coming two weeks. If he did intend to move it would be round the period of the New Moon, 26 February. 'And I think that he will move.' The astrologer foresaw the peaceful infiltration of Bulgaria, combined with intense pressure on Greece. The report then turned to Yugoslavia, which bordered both Bulgaria and Greece. He believed Hitler would try to avoid war with Yugoslavia, though he knew the country 'had bad aspects in the second half of this year, especially in August and September.' If there was any time a move against Yugoslavia would be favourable for Germany, it was then.

As far as the later months of 1941 were concerned, de Wohl raised two areas of major British interest: the Suez Canal and the United States. First, he was convinced astrologically that Hitler was contemplating an advance along the 'Great Way East', the route Alexandra the Great took in conquering his empire and a progress Napoleon had set out on at the end of the eighteenth century – through Turkey, Palestine, Syria and Persia to India. 'The underlying idea,' de Wohl wrote, 'is to defeat Great Britain by robbing her of the most valuable parts of her Empire – Hitler from our side; Japan from the other.' He foresaw Axis attempts to put the Suez Canal – a crucial link in Britain's sea route to India and the east – out of action, especially in September or October 1941. As far as the United States was concerned, de Wohl said Hitler viewed the country as 'definitely anti-German' and that he might attempt to drag her into the war:

> It may be in Hitler's interest to <u>get her involved before she is ready</u>. This would probably stop a part of the flow of material for Britain, as it will be needed against Japan. And moreover, it might force <u>President Roosevelt to declare war under bad aspects</u> (February 21st–March 21st, Jupiter square Sun, Saturn square Sun), which astrologically would definitely be an advantage.

De Wohl summed up his advice: Hitler would make no major military move before mid-May; there would be action against Bulgaria – but this did not necessarily mean military – and a threat would be made against Greece; the Suez Canal would be in danger in the second half of 1941; the 'gravitation point' at present was the Far East. The astrologer concluded with a surprising proposal. When Britain was still licking her wounds from disaster in France and Belgium, attempting to rebuild and re-equip an army that had only narrowly escaped from Dunkirk, and the fear of German invasion was constant, de Wohl wrote:

> Hitler knows that he is getting into bad aspects soon … What a glorious answer it would be if we could launch an attack against him in the time between March 11th and April 18th (March 18th or April 1st are the best dates, and the worst for him) so as to spoil his timetable, and to make him fight at a time when he does not want to fight, in the strong belief that he is not lucky!

News in March would have convinced the astrologer that someone had taken his advice. De Wohl continued his gung-ho approach in a

6 March 1941 report titled 'Astrology and the War'.[11] An officer's note on the document – 'Major Lennox brings you the latest effusion' – suggested some sections of Military Intelligence were no longer taking the astrologer completely seriously. Despite this his reports continued to be accepted and read.

In his 6 March report, de Wohl praised Operation Claymore, a raid by 500 British commandos on the Norwegian Lofoten Islands two days previously. The troops destroyed factories and shipping in the harbour, returning to England with 300 resistance fighters, over 200 prisoners, and a batch of captured collaborators. A relatively small-scale event, but one that forced Germany to reinforce garrisons in Norway in case of a repetition.[12] Hitler, the astrologer went on, 'is now closely approaching "decrease-of-power" aspects. How I wish we could attempt the re-conquest of Norway, and a direct raid on Germany's war-ports … What a thing it would be to roll up Hitler's front from the North, whilst he is busy in the South-East.' He said his prediction that Bulgaria would remain at peace had been confirmed but that King Boris remained under 'bad aspects'. De Wohl praised General Archibald Wavell, British commander in chief in the Middle East, whom he said was 'getting into most powerful good aspects again soon'. He concluded: 'Our best time is April, Hitler's worst time the second half of April. But then the decisive blows should be dealt, therefore we should start earlier.'

In March 1941, as if anxious to provide convincing evidence of his credentials, de Wohl also sent Military Intelligence a table setting out the future astrological aspects for a range of leading figures involved in 'the great game', as he described the war. 'We can safely assume,' he wrote, 'that a similar table is on Hitler's desk.' He accompanied the chart – composed in black, red and green inks – with a six-page commentary, a rambling, discursive, and in some places animated survey of his past forecasts and future events.[13] What he offered was complex – comprehensible really only to another astrologer – and set out his calculation of the transit aspects from 18 March to 18 May 1941 of Hitler and Goering, King George VI, Churchill, Sir Alan Brooke (commander in chief, United Kingdom Home Forces), Sir John Tovey (commander in chief, Home Fleet), Admiral Raeder (commander in chief, German navy), German generals Brauchitsch and Keitel, Sir John Dill (Chief of the Imperial General Staff), and Sir Archibald Wavell (commander in chief, Middle East).

De Wohl's reasoning in his commentary was that in order to determine Hitler's astrological 'good luck' it was necessary as well to give equal attention to the 'bad luck' of his opponents. 'Astrological timing is a very dangerous weapon, but two sides can use it!' The astrologer set out daily aspects for each of the commanders and leaders he had chosen, denoted by planetary symbols, coloured green for lucky and red for unlucky. He said his table made it possible for any competent astrologer to compare the aspects of German and British leaders on any given day and from that to assess the likelihood of success or otherwise. He added the claim that any layman could easily understand and interpret the table, but one glance at the jumbled handwritten columns of planetary symbols shows this to have been unlikely.

De Wohl repeated his by now familiar insistence that 'since 1923, Hitler has never undertaken a major action unless he had "good aspects" at that time. Whenever, for an undertaking of importance he needed luck, he waited until he knew that he had it. Hence his excellent timing.' The astrologer gave as a clear example of the Führer's reliance on a reading of his horoscope the triumphant conquest of Western Europe, which took the Wehrmacht and Luftwaffe forces six weeks in the summer of 1940. This was followed by a relatively quiet period in which Hitler ordered no dramatic action because of the astrological advice he was receiving. All, the astrologer said, based on guidance he had been given about the significance of transit aspects in his horoscope.

There was a reminder in this of de Wohl's 'prediction' of the loss of the Atlantic liner *Titanic* over two decades after the event, shown to be inevitable, he wrote, when you consulted the horoscope of the ship and its captain, the date the vessel sailed and the time it was launched. The truth was that in March 1940 – weeks before the Germans launched their sweep through Western Europe – de Wohl had forecast Hitler was facing danger and any 'new enterprise' he attempted was doomed to failure. A fellow astrologer at the Harrogate convention – presumably using the same data as de Wohl and Hitler's supposed advisers in Berlin –

had echoed this, declaring that Hitler had passed the peak of his power. Now de Wohl was claiming that Hitler's crushingly triumphant blitz-krieg had come about because he had been guided by a dedicated team of astrologers.

Always fascinated by the relationship between the two dictators, Hitler and Mussolini, de Wohl claimed the German Führer had pushed the Italian Duce into attacking Greece at the end of October 1940. Why? Because he knew Mussolini's aspects were bad at that time and he wished to see Italy defeated. De Wohl had an astrological explanation for this paradox, one that would have puzzled any intelligence officer. 'One of the most predominant features of Hitler's character is his vindictiveness. He never forgets, and he never forgives.' Italy had been a member of the Triple Alliance alongside Germany in 1914, promising mutual support in the event of war, but instead had turned against her friend in 1915 and joined the Allies. Hitler, according to the astrologer, was unable to cast that from his mind and was intent on dragging Italy to destruction. In fact, Mussolini's invasion of Greece took place without Hitler's approval and threatened to undermine the German leader's Balkan strategy, which was one of containment rather than aggression and occupation.

An intelligence officer reading de Wohl's commentary on the multi-coloured table of aspects he had presented would be thinking, 'Yes, very interesting, but what has this to do with today?' The astrologer rambled on with horoscope-based theories on why Hitler had allowed British and French troops to avoid capture at Dunkirk, had ordered his forces to turn instead to seize Paris. He described Hitler's bitter frustration at Britain's refusal to sue for peace on the fall of France, how victory stands already erected in Berlin's Unter den Linden to celebrate Germany's triumph had to be dismantled. Immediate invasion of Britain was ruled out because Hitler's aspects were unfavourable, but he had made military preparations and began the bombing campaign to destroy civilian morale. De Wohl had expected the invasion to take place between late January and 13 February 1941:

He had then still about five weeks of good aspects in front of him. For this is what his astrological advisers were bound to tell him. 'If you want to invade Great Britain, you can only do so between November and the end of February. Afterwards you get bad aspects again. <u>He cannot try it in March. He cannot try it in April. And he cannot try it before the end of May.</u>[14]

De Wohl said that to reach this conclusion he had followed exactly the method Hitler's astrologers would be using 'I have cast and examined all the horoscopes of all the main figures in the great game.' In March, till the end of May, Hitler's, Goering's and Raeder's aspects were bad, while Keitel's and von Brauchitsch's were 'not good'. On the other hand, he had determined that those of the military and naval figures on the British side were 'excellent'. In de Wohl's view, 'To attack these men as long as he has got bad aspects himself would be lunacy.' He went even further, arguing that astrologically a British attack on Germany – her ports in particular – between 18 March and 18 May would be something Hitler must now be dreading. He was still hoping for success through a combination of the U-boat campaign against British shipping and air raids on British cities:

> He may even try to revive the bruised Duce for a while … by helping him in Albania … by threatening Greece. But the last thing he expects is an invasion of Germany. He has had the initiative so long – he does not know that we too check up on astrological aspects. He will not invade us – but it would be the shock of his life to see British uniforms appearing on German soil.[15]

What de Wohl was suggesting about Britain's ability to mount an invasion of Germany (presumably through France and/or the Low Countries) was absurd. British generals and admirals might be 'lucky' astrologically, the aspects in their horoscopes might look good at precisely the time when Hitler's were bad, but more than luck in the charts of two or three officers, however senior, was required to breach the Atlantic Wall and push on into Germany. It was, after all, less than year since a beaten British Expeditionary Force had been driven into the Channel. Was de Wohl being serious? Was he simply militarily ignorant, unaware of the conditions and preparations required to launch a campaign as complex as the liberation of Western Europe? Or was he just playing for time with Military Intelligence, keeping his 'niche' open for as long as possible?

3

Had de Wohl's astrological interpretations in late 1940 and early 1941 been of any real value to British Intelligence? How did his forecasts measure up in reality? The first question had been Hitler's plans for the invasion of Britain, feared as inevitable in the months after the lightning Nazi campaign had subdued France and the Low Countries. What were Hitler's astrologers telling him? De Wohl told the Director of Naval Intelligence, Rear Admiral John Godfrey, and through him the War Cabinet, that the astrological advice supplied to Hitler would be that the period beginning 19 October 1940 was the most favourable time to commence the invasion of Britain. This had been taken so seriously by the Chiefs of Staff – the heads of the army, navy and air force – that they had included this in their warning of the imminence of invasion. De Wohl subsequently told Military Intelligence in his report titled 'The Astrological Tendencies of Herr Hitler's Horoscope September 1940– April 1941' that the Führer's 'good luck' would run from the end of October 1940 to February 1941 and this would be the period for him to 'finish us off'.

In January 1941 de Wohl told his MI5 handler Major Lennox that a 'major action' could be expected from Hitler – again acting in tune with astrological advice on favourable aspects – by March 1941 at the latest. In a 21 February report 'Hitler's Present Military Policy', a detailed document, de Wohl reported that as Hitler was 'out of luck' from March to May 1941 – and would be told so by his astrologers – he was unlikely to attempt an invasion before the end of May at the earliest. Unknown to him, the astrologer was revealing the limitations – if not the absolutely fallacious nature – of his science, or craft, or art. While de Wohl was busily making his calculations, shifting and shuffling the date, feeding the information to British Intelligence – who may or may not have accepted what he was telling them – Hitler had already ruled out an invasion. As a leading biographer of the Nazi leader puts it, 'On 17 September he ordered the indefinite postponement – for psychological reasons, not the cancellation – of "Operation Sealion".'[16]

On 18 December 1940, War Directive No. 21 set out definitively what had now become Hitler's overriding military objective: the destruction of the Soviet Union *before* war with Britain had ended. He was abandoning any thought of conquering Britain for some time to come, if ever. Yet de Wohl continued to set out possible dates Hitler – acting on astrological advice – would have in mind for Germany to mount a cross-Channel invasion. Had any of the horoscope-based information de Wohl had been giving British Intelligence on the likely timing of this attack been of any practical use? It is difficult to see what he was revealing to the military and naval authorities that their own experience, instincts and other sources had not already told them. British Intelligence had been in a position to inform the Cabinet that Hitler would launch his campaign against the Soviet Union in the latter half of June. This information come through Ultra, through which teams at Bletchley Park had been decrypting German intelligence codes since the middle of 1940. Despite this, Military Intelligence had not completely dismissed their astrologer out of hand. He continued to receive the pay of a British Army captain and to pass them the results of his calculations via Major Lennox.

At this stage of the war, late 1940 and early 1941, there were two zones of major military action on land: the Balkans (Bulgaria, Yugoslavia and Greece) and North Africa. How far was de Wohl able to provide British Intelligence with a useful astrological perspective on Hitler's intentions in these areas? Hitler's biographer Ian Kershaw points out that Hitler's strategy in the Balkans was to avoid resorting to force. Once he had decided on Operation Barbarossa – the invasion of the Soviet Union – his aim was to safeguard his southern flank by keeping the Balkan states, already economically linked to Germany, under control but in a state of peace.[17] But it was events on the ground rather than movements of the planets through his horoscope that would make it necessary for him to revise this policy.

As far as Bulgaria was concerned, de Wohl told Military Intelligence on 6 January 1941 that the country's ruler King Boris would be 'unlucky' in February and March and that prospects for the rest of 1941 were hardly better. He said the king's horoscope suggested he might even be forced to abdicate. While sympathetic to Germany, Bulgaria had remained neutral on the outbreak of war in September 1939. In his 21 February report the astrologer foresaw a peaceful infiltration of Bulgaria by Germany. This was borne out on 1 March 1941 when, under German pressure, the government signed an alliance with the Axis and allowed German troops passage through the country to invade Greece. None of this would have come as any great surprise to Britain's intelligence services. Bulgaria took no active part in the German invasions of Yugoslavia and Greece in April nor the attack on the Soviet Union in June. King Boris did not abdicate, but his sudden death in August 1943 at the age of 49 two weeks after a tense meeting with Hitler in East Prussia provoked rumours he had been poisoned. De Wohl had clearly seen some signal in Boris's chart: a monarch's unexpected death could be viewed in the nature of an abdication.

The astrologer's forecasts of developments in Greece in 1941 could hardly have been more out of line with the actual course of events. In December 1940 Hitler had decided any British military presence in the country would pose a possible threat from the south when he launched an attack on the Soviet Union. But in his 6 January 1941 report de Wohl doubted Hitler would intervene to help Mussolini in what had turned out to be a disastrous invasion of Greece: the Führer's aspects remaining 'bad' from March onwards would restrain him from any action. De Wohl reported that King George of Greece's horoscope, on the other hand, revealed improving aspects, soaring to 'splendid' in May. A comparison of George and Hitler's horoscopes together, de Wohl said, suggested it was not 'likely that one will suffer through the other'. His 21 February 1941 report said that from March to May 1941 Hitler would be 'out of luck', though he foresaw 'pressure' on Greece. In fact, the form this pressure took was a rapidly concluded invasion of Greece through Yugoslavia and Bulgaria in April, the period when de Wohl said Hitler would be least lucky, and advised as such by his own astrologers. German troops entered the Greek capital Athens on 27 April, completing their campaign by seizing the island of Crete by the end of May.

What contribution had de Wohl's predictions made to those attempting to determine possible future developments in Greece? Very little, it seemed. Under an agreement with Greece as early as April 1939, Britain had pledged military assistance should the country's independence be threatened. British troops had been based on the island of Crete – southeast of the Greek mainland – since October 1940. The Royal Air Force despatched squadrons of aircraft to mainland Greece the following month. British and other Commonwealth troops landed at the port of Piraeus from bases in Egypt on 2 March 1941, following agreement at a meeting between the king and British Foreign Secretary Anthony Eden in Athens on 22 February. It was unlikely de Wohl's reports had prompted this. King George, rather than benefiting from 'splendid' aspects in May, had been forced to flee the mainland to Crete on 23 April, travelling from there to England, where he lived in exile for the remainder of the war. Possibly his escape from the Germans and survival could be interpreted astrologically as 'splendid'. None of this, however, was a testimonial to astrology as a predictive tool.

Similarly with Yugoslavia, which bordered both Greece and Bulgaria. In his 6 January 1941 report on the Balkans, de Wohl implied Hitler would not attack Yugoslavia, though he saw 'bad aspects' for the country in the second half of the year. On 25 April 1941 Yugoslavia formally joined the Axis powers by signing the Tripartite Pact, as Bulgaria had done in March. Air force officers opposing this entanglement with Nazi Germany mounted an immediate coup in Belgrade, repudiating the agreement. Hitler – not wanting a troublesome country to the south two months before his projected invasion of the Soviet Union – ordered his troops into Yugoslavia on 6 April. The ill-equipped Yugoslav army – facing attacks on three fronts – surrendered eleven days later, well before the appearance of the 'bad aspects' de Wohl had seen for August and September. He had, though, complained in January that he had no birth data for King Peter and Prince Paul, the country's Regent. As his method was to draw up horoscopes of a country's leading figures, this was hardly the best recipe for making an accurate astrological reading of Yugoslavia's fate.

The second area of major military activity was North Africa. De Wohl specifically mentioned the Suez Canal as an enemy target in his

21 February report entitled 'Hitler's Present Military Policy'. He forecast particular efforts to put the canal out of action in September and October 1941. It would have taken a particularly incompetent intelligence officer not to be aware of that possibility without the benefit of astrological advice. Italy had declared war on Britain and France on 10 June 1940, as Hitler's sweep across Western Europe was reaching its climax. On 14 June British forces in Egypt launched raids across the border into Libya, an Italian colony since 1912. There followed a run of attacks and counter-attacks by British and Italian armies between Egypt and Libya until the Italian 10th Army was virtually destroyed in Operation Compass in late 1940 and early 1941. Hitler despatched the Afrika Korps to Libya under General Erwin Rommel to bolster the Italians. Disregarding orders simply to hold the line, Rommel instead began an advance against British forces on 7 April, pushing deep into Egypt, threatening the Suez Canal.

In his 6 March 1941 report to Military Intelligence, de Wohl had picked out General Archibald Wavell, commander of chief of British forces in the Middle East, for particular praise. He said Wavell was 'getting into most powerful good aspects again soon'. This – coming after the rout of Italian forces in Libya in Operation Compass, the first British success on land in the war so far – suggested greater things could be expected of him. But with the arrival in North Africa of Rommel and the Afrika Korps, the luck de Wohl forecast would accompany Wavell as a commander began to run out. In February he was ordered by Churchill to despatch his most experienced troops to join the battle for Greece, a move Wavell opposed but had to acquiesce in. Churchill personally disliked Wavell and he was removed from command in the Middle East following his defeat by Rommel in June 1941 in Operation Battleaxe and despatched to India. A few months later Wavell was seriously injured when he fell from a pier. What was British Intelligence to make of these turns of events when de Wohl had forecast 'powerful good aspects'?

What of the biggest story of all, the main event, the German invasion of the Soviet Union? De Wohl's analyses of Hitler's horoscope in 1940 and early 1941 did not reveal that the Führer intended to break the August 1939 pact with Stalin and begin the final struggle with

Bolshevism. The astrologer missed this entirely. As with his failure – along with most astrologers – to foresee the outbreak of war in 1939, there had to be an explanation for this. He had to devise a reason for not having foreseen the attack on the Soviet Union. The answer was simple: de Wohl had not been mistaken, the horoscope had not been wrong, the fault – he explained in *The Stars of War and Peace* – was with Hitler himself:

> We are told that Hitler undertook the war on astrological advice. Yet there is no astrological system that could possibly regard the Russian enterprise as propitious and, moreover, Hitler himself admitted that he had no made use of astrological advice. He said so publicly, but it has been conveniently forgotten. In December 1941, when he dismissed Field-Marshal von Brauchitsch and took over himself, these were his words: 'In future I intend to follow my intuitions again.'[18]

This, de Wohl insisted, confirmed that while Hitler had certainly made his moves on the basis of astrological advice in the past, so far as the attack on the Soviet Union was concerned he had ignored his astrologers, acting against what the stars were telling him. What in fact Hitler was saying was that he no longer trusted his generals – as his dismissal of von Brauchitsch demonstrated – and he would rely in future on his own military assessments, the intuition that he believed had guided him since his confinement in Landsberg Prison.

If astrology had the validity de Wohl was claiming, there would have been some recognisable clue in Hitler's horoscope that the invasion of the Soviet Union would result in disaster, as it did. According to de Wohl, Hitler's astrologers had seen the portents, but the Führer had chosen to ignore their advice. If de Wohl too had seen what was coming, why had he not shared this with British Intelligence? Had he missed the signs? The irony was that (despite de Wohl) the British Intelligence and Churchill's government did know what Hitler planned and Stalin would have too had he been prepared to listen. 'Warnings from the British (who knew the date fixed for the invasion before the end of April) were dismissed by the Russians as troublemaking.'[19]

4

If Louis de Wohl had been given the opportunity to read his MI5 personal file, PF49321, he would have been surprised – even flattered, given how fond he was of attention – by the constant background conversation around him. His connections with the Special Operations Executive (nominally his employer and paymaster), with the War Office, with former Romanian ambassador Tilea, with the clients of his private astrological practice, with his wife and other women, were dissected and mulled over by intelligence officers, sharing their hunches and opinions about this mysterious man, his habits, and his usefulness or lack of it. How dare he claim to be Hungarian, one sneered, because when he was addressed by a Hungarian he was unable to speak a word of the language. In his enthusiasm for denunciation, the officer had not studied the file closely enough to take in the number of times it was explained that, although he held Hungarian citizenship, de Wohl had been born in Berlin, was educated and lived his life in Germany until he left in 1935.

De Wohl's existence in London was a complex web of activity – watching and being watched, reporting and being reported on. He was wearing three hats: attached to the Special Operations Executive to undertake propaganda work and producing, as he put it, 'essays on the psychology of leading men of the Third Reich'; passing assessments gleaned from his analysis of horoscopes, Hitler's in particular, to Military Intelligence via Major Lennox, his MI5 contact; and continuing in lucrative private practice as an astrologer. In that latter capacity he was feeding MI5 information about conversations with clients and their horoscopes, with names and personal details passed to Lennox under what the latter called a 'private arrangement'.

One such client was an officer in the Free French Forces, Commandant Janvier. De Wohl wrote to Lennox on 20 January 1941 to say Janvier had been introduced to him by a woman who had been his client for some years, Eve Lewis Bailey. The astrologer was acting as a spy – as agreed with Lennox – carefully extracting information from Janvier about his forthcoming posting to Libreville in French Equatorial Africa. Janvier also said he had family in German-occupied France and was concerned about them. De Wohl may have thought MI5 would be interested in what Janvier had to say for three reasons. The first was that they were concerned at lapses in security and with the political sympathies of some of the staff at the London headquarters of General de Gaulle's Free French Government in exile. Lennox had been present at meetings where these concerns were discussed and may perhaps have mentioned the matter to de Wohl. Then there were the almost permanently strained relations between the British Government and de Gaulle, described by one senior MI5 officer who met him as 'truculent' and known to be sensitive about his position.[20] Finally, Janvier's worries about the safety of his family in France might make him vulnerable to pressure from German intelligence. However, when writing the same day to a colleague, Lennox dismissed what de Wohl had to say about Commandant Janvier as of no interest – there was 'nothing mysterious' about his posting or for MI5 to be concerned about. The letter was nevertheless revealing about de Wohl's willingness to continue to act as an MI5 informant, as well as providing astrological services.

De Wohl had also said in his 20 January letter to Lennox that Mrs Bailey – whom he described as 'very clever, much travelled … very patriotic, politically rather right wing, almost moderately fascist' – was eager to help MI5 but at the moment was trying to get work with the Free French. The suggestion about Mrs Bailey – on whom MI5 already had a file – left Lennox 'very cold', particularly as it came from de Wohl. Lennox would surely also have been unhappy about de Wohl bringing MI5 up in conversation with Mrs Bailey and, by implication, with everyone he met.[21] Lennox was dismissive of de Wohl in a letter to MI5 colleague Major Younger, even contemptuous, describing him as 'a tame astrologer … employed by S.O.2 for their own fell purposes'. This was despite the fact that Lennox was acting as a go-between, passing reports composed by his 'tame astrologer' to Military Intelligence.

If Lennox had such a low opinion of de Wohl, what did other elements of British Intelligence actually make of him? The Director of Naval Intelligence, Godfrey, had found him convincing at first, impressive even, until his superiors at the Admiralty warned him off, as obviously they had. De Wohl's boss at the Special Operations Executive, Charles

Hambro, believed he was a 'perfectly splendid chap', but this opinion did not seem to be widely shared. Lennox, who was perhaps closest to de Wohl, had what looked like a bantering relationship with him, lunched with him regularly, but described him to Younger as 'funny', meaning odd rather than humorous. Dick White, assistant director of head of MI5's B division, had little time for him, writing de Wohl off as a 'charlatan and an imposter'. White scrawled by hand across one note on de Wohl's file, 'I don't like having decisions of this kind made by reference to the Stars rather than MI5.'[22] SOE officer Eric Maschwitz, who was involved with the astrologer when the two were in New York in 1941, was equally scathing, dismissing him as 'a right swindler ... you never met such a character'.[23] Colonel Chambers, the security officer at the Political Warfare Executive, to which de Wohl would be attached later in the war, was just as cutting. He took an instant and intense dislike to the astrologer and was heard to have described him as a 'complete scoundrel'.[24]

MI5 were keen on the flimsiest gossip as a source of intelligence and one report coming from an unnamed 'reliable source', exchanged between officers in counter-espionage, was attached to de Wohl's file in April 1941.[25] The report runs over the information about de Wohl's early life of which MI5 would already have been aware – son of a Hungarian, born and living in Germany as Ludwig von Wohl, bank clerk, novelist, screen writer – and then moves into an area that is of great interest to the informant, obviously anxious to dig out any evidence he believes discredits the astrologer. 'He claims in his books to have travelled widely in the East in Arab disguise, and to have often frequented cafes in Berlin in feminine ~~disguise~~ [word struck out in document] attire.' MI5's informant had continued:

De Wohl claims amongst his friends that the flat at Grosvenor House was taken for him by the War Office and was furnished for him by the War Office under the supervision of some woman. This woman seems to be invested with some mystery in view of the fact de Wohl who rather blatantly flaunts his effeminate [sic] inclinations and habits, has of late made rather a close companion of the woman referred to above.

The informant was dismissive of de Wohl's ability as an astrologer, saying that none of his 'pronouncements and predictions' have materialised, apart from his forecast that Italy would enter the war in June 1940, which any person with a basic understanding of international affairs would have seen coming. Who was this informant? Someone, presumably, with access to each of de Wohl's reports to Military Intelligence, either before or after they arrived at the War Office, and, by the sound of it, a man with a distinct grudge. What was his purpose in trying to damage de Wohl as an interpreter of horoscopes, ridiculous as he may have thought astrology was? More ominously for de Wohl's reputation, the informant had told his MI5 contact:

> … that in de Wohl's press cutting books he saw numerous cuttings from German newspapers containing references to the leaders of the Nazi regime couched in the most fulsome terms of adulation. These cuttings were from articles and astrological predictions that appeared in Germany under the signature of Louis von Wohl.

Was there any truth in this particularly serious accusation? The charge did seem unlikely. For a start, de Wohl was not known as Louis de Wohl in Germany but Ludwig von Wohl, something the informant had brought up earlier. Was this a clumsy slip or a clue the story was a fabrication? Secondly, there is nothing on de Wohl's MI5 file to suggest that what purported to be evidence of any Nazi sympathies he may have had was ever put to the test. It would have been an easy matter for MI5 officers to examine the press cutting books, with or without de Wohl's permission. There is no sign they ever took the trouble to do so. Rumour was added to rumour, bringing in British Intelligence's office politics and apparent mutual antagonism between the various agencies. An MI5 officer wrote a file note on 12 May 1941 setting out what a Captain Hope, formerly of the Special Operation Executive's SO2 section – to which de Wohl was nominally attached – had told him:[26]

> Hope said that de Wohl was a homosexual and it therefore becomes rather difficult to explain his interest in the woman who, as reported

by B.24, helped to furnish his flat in Grosvenor House. This also disposes of the theory that has been held that June Bainbridge is Louis de Wohl's mistress. He is much given to boasting about his connections with the War Office, Admiralty, etc. and would appear to be an unsuitable type to be employed in any kind of secret activities … Hope is convinced that de Wohl is really an Englishman and has a German Jewish mother.

When MI5 and MI6 had been concerned about payments de Wohl was making by bank transfer from London to his wife in Chile and about her contacts with Germans there, whether they were merely social or whether they had any espionage significance, June Bainbridge – Hambro's secretary at SOE – had provided evidence confirming the arrangement was above board. 'The method of payment is a perfectly normal one,' she wrote to Major Lennox, 'Our friend has apparently been doing this since March, 1939, without any trouble … So he is quite safe on that point.'[27] Within a few months, Bainbridge would be playing an even more significant part in the astrologer's life.

Captain Hope – the MI5 officer went on in his file note – was satisfied that a rumour de Wohl's real name was Lawrence Wells was true. (Unfortunately, the paper in de Wohl's file dated 27 March 1941 with the source of this bizarre story was removed and presumably destroyed during weeding.) The hysteria was palpable. What could be done about him now he held an army commission, the MI5 officer asked. 'My informant tells me that he has himself seen the official War Office appointment …' But there might possibly be a way of dealing with de Wohl: 'Hope suggested that the best means might be through S.I.S. [Secret Intelligence Service, MI6], who have been at daggers drawn with S.O.2 for some time.'[28]

De Wohl was being squeezed – almost certainly without his knowledge – between the institutional paranoia endemic to intelligence on one hand and the demarcation disputes and jealousies among the different agencies on the other. Or perhaps the astrologer was aware and believed it was to his advantage to play them off against each other. A prime example came over his continuing contact with the former

Romanian ambassador to London, Tilea. He had been instrumental in arranging the contacts that had drawn the astrologer into working for British Intelligence. It was Tilea who had been sure Karl-Ernst Krafft was Hitler's personal astrologer and convinced de Wohl, who in turn used this as the card to play with Naval and Military Intelligence. De Wohl had encouraged Tilea to remain in Britain when he resigned as ambassador, partly through advice based on his horoscope. Tilea was given political asylum and was now active in the anti-Nazi Free Romania Movement with, as he complained to de Wohl, little help or encouragement from the British Government. After initial neutrality in the war, Romania had allied with the Axis powers in November 1940 under the Antonescu dictatorship and would join Germany in Operation Barbarossa, the June 1941 strike on the Soviet Union.

De Wohl mentioned in passing in his 20 January 1941 letter to Lennox that Hambro of SOE had instructed him to advise Tilea to postpone his plans for six months. What these plans were de Wohl did not say, but they would presumably have involved the activities of the Free Romania Movement. There were two rival Romanian anti-German organisations in London competing for British Government recognition and support. Tilea's movement had only fifty or so members and the rival Romanian Democratic Committee, headed by Victor Cornea, even fewer. Tilea believed – probably correctly – that there were two camps in the Foreign Office, one for him and one against him. But government reluctance to officially acknowledge either derived partly from reservations over whether they actually represented opinion in Romania itself – which was seen as generally anti-British – or that either of the organisations' leaders were politically experienced enough to operate a government in exile.[29] Exchanges recorded in de Wohl's MI5 file revealed the irritation the Foreign Office were feeling about his and SOE's involvement with Tilea.

The astrologer's brief reference to Tilea, and his subsequent 'Special Report' to Hambro about other Romanian exiles, which Lennox had managed to procure, generated a flurry of concern in MI5. How had Lennox acquired a copy of the report? There was more murky behind-the-scenes business, of which de Wohl would certainly have been ignorant. Lennox had yet another 'private arrangement', this time with Hambro's secretary June Bainbridge 'who brings me the reports from Louis that we are very interested in knowing about …'.[30] De Wohl wrote in his 'Special Report' that he had acquired two new clients, both former Romanian diplomatic representatives in London – one was Florescu, who had replaced Tilea as ambassador when he resigned in 1940.[31] Both had sought his advice over whether they should return to Romania or break with their government and stay in Britain. De Wohl reported that he gathered from an SOE liaison officer 'that the matter was left to my own decision'. He went on:

> I have advised both to stay. Quite apart from their planetary tendencies, it seemed to me that an opposite advice would subconsciously mean to them that I believed in Hitler's victory. Besides, the psychological effect on:- A) the Germans B) the Roumanians had to be considered … The psychological impression on the Germans and certainly on the Roumanians must be that 'the atmosphere' in London firmly believes in a British victory in the end.

De Wohl was now getting into far deeper waters than merely passing astrological interpretations to Military Intelligence. These were sensitive matters with possibly serious political consequences, as the two groups of Romanian exiles competed for official British attention. Lennox passed de Wohl's report to Dick White. An obviously angry White asked Toby Caulfield in MI5's B3 division (which had an interest in the Balkans) to comment, remarking, 'I don't like having decisions of this kind made by reference to the Stars rather than MI5.'[32] Caulfield was more measured in his response. He felt no real concern about 'the stars' side of the case, though he agreed MI5 'should be allowed a look in'. Caulfield said he would ask Lennox to provide a full list of de Wohl's clients and ensure he arranged with the SOE liaison officer that MI5 were informed before matters were left 'to the decision of the astrologer'.[33] Caulfield wrote again to White two days later. He said he had spoken to Lennox, who had passed him a copy of a further report on Tilea that de Wohl had submitted to Hambro. Caulfield added that he was not 'in the picture' about the Foreign Office/Hambro aspect but it did seem a delicate matter:

> Obviously F/O [Foreign Office] ought to know about de Wohl's activities and have an opportunity of giving guidance jointly with us. It hardly seems Hambro's province at all. May I have your comments as to an approach by us to F/O. Nicholls would be the man I think ... taking it for granted that Nicholls knew all about Hambro's activity with de Wohl.[34]

It was in his covering letter to Caulfield that Lennox revealed he had been going behind de Wohl's back to secure copies of the reports he was making to Hambro at SOE. He added to Caulfield that he would feel no concern about de Wohl's involvement with Tilea and other Romanian exiles if he was confident 'Hambro was definitely working under instructions from the Foreign Office, but I am not at all sure of this'.[35] De Wohl's new report, on Psychological Research Bureau headed paper and titled 'Tilea', ran to three pages of single-spaced typing.[36]

The astrologer reported that he had gone to Tilea's room at the Berkeley Hotel on 20 March, about 5 p.m., and found him engaged in a heated telephone conversation with what de Wohl described as 'a man of importance'. This, Tilea told de Wohl, was Sir Orme Sergeant, deputy undersecretary at the Foreign Office. Tilea was complaining about the threat to intern one of his colleagues in the Free Romania Movement. The conversation over, an agitated Tilea turned to de Wohl and complained about the time being wasted. 'I know you gave me the astrological advice to wait, and I have waited,' de Wohl reported Tilea as saying, 'but now things are different, and I must act. If I do not the damage will be immeasurable.' Tilea's imagination, his capacity to build fantasy on fantasy, seemed as active as de Wohl's. He described the liberation army the Free Romania Movement would recruit. There might be no more than seven hundred Romanians in London but, he went on, according to de Wohl:

> There are almost 70,000 in Canada alone, and many thousands in the United States. From the Canadian Roumanians alone I could form

three battalions. The Roumanians in the States could form air force units. I must send someone over to organise this, and it must be done quickly. I am getting letters over letters from America, spurring me to act. Why don't they let me act?

Tilea complained again there were the two competing schools of thought in the Foreign Office, one in favour of his movement, the other against. Had de Wohl promised Tilea he would use his influence to help with his plans, that he would persuade the Special Operations Executive – and through them the Foreign Office – to give him the backing he sought? Was it a case of one fantasist egging another on? Who was playing whom? Action was required now, Tilea declared. 'In the meantime the Germans are getting busy … the Nazification of the Roumanians in America is intended. We must get there first and win the youth.'

Having reported what Tilea had said, de Wohl asked Hambro, his boss, why 'we' were opposing what Tilea was trying to achieve, an effective resistance to the Nazis and their allies in Romania. 'As you remember, I have been able to stop his activities when you first wanted me to.' How had de Wohl been able to do this? Through astrology, by telling Tilea the time was not yet right, the aspects were for now unfavourable. But, wrote de Wohl, the situation had changed. German troops were occupying Romania. The astrologer came up with what he obviously believed to be a sophisticated plan that would satisfy everyone, while at the same time fishing for clues from Hambro on the extent to which SOE was encouraging resistance activity in Romania. As so often, the astrologer's activities seemed like scenes from one of his novels.

De Wohl's proposition to Hambro involved telling whatever resistance force in Romania SOE might be backing now or would in the future that Tilea was being 'tolerated' in London merely as a figurehead. This would act as cover for the underground movement in the interior carrying out far more worthwhile activities than intriguing in London. It would have the additional benefit of confusing the enemy about which group actually had British political backing. Tilea, meanwhile – de Wohl suggested – should go as soon as possible to the United States 'where he could influence the American Roumanians in our favour, collect their money, and form his units for their fight for freedom, before the Germans can do anything of the kind!' De Wohl had not lost his talent for an imaginative blending of fact and fiction.

It was not difficult to see why MI5 officers were so concerned about de Wohl's relationship with Tilea. The man who in their eyes was merely an astrologer was going way beyond his remit by engaging in freelance diplomacy, attempting to exert influence in a difficult and dangerous wartime situation. What was worse, he was basing his actions on a combination of inspired fantasy and the movements of the planets. 'This is a rather delicate matter,' White wrote to his MI5 colleague Caulfield on 7 April 1941. 'I should try to find out if the Foreign Office know about Hambro's activities through de Wohl, but watch your step and go carefully.'[37] There were sporadic written exchanges between MI5 officers about what exactly de Wohl, Tilea and Hambro were up to in April, May and June 1941, but as these were destroyed when the astrologer's file was weeded their activities remain a mystery.

De Wohl's efforts to place pressure on Hambro and through him on the Foreign Office in favour of Tilea's Free Romania Movement came ultimately to nothing. As the historian of SOE bluntly put it, 'SOE was much concerned with what was going on in Romania during the war, but was able to do little about it.'[38] Within months the issue had become largely academic. On 22 June 1941 Romanian troops joined German forces in the attack on the Soviet Union and on 7 December Britain declared war on Romania, Finland and Hungary (incidentally making de Wohl – still despite his efforts a Hungarian national – effectively an enemy alien). The British Government recommended Romanian exiles in the country gave up organised political activity and instead assisted in the Allied war effort as individuals. As for de Wohl, it would soon be he rather than Tilea going on a journey to the United States, using his claimed mastery of the stars to exert an entirely new form of influence on events.

5

HITLER FEARS DEATH

I

In *The Stars of War and Peace*, published almost a decade after the events de Wohl was describing had taken place, he set out the main difficulty facing him in his role as what amounted to astrological adviser to British Intelligence:

> No single man could undertake the task of making a complete astro-logical analysis of 'things to come', even if he worked eighteen hours a day. There is too much purely technical work. It would take about a dozen good men, working full time, to get somewhere near a com-plete result. And I was alone.[1]

Why were no other astrologers recruited to work alongside him? He never explains, though he believed a group would have been more effec-tive, as well perhaps as more flattering to his ego: heading a team, even promoted to the rank of major to recognise his responsibility. But when Naval Intelligence had taken an interest in de Wohl's proposals and Ewen Montagu was despatched in October 1940 to round up likely recruits from among London's astrological fraternity, either none were willing to give their services or they turned out to be unimpressive. Perhaps some had seen attempting to read Hitler's mind as a hopeless task. It would certainly be fraught with complications absent from a comfortable pre-war practice, among them the danger of having the 'science' officially exposed as valueless. In the end British Intelligence saw de Wohl, their solitary 'tame' astrologer, as enough to be going on with, in more senses than one.

In *The Stars of War and Peace*, de Wohl presents the naval battle of Cape Matapan in March 1941 as an example of how he went about his work. He had no doubt he could claim it as one of his major war-time successes.[2] What is interesting is the story the astrologer tells has nothing to do with the task he had originally set himself to perform: revealing Hitler's intentions by studying his horoscope. What de Wohl claimed he had achieved in this case was to foresee a decisive naval clash in the Mediterranean and to prophesy a British victory over the Italian fleet. Furthermore, he said, he had achieved both these things 127 days before the encounter at sea actually took place. While casting a horoscope in November 1940 he said he had spotted there would be a trine, an angle of 120 degrees, between the planets Mars and Neptune on 27 March 1941.

The astrologer considered all the possibilities the aspect might signify. He wondered at first whether the link of Mars with war and Neptune with the sea was a sign of Hitler's invasion of Britain, the crossing of the Channel by his army for the final battle that would end the war. Or did the combination signify oil and the wells in Romania, sought after by Germany? As he deliberated more intently he ruled out both, and after turning to the astrological charts of a selection of British, German and Italian admirals he concluded he was foreseeing a clash between fleets at sea. He dug deeper and was excited to find what he believed was 'a horoscope of outstanding quality, belonging to a man born on 7 January 1883'. This was Admiral Sir Andrew Cunningham who, de Wohl calcu-lated, would have Jupiter trine (that is, at 120 degrees to) his natal Sun on 27 March 1941. 'This was worth following up a little further,' de Wohl recalled.

The astrologer knew already from his previous dealings with the Directorate of Naval Intelligence that Cunningham commanded the Mediterranean Fleet. The Director, Rear Admiral Godfrey, had even supplied him with the birth details of senior naval officers, much to MI5'a consternation when they became aware of this. As Cunningham was based in the Mediterranean, de Wohl assumed it was more likely that when the admiral led his ships into action he would be battling an Italian rather than a German opponent. He proceeded to construct and explore the horoscopes of the two senior Italian naval commanders. De Wohl found both had 'negative' transits for 27 March and, just as significant for his purposes, the charts of Italy's King Victor Emmanuel and the country's dictator Mussolini were similarly unfavourable over that period. 'The Lunation chart for Italy (Rome) showed negative aspects concerning "those who serve".' The stars were all pointing in one direction for Italy and her fleet. To complete the picture, King George VI's chart, the astrologer found, showed 'strongly positive aspects in various respects …'

> That did it. I wrote my report – dated 20 November 1940 – and mentioned that the Admiral … was most likely to achieve a great success between 27 March and 5 April … It was – or could be – of particular importance for the commander in the Mediterranean to have some foreknowledge of his chances. A V.I.P. – a Very Important Naval Person – assured me in writing that word would be passed on to Sir Andrew, though whether or not this was done I shall probably never know for certain. Certain it is that he was ready to seize his opportunity.

The astrologer recalled that the British fleet in the Mediterranean was made up largely of 'slow old battle wagons', while Italian ships were speedier but carried less armour. This was a critical consideration in the event of a confrontation – the relative values of weight versus swiftness – and it was therefore 'vital for the British admiral to be out and about when the Italians came out of their holes, or else he would never be able to catch them'. De Wohl was satisfied he had given the message and all he could do now was wait. There was a minor clash between British and Italian ships on 27 November 1940, which the astrologer said he had also forecast, but the major battle he had foreseen was yet to take place.

Then on 30 March 1941, de Wohl said, came the headlines, 'Mussolini's Fleet Caught and Smashed'. The newspaper stories reported that on 27 March British reconnaissance aircraft spotted Italian vessels sailing east in the Mediterranean, apparently to intercept a British convoy en route from Egypt carrying supplies to British troops in Greece. The next day Royal Navy light cruisers sighted an Italian battleship and several cruisers. On realising they had been observed, the Italians turned westward. Cunningham ordered his ships on, making an unprecedented combined sea and air night attack. The Italian fleet lost three heavy cruisers and two destroyers sank, a battleship and a destroyer damaged, with over 2,000 seamen killed. The British fleet suffered three dead and minor damage to vessels. The British victory effectively prevented further Italian naval operations for the remainder of the war, a blow to Mussolini's long-proclaimed hopes of dominating the Mediterranean, *Mare Nostrum*. 'Needless to say,' the astrologer recalled, 'I was jubilant.'

But de Wohl was also worried. 'I had not given sufficient consideration, in this case, to the chart that mattered most in any European theatre of war: Hitler's chart.' The German leader's astrologer, de Wohl reasoned, would surely have made the same calculations as he had and would have foreseen the possibility that Cunningham could overcome the Italian fleet. In which case, why did the Germans fail to do what they could to avert the disaster by warning the Italians? 'They knew perfectly well if Cunningham made use of his good aspects he would intercept their ships and defeat them. But they knew also that he would have his hands tied. He would be extremely busy.' Why did the Germans want the British Mediterranean fleet out of the way and otherwise engaged? Because, de Wohl said, they were planning to ferry Rommel's Afrika Korps across to Libya from Sicily and needed to ensure their own ships would be safe from attack by Cunningham's fleet.

Two good stories, but they do not entirely stand up. First, the initial elements of the Afrika Korps began moving into Libya on 10 February and the final formation had landed and was ready for deployment by 12 March 1941, two weeks before the battle of Cape Matapan. Second, the astrologer may very well have seen a British victory at sea on or around 27 March 1941 in Admiral Cunningham's horoscope. But if he did make his report on 20 November 1940, there is no copy in the archives to confirm this. Nor is there any reference to a possible victory at sea around March 1941 in de Wohl's 'Quotations from my reports on astrological lines during 1941/42'. As he presented this in November 1942 to underline his successes, surely he would have been keen to draw attention to this outstanding prediction.[3] If he did indeed forecast the outcome, there is – as de Wohl himself admits – nothing to show that anyone at the Admiralty informed Cunningham of his coming period of good luck. And if he had been told in advance, then what? De Wohl's astrological interpretation would not guide the admiral to the Italian fleet's position around 27 March or tell him where to deploy his ships to ensure the successful interception and destruction of the enemy.

A far more crucial point is that de Wohl was not aware, and could not have known at the time, of the part the highly secret Ultra project was now playing in British naval operations. Codebreakers working on German Enigma machine decrypts at the Bletchley Park Government Code and Cypher School had cracked the Italian naval code in September 1940, over six months before the battle and some time before de Wohl's astrological revelation in November. One historian of British Intelligence describes Cape Matapan as, 'the first important operation in the Mediterranean to be based on Sigint'.[4] A former member of Military Intelligence summed up the situation precisely: 'Mavis Batey decyphered the Italian Fleet signal that told Admiral Cunningham what he needed to know to win the Battle of Matapan.'[5] By this means, Cunningham was aware from intelligence the Italian fleet was setting out to sea before it had even left harbour. The British reconnaissance aircraft de Wohl referred to had been a decoy, a flying boat ordered into the air to mask the fact that the Bletchley Park codebreakers had given Cunningham forewarning of the Italian fleet's every move and were able to tell him where each enemy ship was positioned.

Final confirmation that it had been Bletchley Park and not de Wohl's interpretation of the stars that had been instrumental in Cunningham's success against the Italians came almost immediately after the battle had been won. Godfrey, the Director of Naval Intelligence who had initially been so impressed by de Wohl, telephoned Bletchley Park to congratulate Dillwyn Knox, who led the team that had deciphered the crucial message. 'Tell Dilly that we have won a great victory in the Mediterranean and it is entirely due to him and his girls.' Cunningham went to thank 'the girls' personally a few weeks later.[6] What need was there for the services of an astrologer when reliable hard intelligence was available? But British Intelligence would still find a use for de Wohl and continue to pay him an army captain's wage.

2

Officers of the Directorate of Military Intelligence were not always entirely enthusiastic when a report from de Wohl arrived via Major Lennox of MI5. They revealed their attitude with file notes, describing him as 'our friend', giving the impression they were beginning to doubt the worth of his contributions. This was the initial response when Lennox presented a six-page closely typed document headed 'The Orchestra of Hitler's Death' early in 1941. The receiving officer wrote, 'Major Lennox has just brought up these effusions of our friend.' But having read the report, one unnamed Military Intelligence officer was far more complimentary. He added to the document's covering slip, 'The top paper is worth reading & keeping in mind. The writer has a good knowledge of German mentality. What he has written agrees with much that we have heard.'[7]

The style of 'The Orchestra of Hitler's Death' was vivid and dramatic, the work of a professional writer, someone with long experience of producing novels and screen plays, far from the colourless wording of the typical bureaucratic report. The six pages read like the scenario for a particularly sensational film or book, the type that ensured de Wohl had prospered in pre-Hitler Germany. What is startling is that such a document should find its way into a Military Intelligence file, not only read but eventually receiving serious consideration from case-hardened wartime officers. Or, given the desperate temper of the times, perhaps not so surprising after all. Hitler's death had been de Wohl's preoccupation for some time and its forecast a regular occurrence, even at the outbreak of war. An experienced astrologer reviewing de Wohl's book *Commonsense Astrology* in 1940 declared 'a certain Mr. H. seems to be his *bête noire*. Writing in September 1939 he informs us that Hitler is "as good as dead".'[8]

De Wohl began 'The Orchestra of Hitler's Death' theatrically with what he described as 'The Overture':

> We are up against a formidable adversary. His personal magnetism is so strong that its emanations can be felt in all countries of the globe … The numbus [*sic*], the magnetic power of this man must be broken. To break it, we must not only influence the peoples all over the world: we must also influence the centre, from which the magnetism emanates. We must influence Hitler himself. This is not at all beyond our power. For, although obsessed, Hitler is still a human being, and as such subject to certain hopes, and certain fears. We must therefore disappoint and destroy these hopes. And we must increase, and a hundred times increase, those fears.[9]

The astrologer's objective in his work for British Intelligence was now not solely to read Hitler's mind but to break it, to insinuate a sense of dread and panic in the Führer that would undermine his psychological balance and ultimately succeed in destroying him. Along with this, the German people were to be pushed into abandoning any confidence they might have that the war would end with their victory. 'Hitler fears death,' de Wohl wrote. 'I know his character well enough to describe exactly what sort of fear it is.' He said Hitler loved life – which only served to heighten the anxiety he felt about dying – and feared for the fate of what he believed to be his mission if it passed into other hands.[10] De Wohl had no doubt Hitler would have asked his astrologers to forecast the date of his death, as he himself had once done in India. 'I must know how long I shall be able to work for the German people,' Hitler would tell them. They would have to answer truthfully, de Wohl said. 'They would have to warn him of a dangerous aspect, threatening his life within the near future.'

> By his astrological advisers he is told this: 'Your death will be Neptunian. This means that it will be mysterious and strange, you will

disappear, and the people will not for a long time, if ever, actually know how you have died ... Under certain passages of your horoscope there is danger from men in your environment.'[11]

The astrologer said bad aspects in Hitler's horoscope were falling inescapably into place, with their greatest impact in the second half of March 1941, all of April, and the major part of May.

> Therefore we must begin to play the symphony of his death in the first week of March, and go on playing it for at least ten weeks. From all parts of the world our instruments must play the melodies of his approaching death. He is sensitive, hypersensitive. They will try to keep the sound of our orchestra away from his ears. We shall see to it that they don't succeed and I know how ... This composition must be played in all countries of the world ... It is impossible that the whole world speaks of the death of one man, without this man becoming aware of it. <u>It will haunt him</u>.[12]

De Wohl then moved on to second phase of his proposed project: 'The Work to be Done'.[13] The campaign, he proposed, must begin abroad, not in Britain. The British press should come into play only later, repeating what astrologers in other countries were forecasting, once the latter had been persuaded to do so. Leading astrologers in Egypt, India and Ceylon (now Sri Lanka) would be approached and asked to present interpretations of Hitler's horoscope that pointed to his death, the fate awaiting him not in years to come but soon. 'They are mostly natives,' de Wohl said, and suggested 'the Secret Service' were better equipped to deal with them than embassy and high commission press officers. Once the astrologers had made their prophecies, intelligence officers should then 'lead' the press to them.

Were these seers being asked to contrive, make up, forecasts of Hitler's death or did he believe they were genuinely there to be found? De Wohl, perhaps intentionally, did not make this clear. He went on, 'The Secret Service should be informed that we want the rumour of Hitler's impending death to be spread over the bazaars. Bazaar-talk is as quick as the telegraph, as anyone who knows the East will confirm.' The results were first to be published in local newspapers then spread out by telegraphing them to journalists in Australia, Canada and South Africa, where they were to be widely reprinted. Chinese astrologers were also to be called upon to 'chime in' and naturally the form a prediction took would need to have a local complexion.

One type of prophecy that would be useful, de Wohl suggested, would run along the lines, 'A great King is going to die this year. He is more powerful than many others, yet he has never been crowned.' Newspapers would follow this up with their own interpretation of what the prophecy could mean. Journalists in South America were to be provided with material indirectly, apparently derived from neutral sources. What was crucial, he insisted, was that every precaution was taken 'so as not to create the suspicion that it is propaganda material'.

At the heart of the campaign, the astrologer said, should be influence on the United States.[14] He listed twenty-three American astrologers whom he suggested the press should approach to interview about forecasts of Hitler's death. They included Paul G. Clancy (editor of the popular magazine *American Astrology Your Daily Guide*), Grant Lewi (the 'father of modern astrology in America', author of *Astrology for the Millions*), the astrologer to Hollywood stars Nella Webb, the English-born Ellen McCaffrey, Paul Councel (author of *Your Stars and Destiny*), and Frederick van Norstrand (a prolific contributor to astrology magazines), all well known and highly respected in their field. There was also Dane Rudhyar, a French-born musician, novelist and astrologer, author in 1936 of the Jung-influenced *The Astrology of Personality*.

Did de Wohl know any of these people personally? As he had not as yet been to the United States, it seemed unlikely. But as all had published influential and/or popular books, their names would be common currency among professional astrologers. He had misspelt the names of two, Rudhyav for Rudhyar and Levi for Lewi, though given de Wohl's haphazard typing this may have been simply a slip of the finger. He went on to recommend contacting occult newspapers in the United States, arranging with them to print articles pointing in one direction. Private seances should be set up for reporters to attend with, once again, mediums encouraged to concentrate on the inevitability of Hitler's death:

> The more vivid and detailed the occult information is, the better. BUT IT MUST ALWAYS BE FOR THE VERY NEAR FUTURE. If it is not, there will be no fee for the medium. No good having scruples there; we want to accelerate his death (Maximum result) or attempt to make him nervous and afraid (Minimum result) by letting the whole world speak of his death, before it has happened.

De Wohl advised that 'our men' in the United States should be instructed to contact women's societies and clubs – 'a very powerful factor' – offering to organise astrological lectures based on the theme 'Hitler's decline and death'. He said he would prepare addresses lasting from a quarter of an hour to as long as over 2 hours to cover this. Similarly, the heads of religious denominations of all creeds should be encouraged to arrange meetings where speakers could address the congregation on 'Hitler, the Anti-Christ'. Hitler's racial prejudices and policies should be emphasised at meetings of black Americans, who would be drawn into the campaign through use of the slogan 'Freedom with Christ or back to Slavery under Hitler'. He envisaged a programme of activity drawing in not only all Christian denominations but also what he called 'semi-religious orders' such as Theosophical lodges, Christian Scientists and Rosicrucians. His timetable was 'the period from March 13th to the end of May'.

How seriously was de Wohl taking what he had written? Was the 'Orchestra' produced for his own amusement, the pleasure of constructing a neatly plotted story spanning continents? Did he see the plan as he described it to be a realistic contribution to the struggle against Germany and Nazism? Was he trying to impress Military Intelligence with the breadth of his strategic vision, combined as it was with a grasp of the intricacies of astrological calculation? Probably, given the tone and substance of his earlier reports, all of these at once. But not only was his proposal read, it was welcomed and quickly put into effect.

De Wohl set out three specific rumours that he thought the press in the United States should be persuaded to take up and spread.[15] The first, to be published immediately, concerned Emperor Hirohito of Japan. The country was a member of the Axis alliance with Germany and Italy. The story would run that the prior of one of the country's oldest Shinto temples, an 80-year-old man renowned and revered throughout Japan for his clairvoyance, had sought an audience with the Emperor. What he said had been revealed by an indiscreet courtier. The prior had told Hirohito, 'You will lose your most powerful ally during this year through a sudden death.' De Wohl said the Shinto religion wielded enormous power. 'The 'prophecy' of the prior … may well influence the course of political events in Japan.'

The second rumour to be disseminated concerned Hitler's dependence on astrology. A story should be planted in mid-April that not only was it widely known that Hitler employed an astrologer to advise him, but what was significant was that Hitler had never refuted numerous articles in the world's press on his 'keen interest in the stars'. Until now, the latest report would say, it had proved impossible to discover the identity of Hitler's adviser.[16] American newspapers would be told:

> We are in a position to reveal the name of Hitler's astrologer. It is a well-known Swiss expert, Herr K.E. Krafft. It is not surprising that the Führer had to make a foreigner his adviser in these matters, as most of the leading German Astrologers were Jews or at least of Jewish descent. Some of these managed to escape from Germany, others were put into concentration camps.

The final part of the operation would involve prophecies Krafft had allegedly made. The former Romanian ambassador to London, Tilea, was now brought on stage. There would be a reference to a letter from Krafft in 1940 that Tilea still possessed in which Hitler's astrologer 'somewhat incautiously admits that likelihood of the Führer's impending death'. The American press should be encouraged to say that Krafft had admitted to Tilea that British and French astrologers were correct in forecasting 'bad aspects' were coming in Hitler's horoscope in 1941. Krafft should also be reported as having gone on to say that 'when the Führer disappears, the National Socialist movement will go on by its own dynamic force'. How else could this be interpreted – de Wohl said – than Krafft's prophecy that Hitler would meet his end in 1941. 'It is worth wondering,' de Wohl remarked as an aside, 'whether he has been courageous enough to tell Hitler about it.'[17]

The truth was that while there was a letter from Krafft to Tilea, it contained none of these things. De Wohl's imagination was working overtime. The layers of de Wohl's proposal, the step-by-step sequence of events he visualised, were clearly derived from his years of experience plotting novels and screen plays. Fact and fiction were loosely knotted together. An American journalist, he suggested, should be left alone for a moment by the desk of the press attaché at the British Embassy in Washington and be allowed to 'find' a deciphered telegram. The telegram should appear to have originated with an intelligence agent in Zurich and would 'reveal' that Hitler's physician, Professor Ernst Sauerbruch, had told a Swiss doctor the Führer's health was declining rapidly because of the nervous strain he was under. He had aged ten years in the last six months. The reporter would be unable to resist using the story, which would provoke neutral foreign journalists in Berlin to question Nazi officials about the state of Hitler's health. These officials would naturally deny the rumours but the damage would have been done. De Wohl added an additional twist to the plot:

> All those foreign diplomats, industrials [*sic*], society members etc., who are likely to go to Germany or occupied territories for whatever purpose should be asked by our men with a twinkle not to ask any questions regarding Hitler's health, as the Germans were rather sensitive about that. In which case, of course, they will ask questions, and the Germans asked the same thing by every newcomer will become nervous and many will believe in the end that after all there must be something wrong about Hitler's health.

De Wohl now strengthened the web he was constructing, setting out the part for him to play in Britain. He would collaborate with English astrologers, seven of whom he named, including Charles Carter, a leading figure in British astrology. The list did not include R.H. Naylor, the

Sunday Express astrologer who had written to the Home Office opposing de Wohl's application for British citizenship in 1940. De Wohl would
address the Easter 1941 convention of British Astrologers in Harrogate,
which, he said, the press always covered. 'I shall disclose the sensational
news that Hitler's astrologer himself believes in the imminent death of
the Führer – which may easily lead to the elimination of Mr K.E. Krafft.'
By this point, de Wohl declared with an enthusiasm that leaps from the
page, 'the Orchestra of Hitler's death should have reached its forte fortis-
simo in the world, and especially in the United States'.[18]

3

The wheels began to turn, sooner than expected given the extraordinary nature of the venture de Wohl had conjured up. The Special
Operations Executive, to which he was formally attached, adopted the
plan. The process was to follow broadly de Wohl's outline, though not
quite with all the panache of the astrologer's vividly written proposal.
One obvious avenue was to work through officials administering
Britain's overseas colonies. Charles Hambro, deputy head of SOE's
operations section, went to the Colonial Office to speak to Thomas
Lloyd, the assistant undersecretary, on 11 April 1941, setting out the
bones of what was being planned. Hambro wrote to Lloyd the following day in a sardonic tone:

> As I told you yesterday I am always asked to do curious things and
> this is probably one of the most curious I have ever been asked to
> arrange but none the less important. Therefore I have no hesitation in
> introducing Major Sheridan who also does curious things sometimes
> and who will explain to you what he wants the Colonial Office to do
> for him.[19]

Hambro said what Sheridan had to say had been widely discussed and
was being undertaken on a worldwide basis according to a definite plan.
A minute in the Colonial Office file on the mission confirmed that the

scheme had been approved by Hugh Dalton, the Minister for Economic Warfare, SOE's political head since Churchill appointed him the previous year. The matter had not, though, been discussed in Cabinet and in that sense remained semi-official.[20] Major Leslie Sheridan of SOE visited Lloyd on 23 April. Sheridan had had a colourful career before joining SOE, having been a journalist with the *Daily Mirror* and *Daily Herald* before being called to the Bar. Lloyd of the Colonial Office subsequently recounted his initial discussion with Sheridan in a lengthy file note, making plain how uneasy a civil servant outside the murky worlds of intelligence and propaganda felt about the entire project.

Lloyd outlined what Sheridan told him about spreading the rumour that 1941 would be 'the year of Hitler's downfall'. Sheridan described how all SOE missions overseas had been instructed to help with the scheme, including those in West Africa, Singapore, Egypt and Turkey. He suggested to Lloyd that the Colonial Office's role would be to telegraph officials in Hong Kong, Jamaica and Trinidad with directives drafted by SOE, prepared copies of which he handed over at the meeting.[21] Lloyd noted the doubts he had raised with Sheridan, together with the major's response:

> The idea behind this strikes me as fantastic. Major Sheridan (who has no personal belief in astrology) meets all such criticism by admitting it but asking why we should not make such use as we can of the credulity of others. He argues that even if the plan fails no harm will have been done, whereas if it should succeed to the extent of penetrating to Germany it will have had a definite value.

Lloyd said he remained sceptical and that he did not believe propaganda of this kind could 'carry any real weight in the face of present German successes'. The Colonial Office head of publicity, Noel Sabine, commented on Lloyd's minute that he really saw no alternative to doing what SOE were asking for, but he thought that – contrary to Sheridan's breezy confidence – harm would indeed be done if the end of the year came and Hitler were still alive. Opinion was divided among the department's officials, to judge by their comments on the file. One said that having read the exchanges, 'I still find it difficult to take the proposal seriously.' Another wrote that he 'did not see how practical results can be obtained'. This was countered by an official who believed the proposal had 'the merit of novelty and was interesting', though he agreed it would be useful to have detailed information before proceeding.

When Sheridan and Lloyd met again on 28 April, the SOE major told Lloyd in a subtly threatening way that, while he had no authority to impose what he was asking on the Colonial Office, the Minister for Economic Warfare, Dalton, 'naturally hopes that assistance will be forthcoming'.[22] The Colonial Office was in a dilemma. The department's officials had their doubts, but as the Foreign Office had already approved the despatch of SOE telegrams to embassies abroad and the India Office was also co-operating, it was unwise to appear obstructive. The Colonial Office sent telegrams to various governors, one despatched to the Hong Kong governor, Sir Geoffry Northcote, giving a flavour. What Northcote was instructed to do was so – in Lloyd's word – 'fantastic' it is worth quoting in full the telegram of 3 May 1941. De Wohl's fingerprints could be detected on almost every sentence:

MOST SECRET
Your co-operation required in world wide scheme to plug idea of Hitler's downfall this year dated by occult powers.

2. This based on following accurate information.

3. Hitler's fate governed in horoscope by Neptune which will be in opposition to birth sign in April and May.

4. Neptunian fate is always mysterious, usually violent and full of conspiratorial danger from closest associates.

5. Hitler maintains personal astrologer Krafft and fears death before completion of work. His decisions reported to be influenced by portents of stars.

6. Induce soothsayers in your area to cast Hitler's horoscope and to prophesy mysterious downfall for Hitler this year. Hitler's birth date April 20th, 1889.

7. Obtain greatest publicity locally for such forecasts which should if possible be made in dramatic circumstances and please arrange for such reports to be sent also to press of as many other countries as possible.

8. If we can organise and elaborate orchestra of Hitler's fate which will echo round the world result will not only be breaking down of belief that Hitler is superman, but also music may be heard within Germany where astrology now recognised science and even reach ears of Hitler himself, with unsettling effect on his judgment.[23]

The governor – who had only recently returned to the colony from six months leave in Britain – was more than enthusiastic to play his part in the game, adding a twist of his own. In a telegram to the Secretary of State for the Colonies, Lord Moyne, on 14 May Northcote said the 'matter will be set on foot on May 18'. He told Moyne he believed it would be most effective to work the scheme in his territory by using a planchette message supposedly originating from a temple in Macao.[24] Northcote even had a particular candidate for the job in mind, a 'Chinese gentleman whose loyalty and discretion has been amply proved'. The governor would then arrange for the story to be spread by Reuters' Hong Kong correspondent, a man, he said, 'who is very discreet'. Northcote believed there would be no difficulty in channelling the report into Germany via Tokyo, though he preferred the British Embassy in Japan was not told about this twist in the exercise.[25]

Lloyd at the Colonial Office passed a copy of the Hong Kong governor's telegram to Major Sheridan at the Special Operations Executive office in Baker Street. As Northcote had promised, the Reuters correspondent was able to produce a story based on the Macao temple 'prophecy', a version of which eventually made its way into the columns of the *Sunday Chronicle* in London: 'Hong Kong, Saturday. A planchette forecast in China discloses disaster for Hitler this year, followed by his death in 1942. Astrologers say that Hitler's fate is governed by Neptune, which connotes mystery, violence and danger from trusted associates.' This was a small but satisfactory ripple in the 'Orchestra of Death' pond, for which Sheridan thanked Lloyd personally by letter. There were other signs the campaign was developing momentum: a newspaper in Cairo published a report that an Egyptian astrologer had prophesied 'a red planet will appear on the eastern horizon four months hence … this means that an uncrowned emperor will die, and that man is Hitler'.[26]

Another astrologer in London, one not working directly for British Intelligence and so not paid by them for results, was more careful in his interpretation of Hitler's horoscope. This was Charles Carter, editor of the quarterly *Astrology* magazine, one of the seven astrologers de Wohl had proposed in 'The Orchestra of Hitler's Death' discussing the project with. Carter wrote in the June 1941 edition of *Astrology*:

> The possibility of Hitler's death this year has been freely discussed. I regard this as within the range of possibility. A man who lives a dangerous life does of course lay himself open to violence … The only indication of a violent end that I can see in Hitler's map is ascendant par. Pluto in 8th, against which we must place the protective influence of Jupiter.[27]

As one of the Colonial Office civil servants feared when he gave his opinion of the scheme, 31 December 1941 would come with Hitler still alive and well. A possible next step in the project, and one surprisingly that no section of British Intelligence came up with, would have been to say that Hitler had died and had been replaced by a double, that the Nazi Party was pretending to the German people they were still safe in the Führer's hands. Assuming de Wohl had believed what he was saying, he had taken a risk with his credibility as an astrologer in the eyes of British Intelligence by being so forthright. Though he was the originator of the plan, 'The Orchestra of Hitler's Death', de Wohl did not mention it in the memoir of his wartime activity, *The Stars of War and Peace*. Was this evidence of his disappointment with the 'fantastic' and 'curious' scheme's impact once put into action? Had he actually believed the aspects in Hitler's horoscope forecast his likely death by the end of the year? Or had de Wohl already moved away from any attempt at genuine forecasting and into the area of 'black propaganda', using astrological language simply to undermine Hitler in the eyes of the world? Whatever 'truth' he thought there was in astrology would then be irrelevant.

4

While de Wohl's 'Orchestra of Hitler's Death' scheme was falling into place, an even more dramatic event occurred, another he failed to forecast, but one in which there were rumours of astrology. This was the flight of Hitler's deputy Rudolf Hess from Germany to Britain. Hess, having handed his adjutant a letter to take to Hitler, piloted a Messerschmitt Bf 110 from Augsburg in Bavaria to Eaglesham, south of Glasgow, on the night of 10 May 1941, parachuting and breaking his ankle as he landed. Taken to the local Home Guard headquarters, he said it was urgent that he was taken to see the Duke of Hamilton, an RAF wing commander based nearby. The explanation for Hess's demand to see the duke had been set out in his letter to Hitler, which told a confused story about his intention to discuss a plan for peace between Germany and Britain with Hamilton who, he believed, was sympathetic to such an agreement and had access to Churchill and King George VI. Hess ended the letter by saying that if Hitler disagreed with his action he should dissociate himself from his deputy and declare him insane.[28] Hess's psychological state was the line a hurried meeting of Nazi leaders and officials agreed to take, with an additional twist. The 13 May edition of the official Nazi party paper, *Völkischer Beobachter*, reported:

> As was well known, Hess had undergone severe physical suffering for some years, and he had sought relief through recourse to mesmerists, astrologers, and the like. An attempt is being made to ascertain to what extent these persons may have been responsible for the mental distraction which led Hess to take this step.[29]

Propaganda Minister Goebbels wrote in his diary, 'The Führer is completely shattered. What a spectacle for the world: a mentally deranged second man after the Führer. Dreadful and unimaginable.'[30] Once the official version of the story of the flight was released to the German media, a joke began circulating in the country. Hess is taken before Churchill, who looks him up and down contemptuously, then asks, 'So you're the madman, are you?' Hess replies, 'Oh no, only his deputy.'[31] *The Times* in London took a similar line to that of *Völkischer Beobachter*, with every sign that British Intelligence was joining in, seizing the opportunity to strike a blow against both Hess and Hitler, using de Wohl's claim that astrology was foretelling the Führer's days were numbered. A special correspondent said to be based on the 'German Frontier' reported:

> Certain of Hess's closest friends have thrown an interesting light on the affair. They say that Hess has always been Hitler's astrologer in secret. Up to last March he consistently predicted good fortune and had always been right. Since then, notwithstanding the victories Germany has won, he had declared that the stars showed Hitler's meteoric career was approaching its climax. Losing Hitler's favour, Hess … realised that his life was in peril and fled to the only refuge which the Gestapo could not reach.[32]

The acting Australian Prime Minister, Arthur Fadden, neatly drew the type of conclusion de Wohl set out to make in 'The Orchestra of Hitler's Death'. Fadden believed millions of Germans would now be asking themselves, 'If this is what Hess thinks of the war, what are we to think?'[33]

What followed in Germany became known as Aktion Hess. On 7 June Martin Bormann, Hitler's private secretary and Hess's successor as head of the Nazi Party Chancellery, issued a directive to gauleiter – regional party leaders – condemning 'astrologers, fortune tellers and other swindlers'. On 9 June the Gestapo carried out waves of arrests throughout Germany, taking hundreds of astrologers, occultists and faith healers into custody, confiscating books and papers, questioning their prisoners over any links they may have had with Hess. There was irony in the fact that that the head of the Gestapo, Himmler, was himself a fervent follower of astrology. Among those taken into custody at the Alexanderplatz police cells in Berlin was Karl-Ernst Krafft, the man de Wohl (prompted originally by the Romanian diplomat Tilea) persisted in claiming was Hitler's personal astrologer. Part of the 'Orchestra of Hitler's Death' involved discrediting Krafft. Propaganda Minister Goebbels wrote sarcastically in his diary, 'Oddly enough, not a single clairvoyant predicted that he would be arrested. A poor advertisement for their profession.'[34] When Krafft was freed from confinement after a year, his physical and mental state had deteriorated markedly.

To what extent had astrology been implicated in Hess's flight from Germany, perhaps even provoked it? The Nazi leadership, floundering around for an explanation of this outlandish and embarrassing event, and determined to protect Hitler, suggested astrology might have been the cause. They pointed the finger of blame at domestic practitioners, but also gave a hint that they suspected there might have been enemy involvement. The 13 May edition of *Völkischer Beobachter* reported, 'It is possible that Hess has been deliberately led into a trap from the British side.' In London the following day, *The Times* was quick to dissociate anyone – and presumably British Intelligence in particular – from such a charge. 'This suggestion is quite untrue: no one in Great Britain knew that Hess was contemplating his flight and his descent among us.'[35] Who had the *Times* reporter discussed the matter with in the hours since Hess landed to be so certain? Richard Deacon in his *A History of British Secret Service* had no doubt who had been complicit in the flight: not British Intelligence as such, but 'a few individualists' working for the Directorate of Naval Intelligence.[36] The Director, Rear Admiral Godfrey, had earlier been impressed with de Wohl's claim that he could read Hitler's mind through his horoscope, though Deacon was careful to absolve senior Naval Intelligence officers of any knowledge of or participation in Hess's defection.

Deacon's version of events pointed to Ian Fleming (the imaginative and maverick assistant to the Director of Naval Intelligence), a member of another branch of British Intelligence, and a contact in Switzerland who was an authoritative practitioner of astrology. Deacon writes, somewhat suspiciously given that he had been willing to identify Fleming, 'It is not possible to reveal the names of these two friends, both of whom ran grave risks in acting on Fleming's hunch.'[37] According to Deacon, the first stage had been to plant the impression in the minds of Nazi leaders that there was a revival in Britain of the pre-war pro-German organisation The Link (which had been led by a previous Director of Naval Intelligence, Admiral Sir Barry Domville, interned until 1943 as a Nazi sympathiser). This imaginary group was said to include senior politicians, supposed remnants of the 'appeasement lobby', and the Duke of Hamilton. They were, the story went, prepared to oust Churchill's government as a preliminary to making peace with Germany. The next stage was to identify Nazi leaders with interests in the occult and astrology in particular. Hess was selected as the most likely to fall into the trap being prepared. Fleming's contact in Switzerland was able by a complex series of connections to plant an astrologer in Hess's camp. It had long been known among astrologers that on 10 May six planets would line up in the sign Taurus and this would coincide with a full moon, an unusual conjunction believed to be a portent of dramatic events. Hess was to be persuaded this signified he was destined to be the man who, if he acted now, could secure peace between Germany and Britain.

Was it possible that any of this was true? Deacon continued to tell the same story in subsequent editions of his book, despite disagreement and criticism in the letters column of *The Times*. Deacon's book was first published in 1969. As Ian Fleming had died in 1964, he was no longer around to confirm or deny the story. But his brother Peter was. He agreed in a letter to *The Times* in September 1969 that while it was not impossible his brother might have come up with such a plan, he doubted it would ever have been acted upon. 'I am certain that if my brother had had anything to do with Hess's dramatic arrival in these beleaguered islands, he would have told me about it. He never did.' But, Fleming added, what he did know was that there had been an astrologer involved with MI14, the section of Military Intelligence covering Germany. He named him as Louis de Wohl and said he 'was invoked to divine the enemy's intentions and avert national disaster'. Fleming added that he had read de Wohl's *The Stars of War and Peace* and there had been no mention at all of a plan to encourage Hess to flee Germany by means of astrology. 'If any such stratagem was employed, or even contemplated, I am pretty sure that de Wohl would have known of it, and I think it unlikely that, twelve years later, he would have withheld so colourful an episode from his readers.'[38]

Ellic Howe, who was active in black propaganda in the Political Warfare Executive during the Second World War, and was associated with de Wohl in his work, wrote to *The Times* in similar terms to Fleming, dismissing Deacon's version of the events surrounding Hess as 'unconvincing'. Deacon's response to both letters was weak and had the effect of undermining rather than bolstering his story. 'Whatever doubts may be cast on the use of "baited" horoscopes by British agents, the fact remains that the Gestapo suspected this was what had happened.' This was hardly conclusive confirmation of his claim. Deacon added that his book had nowhere suggested de Wohl had been involved.[39] Both Peter Fleming and Howe had been associated closely with British Intelligence during the war – Fleming in military deception in Europe and Southeast Asia, Howe in the Political Warfare Executive. Did either or both have any reason to put readers off the scent by disparaging Deacon's thesis?

Howe had his own version of the background to Hess's flight. He doubted Hess had been directly motivated by astrological prophecy. It was true, Howe wrote in *Astrology and Psychological Warfare During World War II*, that Ernst Schulte-Strathaus – a member of Hess's personal staff since 1935, his adviser on the occult and a known amateur astrologer – had told Hess in January 1941 of a remarkable conjunction of planets due on 10 May. It was also true that during the June 1941 round-up of suspects, the Gestapo accused Schulte-Strathaus of having advised Hess that 10 May would be a fortunate day for his mission. Schulte-Strathaus was held in custody and not released until March 1943. But Schulte-Strathaus denied in an interview with Howe that he had done any more than mention in passing to Hess the interesting conjunction of planets in May 1941.[40]

At the astrologers' annual convention held in Harrogate in April 1941, a month before Hess's flight, the astrologer and businessman T. Mawby Cole forecast to the audience and representatives of the press that a momentous historical event would take place on 11 May – a 'great spiritual force is going to be released on this planet' – as a result of the coming planetary conjunction. This was the convention de Wohl said in 'The Orchestra of Hitler's Death' that he was going to disclose that Hitler's astrologer, Krafft, believed the Führer would soon die. In one of the tragic ironies of war (and of astrology), Cole did not live to see if his prophecy was fulfilled. He was killed in a German air raid on London on the evening of 10 May.[41]

5

There was another prophecy at the Harrogate astrologers' convention in April 1941. This came from a Brighton devotee of the science and a prolific writer, P.J. Harwood, who that year published *When the War Will End: An Astrological Almanac*. He predicted that German parachute troops would mount an invasion of Britain in May 1941, but that the Allies would regroup, counter-attack and win a decisive victory in January 1942.[42] This was a firm prediction but within a few weeks he was proved mistaken: there was no German landing and therefore no riposte.

Could de Wohl claim any greater success for his prognostications? He made an effort to convince the Special Operations Executive and the Directorate of Military Intelligence that he could, at a point he may have felt he was going to be abandoned by one or both bodies. The astrologer sent Hambro – his patron at SOE – a report setting out what he claimed had been his positive predictions over the past two years. Hambro passed a copy to an officer at the Foreign Office's Political Intelligence Department (the cover name for the Political Warfare Executive), describing de Wohl as 'our tame astrologer'. He went on, 'I have no doubt that if I checked up his successes I would see that he had more than an equal number of failures, but I have not the inclination nor the time to do so.'[43]

De Wohl divided his paper into two columns, one headed 'Quotations from my reports on astrological lines during 1941/2', the second 'Events in 1942' (although they actually began in 1941). For the year 1941 he selected two reports, 21 February and 1 April. The astrologer had predicted, 'Up to May Hitler will establish himself as the sovereign master of Europe'. This was true, but it had not required a knowledge of the movement of the stars to see the extent of German military success in the summer of 1940. The rest of what de Wohl wrote under 'quotations' was either so vague as to be of no value, or plainly wrong. He had said confidently that 'Hitler will avoid war against Yugoslavia if possible'. Germany invaded and subdued the country in April 1941. 'If possible' had been a convenient way of avoiding commitment, a useful two-way bet.

De Wohl included one entry from his 1 April report in the paper to Hambro: 'A date in Hitler's horoscope favourable for the invasion of an island is May 10th to June 5th.' When de Wohl had submitted his original report 'an island' had naturally been interpreted as a reference to the long-expected invasion of Britain and, as he later said, the idea was ridiculed at the time by British Intelligence officers. But he had not specified which island and now, under the heading 'Events', de Wohl typed the words 'Conquest of Crete'. This really did expose the limitations of astrological interpretation – Britain and Crete were indeed islands, at different ends of Europe. For a forecast to be so general as to be able to include any island anywhere really had no value for intelligence. But vindicated to his own satisfaction, de Wohl could have added that German troops began their invasion of Crete on 20 May, taking the island over completely on 1 June 1941, remarkably close to the dates he had given.

Regardless of his use or otherwise as a forecaster, the reader of Hitler's mind, British Intelligence were not abandoning de Wohl and plans were being made for SOE's 'tame astrologer'. He was to be despatched across the Atlantic to play a central part in his own scheme, 'The Orchestra of Hitler's Death'. This was to be linked with a campaign to counter Nazi propaganda in the United States that was encouraging the country to remain neutral. De Wohl's role would be to combine the inevitability of Hitler's death and Germany's defeat with the need for the United States to play a part in the struggle against Nazism. In his memoir of his wartime experiences, *The Stars of War and Peace*, de Wohl says very little about the months he spent in the United States. Given the astrologer's fondness for boosting his achievements, his failure to enlarge on propaganda work he carried out is surprising, though perhaps understandable. Did the explanation lay solely in the wording of the Official Secrets Act 1911, or was there another reason for not going into detail about his activity across the Atlantic?[44] Either way, soon after his return to London, Hambro at SOE, de Wohl's patron and the man responsible for sending him to New York, told the astrologer he had 'done an excellent job of work in America'.[45]

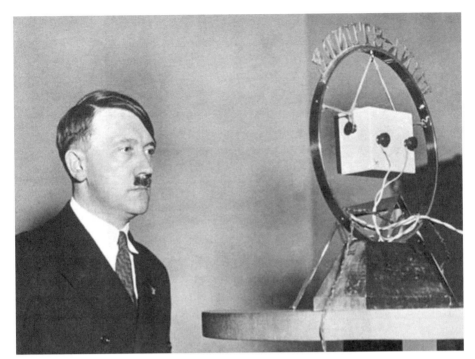

Hitler addressing the nation on radio, 1 February 1933, after he became German Chancellor. (Source: Unknown photographer. Bundesarchiv. Bild 183-1987-0703-506/CC-BY-SA 3.0)

Alexanderplatz, Berlin, in 1903, the year of de Wohl's birth. The astrologer, though a citizen of the Austro-Hungarian Empire, was born and lived in Berlin until he fled Germany in 1935. (Source: Unknown photographer. Wikimedia Commons/Public domain)

Louis de Wohl aged 36 in a vaguely sinister pose not long before he offered British Intelligence his services as an astrologer. (Source: Hulton Deutsch. Getty Images)

Viorel Tilea, the anti-Nazi Romanian ambassador in London in 1938–40, who believed, and told de Wohl, the Swiss-German Karl-Ernst Krafft was Hitler's personal astrologer. (Source: Unknown photographer. Biblioteca Centrală Universitară, Romania)

Prime Minister Winston Churchill and Foreign Secretary Lord Halifax. De Wohl impressed Halifax with his spontaneous 1-hour analysis of Hitler's horoscope in August 1940. (Source: Unknown photographer. Wikimedia Commons/Public domain)

ADOLF HITLER

April 20th, 1889, 6.30 p.m., Braunau, Austria

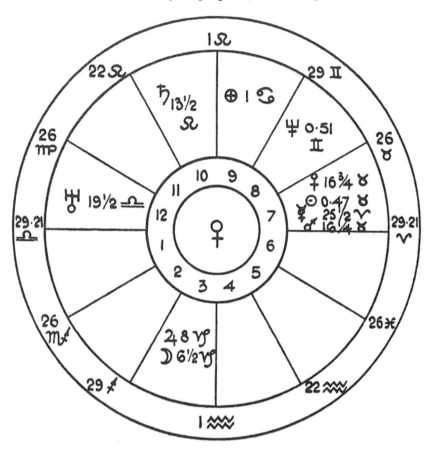

MAIN ASPECTS.

Hitler's horoscope, drawn up by de Wohl, by using which the astrologer told British Intelligence he could read Hitler's mind and intentions. (Source: Louis de Wohl, *Secret Service of the Sky*)

Rear Admiral John Godfrey, Director of Naval Intelligence, was particularly interested in 1940 with de Wohl's proposed use of Hitler's horoscope, though senior naval officers had doubts. (Source: Wales Smith, Royal Navy photographer. Wikimedia Commons/Public Domain)

Grosvenor House Hotel, Park Lane, London, where de Wohl was given a suite in which he lived and operated his one-man Psychological Research Bureau in 1940–41. (Source: Postcard, unknown artist. Wikimedia Commons/Public Domain)

British fleet viewed from the air during the Battle of Cape Matapan, 25 March 1941. De Wohl wrote in *The Stars of War and Peace* that he forecast a British victory 147 days before the clash with the Italian fleet. (Source: Unknown photographer. Wikimedia Commons/Public domain)

Eighth Army Commander General Bernard Montgomery observing British tanks going into action at El Alamein, November 1942. De Wohl claimed he predicted Montgomery's victory over the German Afrika Korps commander Erwin Rommel by comparing unnamed horoscopes. (Source: Unknown photographer. Wikimedia Commons/Public domain)

Hitler Will Die Soon, Stars Inform Visiting Astrologer

Hungarian Also Predicts Germans May Try Move Through South America

Adolf Hitler has not long to live.

He is mentally ill.

If Germany wins the Russian campaign it won't be with the help of Hitler's favorite stars.

Germany may well try an invasion of the United States—through South America.

The "golden age of peace will start in 1948, although the present world conflict may" not last that long.

'NOTHING MYSTIC'

There's absolutely nothing mystic about predictions such as these from Louis De Wohl, Hungarian astro-philosopher now visiting friends in Los Angeles.

As a matter of fact, if you're any illusions about the way an astrologer should look and act, De Wohl will erase them.

Chubby, blue-eyed, curly-headed and bespectacled, De Wohl hopes to see the day when astrology will be recognized as a science.

COLD LOGIC

Already he has astounded editors and the general public with predictions. A book written in 1938 foresaw many of the things which have followed. Recently he predicted the first clash between German and Italian troops, somewhere in Greece, and two days later an item from Athens told of the conflict.

"There's nothing supernatural or uncanny about it," he insists. "It's just cold logic. Stars can affect our doings only 40 per cent and wills of humans affect the remaining 60 per cent. But you can't ignore that 40 per cent."

SECRET OF PREDICTIONS

He explains the whole science by pointing out that the stars, sun and moon are made up of chemical elements and so are the human bodies. Then, he says, is it not logical that the combination of the chemical elements in the heavens in a given position might have certain reactions on the human systems? Therein lies the secret of it, he believes.

Having once been offered a position in the German Geo-Political Institute at Munich, which employs 1000 experts to plot Hitler's stars, De Wohl points out he turned down the offer and fled Germany but thus knows that Hitler watches astrological aspects.

'HITLER END NEAR'

Hitler's horoscope shows he has not long to live. The mentally ill state explains why he and Mussolini conferred for five days—because Hitler can no longer engage in lengthy conferences and must limit them to short periods.

The Russian campaign, contrary to other campaigns, was started when the aspects were bad for Hitler and was done by the high command's influence against that of the stars.

After next June 11, the aspects for the United States will turn for the worse and after that date, if Germany is still going, an invasion may be started through Brazil, which already has many German colonists, De Wohl declared.

ICELAND MOVE GOOD

But, meantime, the United States has its best period. The move into Iceland came at a high spot for both the United States and the President and both the nation and Roosevelt will continue in a good position until next spring.

De Wohl declared that between now and June 11, 1942, would be the best time for the United States to enter the war.

FORMERLY AN AUTHOR

De Wohl pointed out that he's really more interested in the psychological aspects of astrology than in predictions. He was an author before he took up astrology 12 years ago and has written several motion-picture scripts.

Incidentally, he won't make any snap predictions. Each one requires weeks of study of horoscopes, birth dates, positions of the stars and other technical points. Then, after lengthy consideration, he'll decide what things are most likely to happen.

Los Angeles Times, 9 September 1941. The article was an example of the invariably friendly media treatment de Wohl received during his wartime mission to the United States. (Source: *Los Angeles Times*.)

Sefton Delmer of the Political Warfare Executive with whom de Wohl – a kindred spirit – used astrology in black propaganda in 1942–43. (Source: Kurt Hutton. Getty Images)

To-day the strange story is told of Britain's

STATE SEER

★ **A prophet in Mayfair**

···

relates how he fought

···

Hitler by 'star warfare'

···

wou.d be *h.o—ipyas.or.* he pre-dicted. before May 1941 when Jupiter would be in co.' m 'pon with the position of Ne t n e a: Hitler's birth").

The sea battle of Cape Matapan was Andrew Cunning-ham's triumph. Astr.ogically. it was apparently De'.o' The impending "powerful attack" of Admiral Cunningham i.d im-pressed him, '.c recalls. as early as November 2), 1940. when "I wrote my report and mentioned that the admiral was most likely

Evening Standard, 19 August 1952. An article in the newspaper based unquestioningly on de Wohl's *The Stars of War and Peace*. (Source: London *Evening Standard*)

6

AMERICA WOULD BE 'IN' BY 1944

1

De Wohl wrote in *The Stars of War and Peace* that the question he was asked most often in the first two years of the Second World War was when the United States would enter the conflict as Britain's ally against Germany. He was in no doubt she would and was satisfied he could reveal through his astrological calculations when that would be. He believed the combination of the planet Uranus and Gemini, the sign rising at the time of the country's 'birth' – the day the Declaration of Independence was proclaimed, 4 July 1776 – was the key. Uranus stood at the ninth degree of Gemini at that point. The planet took eighty-four years to move through the twelve astrological signs, which meant Uranus could be found to be in conjunction with its original place in the natal horoscope every eighty-four years. 'In 1776 the States were in their War of Independence,' de Wohl wrote. 'Eighty-four years later, in 1860, the State suffered their Civil War. Another 84 years … There was little doubt that America would be "in" by 1944.'[1]

De Wohl had set out his own typically grandiose vision in 'The Orchestra of Hitler's Death' and the Colonial Office and Foreign Office had already put some parts into action. But the astrologer's move from England to the United States was sudden, with little time to make any firm arrangements. His personal target, however, would always be

Hitler, on whose horoscope he believed himself to be the specialist. De Wohl was to be one element in an official British campaign to draw the United States into the war against Germany, the only way – as Churchill had admitted privately from the beginning – of defeating the Nazi enemy and guaranteeing Britain's survival. The astrologer's explanation in *The Stars of War and Peace* for his mission across the Atlantic was simply that he had asked permission (of whom he did not say) to meet fellow American practitioners in the stars. Far more likely, it was the decision of de Wohl's patron in the Special Operations Executive, Hambro, to send him on this 'astrological mission'. The SOE War Diary was explicit. De Wohl was on a 'sponsored visit to the United States in order to carry out anti-Hitler propaganda'.[2] The 'Orchestra of Hitler's Death' was officially on tour.

German intelligence agents were conducting a vigorous campaign of psychological warfare in the United States, planting stories and letters in astrology magazines predicting the inevitability of Nazi victory. The strategy was to encourage an already significant isolationist sentiment in the population to maintain the country's neutrality in the war. It had, after all, been American entry in the First World War in 1917 that had made certain Germany's defeat. The Nazi operation had to be countered, using their own weapon against them: the horoscope. As far as Hambro was concerned, de Wohl was the perfect – perhaps the only – realistic candidate for this task. Was this just a compliment to the talent he had shown for imaginative black propaganda or was it a convenient opportunity to remove what some in British Intelligence were beginning to see as a nuisance? Probably both played a part.

June Bainbridge, Hambro's secretary at the Special Operations Executive's Baker Street headquarters, was ordered to accompany the astrologer on his mission, deployed to provide administrative support and – just as important – to keep an eye on a maverick who remained an object of suspicion. One SOE officer recorded Bainbridge in her personal file as going to New York with the astrologer to act as the astrologer's 'bear leader'. She had earlier been used by Lennox of MI5 as a source of under-the-counter information on de Wohl's activities with SOE, passing papers Military Intelligence would not otherwise see but might find enlightening. This was yet another example of everyone watching everyone else. She later described Lennox merely as 'a gentleman in the War Office' and may have believed that to be the case. An MI5 officer was even recorded on de Wohl's personal file as saying he had suspected Bainbridge was the astrologer's mistress. Her version of de Wohl's despatch to the United States differed from the astrologer's. She said de Wohl was initially reluctant to leave on the mission because after consulting his own horoscope he decided his 'current planetary "aspects" were unsatisfactory'. He had to be persuaded he had a duty to go when other refugees from the Nazis were actively engaged serving in the armed forces, risking their lives.[3] De Wohl had, of course, been prepared to take that risk. He had offered himself for service in 1939, been rejected, and the stars were all that was left if de Wohl were to play his part.

There was, as so often with de Wohl, an element of unintended irony in what he was doing. Only a few months before, in February 1941, he had been warning that because of the United States Government's aid to Britain through, for example, Lend-Lease, as far as the war was concerned 'it may be in Hitler's interest to <u>get her involved before she is ready</u>. This would probably stop part of the flow of material to Britain ...'[4] That line was now dropped. The intention was that the United States should be drawn into the war against Nazi Germany alongside Britain and the Soviet Union and the astrologer's role would be to help in the task of softening up American public opinion. De Wohl went from England by sea, landing in Canada on 24 May 1941 and travelling on by train to Montreal, where Bainbridge joined him. It was surely no coincidence that the Director of Naval Intelligence, Rear Admiral Godfrey, accompanied by his personal assistant Commander Ian Fleming, travelled to New York in the same month, arriving on 25 May.[5]

In the weeks before Bainbridge left to carry out her task of keeping tabs on the unpredictable astrologer, SOE was embarrassed to find that, so casual had arrangements been when recruiting her as Hambro's secretary in the confused summer of 1940, she was not put through the mandatory security vetting. SOE had to ask MI5 to remedy this quickly before she was able to leave the country. Once Bainbridge had arrived in Canada, she and the astrologer crossed the border into the United

States together, reaching New York on 11 June. The fiction for public consumption was that de Wohl, a refugee from the Nazis, a celebrated Hungarian astrologer and writer, was visiting the country as a private citizen, with Bainbridge accompanying him as his secretary. After New York, the story would go, they would travel cross country to Hollywood for de Wohl to look into the possibility of returning to his previous involvement in the film industry.

The astrologer found what he later described as 'an incredibly peaceful atmosphere' on his arrival in the United States, with most Americans unable to comprehend that they would inevitably be drawn into the war, making it international rather than European:

> They did not understand that Hitler hated them – was bound to hate them, not only because their power had done so much in World War 1 to bring about the downfall of Germany, but most of all because in their unity they were a living example of the complete fallacy of his racial doctrine. A complete mix up of races *could* be complete success! That was something Hitler could not tolerate.[6]

About the time de Wohl had set out on his mission (and, by chance, a few days after Hess's strange descent from the clouds in Scotland), Lord Halifax – now British ambassador to Washington – had warned Americans in a speech in Kansas City, Missouri, of the danger and the impossibility of neutrality, slotting neatly into the campaign the astrologer was crossing the Atlantic to assist. 'I do not believe,' Halifax said, 'that it is possible for you to maintain your way of life if the Nazis ruled the British Commonwealth and British sea power were destroyed … From this struggle there can be only one issue. There is no room for compromise. We must achieve victory or death.'[7] The timing was clearly no accident: Halifax's speech, the astrologer's arrival on American soil, the visit of the Director of Naval Intelligence, all there by chance? Hardly likely. It had been at dinner at the Spanish ambassador's residence in London in August 1940 that de Wohl – at least according to his own account – had impressed the then Foreign Secretary Halifax with his insights into Hitler's character through his horoscope, the first step in the astrologer's relationship with British Intelligence. And it had been the Director of Naval Intelligence who had first taken an interest in the part the stars might play in the war against Germany.

If contemporary opinion polls were an accurate guide, de Wohl had misjudged the popular mood on his arrival in America, while Halifax – as he would have known from his own conversations with President Roosevelt – was pushing at a door already half open. At the outbreak of war in September 1939, United States opinion was almost equally divided, with 42 per cent of Americans questioned backing support for Britain and 48 per cent against, even if she and France were to face defeat at German hands. Within a month, as Germany and the Soviet Union consolidated their occupation of Poland, opinion had shifted dramatically, 29 per cent saying America should aid Britain and France, with 71 per cent opposing any such idea. After German armies had swept through the Low Countries and into France, American public opinion was even more firmly opposed to any form of support, with an almost insignificant 7 per cent in favour and 93 per cent emphatically against.

But with the collapse of France attitudes began to shift. In September 1940, 52 per cent of those questioned by Gallup thought the United States should 'help England win', even if doing so might lead to coming into conflict with Germany. There could be no doubt where President Roosevelt's sympathies lay and – while promising at the 1940 presidential election not to 'send any American boys into foreign wars' – he had been nudging the country step by step to prepare for entry. In 1940 military conscription had been introduced, along with Congressional authorisation to double the size of the navy. Roosevelt pledged to come to the aid of any country on the American continent that came under attack. In a December 1940 radio broadcast the President described the United States as the 'arsenal of democracy', arming Britain in the fight against Nazi Germany. Britain was provided with fifty destroyers – old, but serviceable – in return for the use by American forces of bases in British Caribbean islands. Finally, the Lend–Lease Act authorised the sale, transfer, lease or loan to any government whatever equipment the President deemed vital for the defence of United States interests. When Roosevelt was elected for a third term in November 1940, the proportion of the country favouring actively aiding Britain had risen to 60 per cent and when the Lease-Lend Act came into effect to 67 per cent.

2

De Wohl arrived in New York in June, but there had been a British Intelligence presence in the city for a year pulling together information and working to influence American public opinion. British Security Co-ordination (BSC) was set up in the United States in June 1940 at the instigation of Prime Minister Winston Churchill, when British prospects of survival against Hitler appeared at their most precarious. German forces had occupied much of Western Europe and the invasion of Britain was the next step. So desperate had been the situation that British Intelligence had even called upon de Wohl for astrological advice on Hitler's possible timing. If the worst happened and Britain were to be occupied by the Nazis, the BSC offices would function as British Intelligence's outpost in the Western Hemisphere. The organisation – the name of which was reputed to have been suggested by J. Edgar Hoover, director of the Federal Bureau of Investigation – was headed by William Stephenson, a Canadian steel millionaire, a personal friend of Churchill's who had served as a fighter pilot in the First World War. In the appeasement period of the late 1930s, Stephenson had used his business contacts in Germany to keep Churchill informed of developments under the Nazis. He was drafted into MI6, the Secret Intelligence Service, and sent to New York in the guise of 'Passport Control Officer', the traditional cover used by British intelligence chiefs abroad. BSC was eventually based on the 35th floor of the Rockefeller Center, where it masqueraded as the British Passport Control Office. Stephenson's role was to direct the activities of British intelligence in the Americas, overseeing the multi-faceted work of MI5, MI6 and the Special Operations Executive. At the height of BSC activity, over 2,000 agents were estimated to be operating in the United States.

BSC's central task in the United States was to combine propaganda encouraging popular support for the British fight against the Nazis with espionage and counter-espionage. Much of the organisation's work involved black propaganda and the manipulation of news, planting genuine or spurious anti-German stories in the American press and on radio stations, pushing journalists and editors into taking a pro-British line. As SOE's official historian comments, Stephenson's personality and experience gave him the particular skills required. His 'discreet feelers and suggestions to newspaper owners, columnists and leader writers all over the United States paid off'.[8] BSC also functioned as the link between the British and American intelligence services. Stephenson worked closely, though unofficially given the country's neutrality, with Hoover of the FBI and William Donovan, a former New York lawyer who operated as the country's senior intelligence officer. Donovan subsequently became head of the Office of Strategic Services, forerunner of the Central Intelligence Agency.

De Wohl was to be part of the intensifying BSC campaign to discredit pro-German propaganda and domestic isolationism and to win support for America's active participation in the war. As the astrologer was arriving in the United States, the objectives of the Special Operations Executive, to which he was attached, were broadened. SOE agents were instructed to 'take any warrantable action likely to influence the entry of the US into the war and to discredit the enemies of the Allies in the US'.[9] Although BSC's existence was not officially acknowledged until the United States became engaged in the conflict in December 1941, President Roosevelt was supposed to have laughingly confided to the organisation's head Stephenson in the White House, 'I'm your biggest undercover agent.'[10] One MI6 officer described the head of BSC's relationship with Roosevelt and with Donovan of American intelligence as 'well dug in'.[11] Roosevelt's sympathies were entirely with Britain against Nazi Germany and in March 1941 he reportedly stated 'categorically' that he 'would act to bring the USA in very shortly'.[12] De Wohl's role would be to use his skill as an astrologer to contribute what he could to encourage the American people to follow Roosevelt's lead.

What remains remarkable, given the prominence of the astrologer's role in one important aspect of the Special Operation Executive's American campaign, is how little he has to say in *The Stars of War and*

Peace about his involvement from June 1941 to February 1942, the period he was in the United States. In a book in which he devoted pages to rambling commentaries on small and relatively insignificant incidents, he deals with his stay in no more than two pages, much of the text made up of quotations from what American astrologers were saying in 1941 about the likelihood of the country entering the war. His only specific comment is, 'I conferred with American astrologers, first in New York, then in Cleveland, where I spoke at the Astrological Congress.'[13]

Either de Wohl considered he had added nothing of significance to the war effort – which was unlikely given the fact that his activity in the United States traced almost step-by-step the outline of his 'Orchestra of Hitler's Death' – or his work was so sensitive or potentially embarrassing to British Intelligence that MI5 officers vetting the draft of his memoir had ordered him not to reveal any of it. As De Wohl's involvement with Rear Admiral Godfrey and Naval Intelligence in 1940 had similarly been excluded from *The Stars of War and Peace* in this way, that is also a possible explanation. A third is that he realised that his propaganda activity in the United States could be seen by his peers as a misuse of astrology, a prostitution of the craft, however good the cause.

3

De Wohl was officially in the United States as an astrologer, a civilian, so his rank as a British Army captain (however dubious that might be) and his involvement with the Special Operations Executive and Military Intelligence had to be hidden. According to one SOE officer, American intelligence wondered whether 'the de Wohl mission was a cover story for something infinitely more sinister'.[14] But the close co-operation between Stephenson of BSC and Donovan ensured they had a good idea of the actual reason for the astrologer's stay. To bolster the subterfuge, de Wohl acquired a press agent, a self-styled 'personal representative', Martin Starr – an apt surname – based at Chanin Building in Manhattan. Starr (or was this de Wohl himself in yet another guise?) produced a four-page biography of de Wohl for circulation as publicity material. A copy eventually found its way into de Wohl's MI5 file. Describing the astrologer as a 'distinguished author, astro-philosopher and exile from Hitler's Geo-Political Institute', Starr went on, 'This world renowned astrologer, famous author, fine speaker with an innate sense of the timely-tempoed [*sic*] dramatic is the news interest of the hour. Verily, it is no wonder that reporters in their stories, respectfully refer to Louis de Wohl as "the modern Nostradamus".'[15]

De Wohl offered a programme of four lectures, each of which he delivered in a tour of major American cities. Starr listed them in ad man's overblown language, perfectly pitched for a country still at peace but avid for news of the war. Number one was 'Hitler and Napoleon ... Yesterday's bloody pages of history are mirrored against the tumultuous happenings of today with ironic parallel. The subject is more dramatic than drama itself.' Next came 'Weathering the Early Blitzes ... Those terrible days that followed the fall of France. The unbelievable terror that struck from the skies ... the smouldering ruins of cities, hospitals, churches.' Then, 'Hitler's Geo-Political Institute in Munich ... The untold tale of the school of the stars that plays so dominant a part in the field operations of Hitler and his generals ... Why de Wohl refused to become part of the Institute.' Finally, 'Things to Come ... The news of the day in the theatre of war. The probable outcome of the morrow. Prognostications, prophecies and predictions bearing on international situations.'

The astrologer's lectures ran parallel with newspaper interviews, all intended to persuade the public the defeat of the Nazis and Hitler's death were inevitable and that America's participation in the war was essential. De Wohl's companion on the mission, June Bainbridge, later described the form the astrologer's interviews often took:

> De Wohl worked out astrological 'maps' of various people he thought were of particular use to Hitler and then told selected gatherings of journalists all the 'astrological bad aspects' to which his selected victims would be subject during the near future, in the hope of giving the said victims an aura of 'bad luck'.[16]

Given de Wohl's mission, it is interesting to return to what he had written in June 1938 in *Secret Service of the Sky* when he analysed President Roosevelt's horoscope. Roosevelt, he said:

> has the Moon (people) in the House of Career and also Mars (energy, power, war). But as the Moon and Mars are only well aspected, America under his government should not be involved in an unfortunate war ... The constellation of the House of Foreign Countries (ninth) does not look too good, with Neptune and Jupiter therein, both in bad aspects to the Sun. Here in itself lies the danger of conflict with a foreign power – although not necessarily war.[17]

So, according to de Wohl in 1938, it was possible to foresee from Roosevelt's horoscope the United States becoming involved in a conflict of some kind, but not an unfortunate war. Whether this meant no war or a war the country was destined to win the astrologer could not determine at the time (nor with whom) or preferred not to say.

The 'project' – as Bainbridge herself described de Wohl's mission in the United States – was originally intended to last only two months but in the event was continued until after the country had entered the war in December 1941. To maintain the illusion he was simply a Hungarian civilian and Bainbridge his personal secretary, the astrologer had no direct contact with British Security Co-ordination in New York, nor with any other British officials. Bainbridge served as his liaison with BSC, passing him instructions and information from SOE in London. While he was in New York, de Wohl stayed in an expensive hotel suite, equivalent to his relatively lavish quarters at Grosvenor House. Eric Maschwitz, composer of the contemporary popular song, 'A Nightingale Sang in Berkeley Square', at the time an SOE officer, had the job of delivering de Wohl's wages in 'untraceable greenbacks'. During their meetings Maschwitz took an intense dislike to the astrologer, describing him as 'a right swindler ... you never met such a character. He was up to everything and he was paid a lot of money and I know because I used to have to go and pay him once a week.'[18] As with SOE in London, there seemed to be substantial amounts of money sloshing around. A merchant banker on wartime attachment to the Treasury who visited BSC's New York headquarters complained on his return that 'on the thirty-fifth floor of the Rockefeller Building there were a large number of people drawing $800 a month for doing absolutely nothing'.[19]

American intelligence took de Wohl's role seriously enough for Ernest Cuneo – formerly legal adviser to the New York mayor, now operating as President Roosevelt's secret liaison officer with British Security Co-ordination – to be given the task of launching the astrologer in the country. Cuneo recruited a publicity agent from the film company Metro-Goldwyn-Mayer to set up meetings with the press soon after de Wohl's arrival. In his paper 'The Orchestra of Hitler's Death' a few months previously, de Wohl had recommended a concentrated publicity campaign in the United States to ridicule, undermine and discredit Hitler, the Nazis and their collaborators. The newspaper interviews began to appear within a few weeks.

The *New York Sun* on 24 June, under the headline 'Seer Sees Plot to Kill Hitler', quoted de Wohl as prophesying the German leader would be dead by the year's end, that he was a doomed man, that he was slowly going insane, and that his astrologers were afraid to tell him the truth about his fate. This story had two purposes. The first was to undermine any idea in the United States that Hitler had super-human ability, an irresistible quality that would lead Germany to inevitable victory. The second was for the prophecy of Hitler's vulnerability to find its way to Germany, panic the people into believing the Nazi leadership was ill-fated, and – on the assumption the dictator relied on astrologers – encourage him to suspect they could not be trusted.

Hitler's demise was for the future. De Wohl also had news for the present. 'A strong collaborator of Hitler who is neither German nor a Nazi will go violently insane,' he forecast. 'He will be in South or Central America, probably near the Caribbean Sea.' The story was published in the *New York Sun* on Tuesday. By Friday, the *New York Post* was reporting that Admiral Georges Robert, the Vichy High Commissioner of the French West Indies, based on the island of Martinique, had gone mad and had had to be restrained by his aides.[20] The *New York Sun* followed up with what was said to be 'confirmation' of the story the next day. In fact the admiral had not gone insane but had had an attack of sunstroke and there was no independent reporter in Martinique able to check the story. Primed by British Security Co-ordination and Special Operations Executive via Bainbridge, de Wohl could claim he had forecast the event by consulting the stars.[21] De Wohl's tale was, in any case, more entertaining than the banal reality and so it stood.

Another seed to be planted in American minds, and indirectly in those of the German people, was the possibility of the Führer's political death or his overthrow or possible assassination by anti-Nazi conspirators in the armed forces. The 18 July 1941 edition of the *New York Post* contained an interview in which de Wohl forecast that 'within a few days' Hitler would dismiss two senior army commanders, Keitel and von Brauchitsch. The Nazi invasion of the Soviet Union had opened a month before, but – after an initially rapid German advance – there were already signs the attack was faltering. This might be seen as a reason to sack the generals, de Wohl said, but their disappearance would not result from any inefficiency on their part. 'Frankly, Hitler was in fear of these two men.' Hitler believed, the astrologer implied without directly saying, they were plotting to depose him. The short biography produced by de Wohl's agent in New York claimed the astrologer's prediction that Hitler would sack the two generals had been proved correct, wrongly citing confirmation in New York newspapers a few days later.[22]

De Wohl had originally produced astrological pen portraits of the generals von Brauchitsch and Keitel in 1940 for MI14, the German Section of the Directorate of Military Intelligence. His forecast then had been that Keitel would remain in post for some time to come, as would von Brauchitsch, though for the latter he predicted a 'very good' July 1941 followed by a 'dangerous' August.[23] Hitler did not dismiss Keitel in summer 1941 and he remained chief of the armed forces high command until the war's end in 1945. Von Brauchitsch was not removed from command until December 1941, not for conspiracy but after he had suffered a heart attack. As with Admiral Roberts in Martinique, the American press apparently made no effort to check, allowing de Wohl to lay claim to an uncanny prescience. The *New York Post* reported newspapers across the country were besieging him for exclusive stories because of his proven record as a seer. For the purpose of Wohl's black propaganda mission, the truth was unimportant. What mattered was what the American people could be made to believe.

De Wohl's proposal in 'The Orchestra of Hitler's Death' to ensure a persistent drip-drip of bad news about Hitler had now taken off. A former SEO officer writing after the war was out in his timing when he said that 'soon after de Wohl arrived in the USA he asked for "world-wide" backing for his astrological propaganda campaign. It was at his request that we arranged for "predictions" to be made ...' The officer had in retrospect a low opinion of the project which, he said, 'seemed to me to be too complex, too expensive, and too much open to charlatanism, to justify the time spent on it'.[24] The Colonial Office, Foreign Office and India Office had co-operated with the SOE in encouraging soothsayers across the world to make prophecies about Hitler's imminent demise, echoing and confirming the predictions de Wohl would be making in the United States. There were reports of forecasts in Nigerian and Egyptian newspapers of red planets on the eastern horizon, of a monkey-faced man falling from a rock, presaging the death of a tyrant. As one writer on British Intelligence activities in the United States colourfully describes it, 'Such stories were echoed by muezzins from their minarets in Malaya, the Chinese in their temples in Hong Kong, and wherever else the British propaganda warfare could orchestrate prophecies that would confirm de Wohl's eminence in his field.'[25]

An interview de Wohl gave to reporter Ruth Reynolds of the *New York Sunday News*, published on 21 July 1941, drew all the instruments of his orchestra together: 'Hitler's Stargazer Sees Heavenly Stop Light'.[26] The article painted a picture of de Wohl as a 'Berlin-born author, astro-philosopher and voluntary exile from the ideology of National Socialism ... now in New York making a few astounding predictions of his own about international affairs, prior to a journey to Hollywood and film work.' De Wohl first brought up Karl-Ernest Krafft, whom he continued to maintain was Hitler's personal astrologer. He quoted from what purported to be the letter Krafft wrote to the Romanian ambassador in

London, Viorel Tilea. De Wohl said in this Krafft had as much admitted as far back as 1940 that Germany would lose the war and Hitler would disappear. The truth was (as Tilea later confirmed) that Krafft had written nothing of the kind, his letter to Tilea containing mainly pro-Nazi propaganda. But de Wohl went on to embellish his familiar tale with some new elements. The *Sunday News* reporter wrote:

> The letter was sent to de Wohl by Tilea when the latter learned that de Wohl's dislike of the present German regime was so great that he had applied for service in the British army. When and if he is accepted he will become a British subject and return for duty against his Fatherland. De Wohl's intense dislike of Krafft, a fellow professional, springs from his belief that astrologers should never apply 'their supernormal knowledge for evil ends'.

'His Fatherland' was a clumsy but apparently unnoticed slip when the astrologer was supposed to be stressing he was a Hungarian, not a German. De Wohl repeated the now persistent story that Hitler based all his actions on readings of his horoscope, had first become involved with astrology in 1923, and had developed his interest when he shared a prison cell with Rudolf Hess in 1925 following the failed 'beer hall putsch' in Munich. 'Now Hitler depends on the work of two personal astrologers,' de Wohl told the reporter, 'plus a group employed at the Geo-Political Institute in Munich. The predictions of each are checked against the others.' He said he had been invited to work at the Institute and had refused on principle. '"I had three years of Hitlerism and I knew it was wrong," says de Wohl, who is as "pure Aryan" as Hitler could wish.' The article repeated without question the astrologer's 'predictions' on his arrival in the United States in June that the French West Indies High Commissioner, Admiral Robert, would go 'violently insane' (it was temporary sunstroke) and that Generals Keitel and von Brauchitsch would shortly be dismissed (they were not). Finally there came the purpose of de Wohl's presence in the United States and of every interview he gave: 'His latest prediction is that Hitler will be assassinated within a year.'

4

De Wohl wrote in *The Stars of War and Peace* that what had struck him most forcefully when he arrived in the United States in June 1941 was the 'incredibly peaceful atmosphere ... the fact that some Americans seemed to regard peace simply as one of their natural possessions.' But at the same time, he said, many American astrologers were aware of the actual situation and recognised the danger their country was facing. Quoting their predictions and to show their prescience, he emphasised that they would often have been composed months before their appearance in astrological magazines.[27] One in the summer issue of *Astrology Guide* warned, 'On guard, America! Uranus is the planet of sudden changes.' This was a forecast that could obviously be turned to meet almost any situation. But *American Astrology* said in its September 1941 edition, 'The Southern Pacific could become the centre of war activity within the next few months.'

George Llewellyn's prediction in the autumn edition of the *Astrological Bulletin* went as far as naming the immediate enemy: 'The Japanese will tend to take drastic action.' Sydney Bennett in *Wynn's Astrology* could hardly have been more clear about the surprise attack on 7 December 1941. 'Japan now starts a four months period when it will probably attempt some military sleight-of-hand – the horoscope of the Emperor shows him to be ... too sure of the quick success of Japanese arms and diplomacy to hold back the warmongers.' Finally, the November issue of *American Astrology* almost named the day: 'Japan ... is unwilling to withdraw to her own Island kingdom ... hotheads who have been agitating for war at any price will become unmanageable, with December highly explosive and a great possibility of them having their way.'

It was to his fellow professional astrologers that de Wohl turned next, the only activity in the United States that he was prepared – or perhaps allowed – to admit to when he came to publish *The Stars of War and Peace*. His cover for his stay was that he was a visiting Hungarian astrologer, lecturing, giving interviews and writing newspaper articles. In addition, he told the *New York Sunday News* reporter in July, he also proposed to travel across country to Hollywood, where he had friends among fellow refugees from Nazi Germany, to discuss ideas for possible future film work. The actor and director Fritz Lang, for example, shared de Wohl's interest in astrology. Among others de Wohl had worked with in the pre-Nazi German industry and now in Hollywood were the actor Conrad Veidt, directors Curtis Bernhardt and Henry Koster, and screenwriter Carl Mayer.

De Wohl was also booked to address the annual convention of the American Federation of Scientific Astrologers in Cleveland, Ohio, which opened on 6 August 1941. His theme was a comparison between the horoscopes of Napoleon and Hitler. Two writers on the subject have suggested the Federation was a front organisation set up by British Security Co-ordination from New York solely to provide their astrologer with another platform for anti-German propaganda.[28] An interesting idea, but the Federation had been established in Washington DC in March 1938 by Ernest and Catherine Grant, two well-known and long-standing practitioners of astrology. This was over two years before BSC (and, for that matter, the Special Operations Executive) were set up.

Ostensibly an astrological comparison of two European tyrants, one nineteenth century and the other twentieth century, de Wohl's address was a variation on what he had been saying in interviews with the press since his arrival in the United States.[29] The astrologer first entertained his audience with a short exploration of Hitler's sex life, forecasting – though nothing was then known officially outside the highest Nazi circles about the existence of Eva Braun – the violent death of the Führer's mistress. Hitler could call on the service of Germany's finest astrologers, de Wohl said, but he had obviously ignored their advice by invading the Soviet Union in June, 'a great mistake'. The stars had warned against such a move. He condemned American isolationists, in particular their leading figure, the aviator Charles Lindbergh, saying that because a man knew how to handle machines that did not make him an authority on everything else. By chance, Lindbergh was appearing in the same city that week, addressing a meeting of the anti-interventionist America First Committee. In 1932 his 20-month-old son had been abducted and murdered. De Wohl told the astrologers' convention that the boy was not dead but was 'being raised in a Nazi school in East Prussia to become a future führer'.[30] This truly was the deepest black propaganda and the astrologer had perhaps been carried away and gone further than he had intended. That Lindbergh was in Cleveland at the same time as de Wohl made the attack all the more inflammatory.[31]

Turning to the comparison between Napoleon and Hitler he had frequently made before, de Wohl described to the audience the distinct parallels in the two leaders' horoscopes. Both had Saturn in an adverse position in the tenth house, the section of the horoscope signifying an individual's status in the world. This 'detriment', the science of astrology said, forecast 'rise, but danger of downfall'. What would be the reason for that downfall? 'Overstepping the ambitions, using questionable methods, dishonourable conduct ...' Both also had the Moon in Capricorn, 'the worst position of the Moon for decisions on an emotional basis'. This, de Wohl said, explained Hitler's decision to turn to attack Paris in 1940 rather than crossing the Channel to put Britain out of the war immediately, a move that doomed him and Germany to certain defeat.[32] De Wohl was not alone in making the connection between the horoscopes of Napoleon and Hitler. In 1931 – two years before Hitler took office as Chancellor – the president of the Berlin Astrological Society was quoted in the *New York Times* as saying Hitler would rise to power 'but in that moment, even as it happened to Napoleon I and Napoleon III, power will be wrested from his hands by others'.[33]

De Wohl went on to warn that Hitler had every intention of bringing the war to the United States. Germany would invade Brazil, where there was already a substantial German population, and would use the country as a springboard for an attack through the Americas. Astrologically, he said, the United States was vulnerable when the two major malefic planets Saturn and Uranus transited the country's ruling sign, Gemini. This would be the position until the spring of 1942. But, threatening as the situation stood, there was hope. 'President Roosevelt's horoscope is perfectly beautiful,' the astrologer told his audience. 'He towers above all others. A yogi once told me a man born on the date Hitler came into power would cause his downfall. Hitler rose to power on January 30, and that is Roosevelt's birth date.' No astrologer could predict precisely when the Nazi leader's downfall would come, but come it undoubtedly would. 'Hitler is on the downgrade … If the United States enters the war before next spring, he is doomed.'

Was there any way of assessing the impact of de Wohl's activity in the United States on public opinion, combined as it was with the stories carefully being planted round the world as part of 'The Orchestra of Hitler's Death'? The astrologer was undoubtedly busy during his months in America and both he and Bainbridge were congratulated on their work on their return to London. Bainbridge, however, later said they had received little of the practical help they had been promised from British Security Co-ordination in New York. 'It seemed to me,' she wrote, 'that what could have been an excellent piece of psychological warfare turned out, from lack of co-operation, into a fair flop.'[34] But, of course, the idea had been from the start that de Wohl should never be identified as having any direct connection with Britain. He was in the country in the guise of a neutral astrologer giving objective interpretations of what the stars foretold.

Despite Bainbridge's misgivings, BSC's head, Stephenson, was impressed with the impact de Wohl was having. Stephenson wrote in a memorandum to London, 'An ever-growing audience [is] becoming convinced of his supernatural powers.'[35] If BSC were not helping de Wohl, as Bainbridge later complained, the astrologer was certainly helping BSC, supplying the organisation with material in the form of 'prophecies' – invariably of Hitler's imminent death – which were then broadcast throughout the world in a range of languages, to be subsequently regurgitated in American newspapers in a propaganda loop.

Following de Wohl's successful and widely publicised appearance at the astrological convention in Cleveland, the *Los Angeles Times* printed a front-page interview in September that enabled him to run through his well-rehearsed routine.[36] The newspaper reported that he was in the city 'visiting friends'. The astrologer was ostensibly in Hollywood, as he had told the *New York Sunday News* in July, to return to the 'film work' he had abandoned when he fled to Britain in 1935. His actual mission was to meet German and Austrian refugees from the Nazis – many of them former colleagues and personal friends in the industry – to encourage them to play their part in anti-Hitler propaganda activity and creating an atmosphere to encourage America's entry into the war. The *Los Angeles Times* reporter co-operated completely, as the bulk of the country's unquestioning press could now be guaranteed to do:

> Chubby, blue-eyed, curly-headed and bespectacled, de Wohl hopes to see the day when astrology will be recognised as a science. Already he has astounded editors and the general public with his predictions …
> How does he do it? 'There's nothing supernatural or uncanny about it. It's just cold logic,' he says. 'Stars can affect our doings only 40% of the time and wills of humans affect the remaining 60%. But you can't ignore that 40%.'

Hitler was mentally ill, de Wohl told *Los Angeles Times* readers. He no longer had sufficient concentration to get through lengthy meetings. If Germany was able to survive past June 1942 – when the aspects for the United States would take a 'turn for the worse' – the Nazis would attempt to invade the Americas through Brazil. 'De Wohl declared that between now and June 11, 1942, would be the best time for the United States to enter the war.' He explained to the newspaper that he was more interested in the psychological aspects of astrology than in snap predictions, which he claimed a number of times he was never willing to make. 'Each one requires weeks of study of horoscopes, birth dates, positions of the stars and other technical points,' de Wohl confided. 'Then, after lengthy consideration, he'll decide what things are most likely to happen.'

The wind was definitely blowing in de Wohl's favour. He wrote a syndicated astrology column, 'Stars Foretell', which was printed in state and small-town newspapers throughout the country, hammering home the same messages: the United States must enter the war voluntarily or she will be forced to, Hitler was doomed, Germany will go down to defeat. The Federal Communications Commission, which until now had banned astrology from the radio waves, allowed the country's three networks – Columbia, the Mutual and the National Broadcasting Company – to interview him during the course of the Cleveland convention. At the end of August, Pathé News released the first ever interview with an astrologer to appear as a newsreel on cinema screens. De Wohl's agent in New York boasted that this was a 'plunge into prophecy with a nation-wide audience of 39,000,000 sitting in as judge, jury and witness'.[37] Bainbridge, de Wohl's SOE companion on the mission, was less impressed with both the astrologer's appearance and the results. 'De Wohl made one short piece for a newsreel, which cut no ice,' she wrote. 'He looked like hell on the screen and the effort was not repeated.'[38]

De Wohl was more successful with his radio appearances. An interview on WRUL based in Boston not long before he left the United States followed the now familiar pattern.[39] He was introduced as a 'distinguished historian, author and astrologer' and claimed that he knew 'from personal contact and experience that Hitler follows the advice of some of the most learned astrologers in Europe'. It was their careful guidance that had been instrumental in his achievements so far. When he ignored them, he failed. The Führer's end was on the horizon, that of Japan too:

> The time is coming nearer and nearer when the stars will not help him anymore. Hitler's astrologers know it too. They will have to lie to paint a rosy picture for the former housepainter. Hitler's stars are setting, and the Rising Sun in the Orient will set also. Let us work for that day, and as sure as the stars are moving in their rightful courses, the time will come when the two great democracies will stand on 'Friendship Bridge' and watch the dawn together.[40]

5

And then, suddenly, the mission was finished. A Gallup opinion survey polling Americans in November 1941 asked, 'Do you think the U.S. will go into war in Europe sometime before it is over, or do you think we will stay out of the war?' The response was, 'Go to war sooner or later with Germany: 85%.'[41] But despite de Wohl's relentless anti-Hitler campaign, it was Japan with which the United States was first at war. On 7 December 1941 Japanese carrier-borne aircraft mounted a surprise attack on the navy and army base at Pearl Harbor, Hawaii. Next day, both houses of Congress meeting together in President Roosevelt's presence declared war on Japan. Britain finally had the powerful ally Churchill had understood since the dark days of 1940 she would depend on to avoid defeat. Churchill recalled that on hearing the news of Pearl Harbor, 'I went to bed and slept the sleep of the saved and thankful.'[42] On 11 December, Hitler declared war on the United States, followed at once by his Italian ally Mussolini.

De Wohl returned to England from New York in mid-February 1942. Bainbridge had left a few weeks earlier, in January, only to face a not entirely happy fate. She had been first employed as a secretary at the Special Operations Executive offices in Baker Street 'some time in December 1940', as her personnel file noted. It had in fact been October. Procedure had been lax enough for her to start work in this highly secret organisation without the necessary MI5 vetting, a mistake that was not noticed until shortly before she was despatched to New York to keep an eye on de Wohl and act as his liaison with British Security Co-ordination. She passed vetting and signed the Official Secrets Act on 28 March 1941. Bainbridge originally expected to be in the United States for two months, three at the outside. But, she later complained, 'Seven months after leaving England I began to get a bit restless because it seemed to me that it had ceased to be of much use to the war effort.'[43]

On her return to London her superiors had difficulty in deciding where to place her next. There was a suggestion that as she had performed so well in her United States mission and was obviously a 'go-getting type', she should be sent to India to undertake propaganda work spreading rumours useful to the Allied cause. A senior SOE officer wrote in her file, 'I should have thought that a slightly tough female wandering about inhabited cities of India with a certain amount of money to spend would be an admirable way of releasing rumour and incidentally of collecting opinion.'[44] Turned down for this, she was put to work supervising the domestic arrangements for SOE accommodation outside London, a drab routine after the whirlwind excitement of the early months in the United States. There could be nothing again to equal 'bear leading' an astrologer around New York.

Then it was discovered in New York that she had been using the internal confidential post to send letters from London to a friend, a secretary at British Security Co-ordination in the Rockefeller Center. She was dismissed from SOE on 11 May 1942 with a month's pay in lieu of notice. A senior officer warned Bainbridge that had it not been for 'the good work she had carried out in America', she would have faced certain prosecution under both the Official Secrets Act and Defence Regulations for some of her remarks in the letters. Although, Bainbridge was told, her actions had 'reduced confidence formerly held in her', there would be no bar on her working in another government department. The recently established Political Warfare Executive was mentioned as a possibility.[45] This, by coincidence, was where de Wohl would eventually find himself employed.

The astrologer was unable, perhaps predictably, to leave New York without placing himself at the centre of a drama, one he later described.[46] When he arrived at the harbour pier about midday on 9 February 1942 he was disappointed to discover the vessel arranged for his journey to Britain – the SS *Cairn Esk* – was not the liner he had been led to expect, but a small and old hulk resembling a ferry boat. Moored beside it was an actual ocean-going liner, SS *Normandie*, a French ship seized by the United States Navy in 1940. 'How I wished,' de Wohl wrote, 'that I could sail in her instead of in this nutshell of mine.' An hour or so later a steward rapped on his cabin door to tell him the *Normandie* was on fire. As with the fate of the *Titanic* in his *Secret Service of the Sky*, de Wohl turned to astrology to make a reverse prophecy. 'I made a few calculations later on and it became clear to me that this was not simply an accident. The enemy was near.'[47]

What the astrologer did not know as his ship steamed through the North Atlantic towards England was that discussions were taking place between MI5 and the Special Operations Executive – his nominal employers – over what to do with him when he returned. There were even questions about whether he should be allowed back into the country at all. A senior officer in SOE's security section, Major General John Lakin, wrote to MI5's deputy director general 'Jasper' Harker on

14 February. Lakin opened his letter with the comic opera-sounding heading 'Captain Count Louis de Wohl'. He told Harker SOE had no intention of offering the astrologer further employment. He agreed de Wohl's work in the United States had been 'quite satisfactory', but went on, 'He is, however, an enemy alien and, as such, his fate will no doubt be decided by you.'[48] Two days later MI5 authorised immigration officers to allow de Wohl to land but Harker asked Dick White, deputy head of counter-espionage, for his opinion on what they should do next. White said that as far as he was concerned de Wohl was a 'charlatan and an imposter' and regretted that he had ever been allowed to exercise influence over 'highly placed British Intelligence officers through his star gazing profession'. He agreed the astrologer as a Hungarian citizen certainly fitted into the category of enemy alien, but was not sure it would be wise to treat him as one:

> I do not think that the case against de Wohl has ever been such as to justify his name being placed on the Hungarian Black List for internment. Moreover it would seem to me to be somewhat inappropriate to intern him immediately after his arrival back from the United States, where he has been carrying out …

Here the remainder of White's file note has been obscured, blanked out to remove any clue as to what exactly de Wohl had been 'carrying out' while he was in the United States.[49] It is, of course, not difficult to piece together de Wohl's activities when he was away, unless in this case the weeder was hiding something particularly juicy.

As minutes and memoranda passed back and forth between MI5 officers – accompanied, no doubt, by conversations and snatches of gossip in corridors – de Wohl did not realise the perilous position in which he might find himself. Toby Caulfield, an officer in E branch dealing with control of aliens, wrote on 27 February that de Wohl was 'a thorn in my side' with a 'mysterious, if not murky, past'. He complained that the way astrologer 'struts about in the uniform of a British Army Captain' was annoying many people, including 'agents of foreign origin'.[50] He went on:

De Wohl is clearly potentially highly dangerous; there is no guarantee whatsoever of his loyalty and he is likely to be guided solely by his vanity and his idea of self-interest. There is no case for interning him, and even if he were interned he would undoubtedly be speedily released and would, moreover, have a justifiable grievance. On the other hand, if he is left at large it is essential that we should keep a close tag on him.

Was Caulfield saying de Wohl would work for the enemy? There was a thread of opinion running through MI5 that positively disliked and mistrusted the astrologer, if indeed they found it possible to place trust in anyone outside a particularly narrow social circle.[51] Caulfield went on to say there were 'two possible ways of dealing with him'. Those two ways have been obscured so as to be unreadable in de Wohl's MI5 personal file. Did one involve dealing with the astrologer by having him removed from the scene in the most drastic way – to have a man against there was only the vaguest suspicion killed? Given Caulfield's obviously deep personal hostility to the 'potentially highly dangerous' de Wohl, it has to be considered a possibility the thought crossed his mind, that he had committed that thought to paper and that MI5 would be embarrassed if such a notion became public knowledge.

De Wohl arrived back in London after his Atlantic crossing on 27 February. Nobody met him and, having no orders and no idea what he was meant to do, he returned to the suite in the Grosvenor House Hotel from where he had operated his one-man Psychological Research Bureau before leaving Britain for the United States the previous May. He found the furniture had been removed only a few weeks before. The hotel management agreed to make the still unoccupied rooms habitable for him. He then sat and waited to be contacted. He told his MI5 handler, Major Lennox, when they met for dinner on 3 March, 'He did not expect to be met "by a brass band, or even one fiddler", but he did expect that someone would pay at least some attention to his return.' He had, after all, been ordered by SOE to leave New York and return to base and supposed they had plans for him. Lennox shared de Wohl's story with Major General Lakin of SOE in a letter, clearly hoping to resolve matters.[52] According to Lennox, de Wohl had assumed he would restart the astrological work he had been undertaking for British Intelligence before he left England. But what exactly did de Wohl mean? Was he under the impression British Intelligence were still interested in his claim to be able to read Hitler's mind? If so, why had they been so keen to pack him off to the United States? Nothing he had done there involved predicting the Führer's next strategic move. The astrologer's task had been to undermine Hitler by the constant repetition of the inevitability of his death.

De Wohl told Lennox that after a few days, and running short of money, he had tried to contact Charles Hambro, who had originally taken him on at the Special Operations Executive. He felt as if he was being constantly rebuffed. 'He said to me,' Lennox wrote to Lakin, 'it was all as if the whole thing had been a dream … his one desire was to get on with his work, but no one was there to tell him what to do, and he did not know where to find out.' The astrologer did not seem to realise he was a small cog in a large machine, unimportant, not the centre of the picture, a bit of an embarrassment. He was being frozen out, treated as an awkward figure from the past. The war had changed its nature since de Wohl had left England in May 1941 – the dark days of 1940 were over, the Soviet Union and the United States were in the fight against Germany and Britain was no longer alone.

De Wohl had met Bainbridge again in London and she advised him to return to private practice as an astrologer and to move back to the Esplanade Hotel (where he had lived after arriving in London in 1935) and his old life. She probably did not realise that one part of his old life had not been purely civilian, involving as it did acting as an inform-ant to MI5 since 1938. De Wohl was clearly hoping something would come of his dinner with Lennox, that the MI5 officer would use his influence to get him a position of some kind. Lennox took pains not to let him down in his letter to Lakin. There was a marked contrast between Lennox's view of de Wohl's character and that of his MI5 colleague Caulfield. They both believed the astrologer was motivated by self-interest, but differed on their assessment of his ability and his com-mitment to the cause. Lennox wrote:

While I hold no brief for de Wohl, he is an extraordinarily clever and astute man, and at the moment I am quite sure that he is all out to help the British war effort. That may be because it is to his own advantage, but none the less it remains true ... So long as he is employed by someone on useful work at a remunerative salary, I do not think we can anticipate any danger from him ... Few people know German middle class mentality better, and he is undoubtedly a brilliant propagandist ... We do not want to find him on our hands and we would regret the making of an enemy if it can be avoided.[53]

Lennox had as good as decided on de Wohl's destination – the Political Warfare Executive, though it would take some weeks of manoeuvring to finally place the astrologer there. While de Wohl was carrying out his mission in the United States, there had been changes in the structure of propaganda and intelligence in Britain. The personnel of the propaganda section of the Special Operations Executive, known as SO1, had been detached in August 1941, combining with selected staff from the Ministry of Information (MoI) and the British Broadcasting Corporation (BBC) to form the Political Warfare Executive (PWE). PWE's Director General, Robert Bruce Lockhart, explained his organisation's objectives at a meeting of the chiefs of staff of the Navy, Army and Air Force in October 1941:

He defined political warfare as activities undertaken to influence the minds of the enemy ... The object was, therefore, to undermine the enemy's morale ... This object might be achieved by instilling fear into the minds of the enemy ... Although political warfare could not replace military successes it would help to tide over the quiet period of the war and could assist in military operations.[54]

To add to the alphabet soup, the highly secret PWE was given official cover by the Political Intelligence Department (PID) of the Foreign Office. The Political Warfare Executive undertook the dissemination of 'white' propaganda – relatively uncontroversial official informational material, often dropped as leaflets by the RAF – and 'black' propaganda.

The latter came closer to the Director General's description: working at a more insidious psychological level, aimed at gradually breaking down enemy military and civilian morale by means of – among a range of activities – radio stations masquerading as German-based, and printed material, once again pretending to originate in Germany. This would be the area into which de Wohl was drafted, using his astrological expertise as a weapon of war in an entirely different way.

De Wohl finally tracked down Sir Charles Hambro – he had been knighted for his work with SOE while the astrologer was away – on 15 March 1942, over a fortnight after his return to London. Hambro told him he had done 'an excellent job' in the United States, that he was to remain on leave on full pay and in the meantime his future would be considered. Reporting this meeting to MI5's deputy director general, Theo Thomas noted on the astrologer's personal file that as long as de Wohl believed he was being treated fairly, he could be relied on.

> De Wohl will be a loyal and useful collaborator but the moment he got a grievance against this country he might become a very dangerous enemy owing to the considerable influence his charlatanism enables him to exert over the superstitious in high places … If possible use should be made of his undoubted talents as a propagandist.

The idea that de Wohl had such influence with people 'in high places' seemed common currency and was believed throughout MI5. Who these individuals were was never spelt out, unfortunately, but the astrologer's possible impact and his ability to use them to his own advantage was obviously a matter for concern. There is one intriguing entry at this point in de Wohl's MI5 personal file. A note says, 'From Major Morton enclosing report by Mrs. Churchill' and refers to an attachment. The typing has been scored through and the attachment destroyed in weeding. Mrs Churchill was, of course, the Prime Minister's wife. Major Desmond Morton was Churchill's personal assistant and his specialist adviser on intelligence matters. Had de Wohl been touting astrological advice to 10 Downing Street on a freelance basis, invited or uninvited?[55] Thomas suggested as possible destinations for the astrologer SOE, the

BBC or PWE, the latter he seemed to consider particularly suitable. He thought Major General Lakin at SOE was reluctant to re-employ de Wohl, that he was feigning interest and would probably be glad to see the back of him.[56] But progress was slow as officers in each of the departments passed notes and comments between themselves. The impression everyone gave was that they wished de Wohl would just disappear.

7

WE MUST NEVER LIE BY ACCIDENT

I

Following his return from the United States at the end of February 1942, de Wohl enjoyed a long leave in London, with pay and allowances appropriate to an army captain, questionable though his entitlement to that rank remained. There had been talk in MI5 of having his commission – if there was one – withdrawn, but how to remove something never formally bestowed was problematic and the topic was allowed to drift. His connection with SOE ending, and the Psychological Research Bureau in abeyance, de Wohl moved from his suite at the Grosvenor House Hotel to a flat in Athenaeum Court, a 1930s apartment block in Piccadilly, 10 minutes or so walk away. As Howe had said, de Wohl was always keen on a 'good address', particularly when someone else was paying. By one of the coincidences that were part of de Wohl's life, a neighbour in the block was Ian Fleming, still working at the Directorate of Naval Intelligence as Admiral Godfrey's right-hand man and as liaison officer with SOE. Fleming had moved to Athenaeum Court at the end of 1941. They soon became acquainted, the two of them making half of an interesting quartet, all sharing a fascination with trickery and deception. Fleming – working on plans to confuse and mislead the enemy

– was already often in the company in London of Sefton Delmer and Ellic Howe of the Political Warfare Executive, the musketeers of black propaganda and deception.[1]

De Wohl drifted through spring and early summer. Though he is vague about his activities, it would have been out of character for him not to have been actively lobbying for a post as well, presumably, as carrying on his private practice as an astrologer, with gambling on the side. One piece of paid work he certainly did undertake was writing a 15-minute script for BBC radio, a Home Service programme on the life of the German Foreign Minister and former ambassador to London, Joachim von Ribbentrop. This was one of a series of broadcasts entitled 'Black Gallery' dealing with Nazi leaders and went out at 6.30 p.m. on Thursday, 2 July 1942. The narrator was Walter Rilla, a German film actor of Jewish descent who had fled to Britain soon after Hitler came to power. The fact that the two worked together on the programme suggested there was no substance to rumours circulating in MI5 that de Wohl had produced pro-Nazi horoscopes in the years before he left Germany. As both de Wohl and Rilla had been involved in the film business, they were surely acquainted in the 1930s. It was inconceivable a Jewish refugee would have been prepared to work with a writer tainted by any connection with the Nazis.

The astrologer tells a story at this point in time in *The Stars of War and Peace* that seems out of place and strangely irrelevant. What he writes only makes sense later in the context of a passing remark made by Sefton Delmer, the Political Warfare Executive's black propaganda chief, in his own memoir *Black Boomerang*. Delmer mentions a 'prophecy' of the defeat of Rommel's Africa Korps at the battle of El Alamein in October 1942, made in a phoney copy of a German astrological magazine, *Der Zenit*, dated June 1942. This edition was actually produced by PWE – with de Wohl's input – in December 1942, after the battle had taken place.

De Wohl writes that 'One day, early in summer 1942' he was approached by an unnamed 'high-ranking officer'. The man gave him two sets of birth data – day, month and year, no more than that, no place or time of birth – and asked which of the two men was likely to meet with success if they were to clash. The birth dates were 15 November 1891 and 17 November 1887. 'That is all Hitler will want to know too,' the officer told the astrologer. 'And his man is not likely to have more information than you have, so it's even odds.'[2] The officer said he would return next day for de Wohl's answer. After studying their horoscopes, the astrologer was able to tell him the two men were soldiers by profession, one British, one German, both with their Sun in Scorpio. The younger of the two was always prepared to take risks, while the older man was more methodical. He too would take risks, but only when he was certain he could afford to. De Wohl said that if pushed this would be the man to put his money on.

The officer then revealed the identity of the two men: the younger man was the German commander in North Africa, Rommel, the older man the British commander Montgomery. De Wohl then tells a rambling tale, one that feels contrived, about the difficulty he had had in determining which of the commanders would be victorious. Despite an intuitive sense that on character alone that Rommel would be defeated, de Wohl had found no 'bad aspects' in his horoscope to confirm this. In his story the astrologer resolves the conundrum by saying that when the battle of El Alamein opened with an artillery bombardment on 24 October 1942 and Montgomery's Eighth Army began its advance the following day, Rommel was not in North Africa but in Germany to receive his field marshal's baton from Hitler. Therefore, de Wohl reasoned, command was in the hands of Rommel's subordinate, von Thoma, and so the defeat had been his, not Rommel's.

There were problems with this strange tale. The first is that a modern battle was not commenced, fought and won or lost in the course of a day. While it was true that Rommel had been in Germany – on sick leave, not meeting Hitler – he returned in the battle's earliest stage. In fact, Hitler had ordered him to return to North Africa as soon as it was clear Montgomery's army was attacking. The defeat was therefore Rommel's as commander, whatever the aspects in his horoscope had said. Why did de Wohl bother telling the story at all – stretching it out over four pages of *The Stars of War and Peace*? The astrologer was engaging in the kind of reverse prediction he had carried out over the sinking of the *Titanic* and the fire on the *Normandie* in New York. He had not written the prediction of the outcome of the clash between Montgomery and Rommel *before* the battle of El Alamein but *after* for the phoney astrology magazine *Der Zenit* he was helping the Political Warfare Executive produce, as Delmer later revealed. And the 'senior officer'? That would surely have been Delmer himself priming his astrologer for the masquerade.

Why did de Wohl go to all the trouble of making up a convoluted account involving an anonymous high-ranking officer and a dilemma over contradictory aspects in Rommel's horoscope? Why not simply say in *The Stars of War and Peace*, 'I correctly foretold Rommel's defeat by Montgomery at the battle of El Alamein,' then go on to present the evidence for this? Surely it was because he was unable to tell the true story of the deceit he was involved in with Delmer and the Political Warfare Executive, the pretence after the event of foretelling the result. In which case, why say anything at all? An odd and inexplicable psychology is involved, an urge to exaggerate and embellish, to assert he really did have the power of prediction. Dick White of MI5 made no bones about this when he described the astrologer as being in his opinion 'a charlatan and an imposter'.[3] Over time, the word 'charlatan' frequently comes up in connection with de Wohl, both of him and by him.

Finally there was some movement and, as in 1940, the astrologer found a niche. On 10 July the Political Warfare Executive sent a pro-forma letter to MI5 asking if anything was known about de Wohl. The reason given for the enquiry was 'Possible employment in German Section on very secret work'. Under particulars of previous employment the PWE enquirer wrote simply 'Commission in H.M. Forces (Army) rank of Captain'. Before MI5 replied, Major Kenneth Younger, asked Major Lennox – the astrologer's long-term handler – for his opinion. 'I presume you have helped de Wohl to contact P.W.E.,' Younger wrote:

> I do not much like the sound of 'very secret work', but perhaps you, with your greater knowledge of de Wohl, may think it all right. As the early volume of his file is destroyed, we do not seem to have very full information about his remoter past. Having read this file I still feel that I know nothing whatever about the man.[4]

In his response to Younger, Lennox gave an outline of what had been going on behind the scenes. It had been agreed within MI5 that 'if a suitable job could be found for de Wohl in P.W.E. we would be relieved'. Lennox said that Sir Charles Hambro, who had encouraged the astrologer's previous activities with the Special Operations Executive, had put in a word for de Wohl with Sefton Delmer. Brigadier Tony Brooks, also of SOE, had no doubt he would be 'very useful' to PWE:

> The outcome is that de Wohl has, in fact, got a job under Sefton Delmer, in which he is to be editor of an astrological monthly paper which is being sent to Germany by surreptitious means. I think de Wohl should be very good at this, and I believe the first copy of which is now being published has pleased P.W.E. very much. At present the job seems to be only a part time one, and the pay small, but knowing de Wohl I think we can leave the rest to him![5]

A secret propaganda department like PWE was, as one who worked closely with Delmer and de Wohl later acknowledged, a magnet for the unconventional, 'never the Establishment's happy hunting ground'.[6] But some people were not at all happy with de Wohl's posting, and with the fact that he continued to stalk the West End streets in army uniform. An unidentified MI6 officer wrote to Toby Caulfield of MI5 on 9 August complaining that he had 'warned off' PWE, with no effect. The MI6 officer claimed one of his seniors had said he could not believe anyone would even consider employing de Wohl, whom he described as a 'dangerous charlatan and confidence-trick merchant'. The senior officer had added: 'Is it really possible that this man is allowed to wear the uniform of a British Officer! Surely it is time the gullible were protected from the creature.'[7]

Sefton Delmer, to whom de Wohl would be answerable at PWE, was far from gullible and needed no protection from anyone. In some ways the two could even be seen as kindred spirits: unorthodox, maverick, imaginative, always in danger of putting on weight. There were similarities in their backgrounds and both had what appeared to be an intimate understanding of the German psyche. Delmer was born in Berlin in 1904 – a year after de Wohl – the son of Australian parents. He was educated at a Berlin *gymnasium* (grammar school) in the early years of the First World War, until the family were allowed to leave for Britain in 1917. After St Paul's School and Oxford, Delmer kept up the German connection. He was recruited by the *Daily Express* proprietor Lord Beaverbrook to head the paper's Berlin office in 1928. In this role he became closely acquainted with many leading Nazis including Hitler, whom Delmer accompanied round Germany in his private aircraft during the 1932 general election campaign. Delmer went on to report from Spain in the civil war and was in Poland in September 1939 when Germany attacked. Attached to the French army as a correspondent when German forces were beginning their lightning advance through the Low Countries, Delmer narrowly escaped from Paris in June 1939 as Nazi troops marched into the city.

By what seemed to be the usual roundabout process in the world of British Intelligence, from lunch at Boodle's in St James's – a prime MI6 recruiting spot – Delmer made his way through work for the Secret Intelligence Service to the BBC as an announcer with the corporation's German service. From there he moved to SOE and in 1941 to the newly established Political Warfare Executive, concentrating initially on setting up a radio station to transmit black propaganda to Germany. His methods were unorthodox and controversial. His aim at PWE, Delmer said in June 1941, 'is subversive … We want to spread disruptive and disturbing news among the Germans which will induce them to distrust their government and disobey it, not so much from high-minded political motives as from ordinary human weakness …'[8]

A wartime colleague of Delmer described him as 'the most imaginative and skilful exponent of "black" psychological warfare techniques that I encountered during close on four years' employment at the Political Warfare Executive'.[9] Delmer was later equally complimentary about de Wohl, with only the slightest hint of irony, saying of the astrologer, 'Undoubtedly he was a great artist in his field.'[10] Delmer understood that on the black propaganda level Nazi trickery could only be countered by the exercise of even more determined deceit. He saw de Wohl as sharing the underlying temperament this required.

2

On 3 June 1942 there were entertaining exchanges on the floor of the House of Commons when Bernard Bracken, Minister of Information since July 1941 and a close confidant of Winston Churchill, was responding to questions from a member about recent astrological predictions in the press. Bracken shared responsibility for the Political Warfare Executive, the body for which de Wohl would soon be working. The questions and answers are worth quoting in full for the picture they paint of the atmosphere at the time:

> Mr Keeling (Twickenham, Unionist.) Has the Minister of Information's attention been drawn to the fact that astrologers were predicting that Germany was on the verge of collapse; and will he stop astrological predictions about the war in order to counteract the risk that addicts of astrology would relax their efforts.

> Mr Bracken: Astrologers seem to have the misfortune to be perpetually in conflict. And as no sensible person takes their predictions seriously, I cannot ask our overworked censors to meddle in their mysteries. (Laughter.)

> Mr Keeling: Has the Minister seen the recent statement in the People that owing to the conjunction of the stars, no invasion of this country can ever take place? (Laughter.) Is he aware that a great many people do treat such statements very seriously indeed?

> Mr Bracken: Yes, Sir, but I must point out that some other papers' astrologers probably state that England can be invaded. It is well known that Hitler dabbles in astrology. May it not be that certain articles are written for him? (Laughter.)

Mr Lawson (Chester-le-Street, Labour.): Is there any reason why Hitler should have a monopoly of astrology?

Mr Bracken: No, Sir. (Laughter.)

Mr Shinwell (Labour.): Is the Minister aware that one astrologer predicted last Sunday a Government crisis this month? (Laughter) Is there any truth in that? (Renewed laughter.)[11]

Did Bracken know in any detail the nature of the work de Wohl had been taken on to carry out? The Minister, as one of the political heads of the Political Warfare Executive, would certainly have had an overview of its propaganda activities, black and white. His answers in the Commons had a touch of knowingness about them, as if a conversation was being conducted in code between minister, members and in the background British Intelligence. 'It is well known that Hitler dabbles in astrology. May it not be that certain articles are written for him?'

In a debate a week of so earlier the subject of astrology had been treated with far more concern and there were no interruptions for laughter. The former Secretary for War, Leslie Hore-Belisha, raised the matter of a column in the 3 May 1942 edition of *The People* by the paper's regular astrologer, Lyndoe. He had forecast that Russia would open a spring offensive against German forces around 10 May. The attack began on 12 or 13 May. 'Some people think that this is a harmless lunacy,' Hore-Belisha told the Commons, 'but I regard it as a rather serious manifestation … I want to ask the Government whether anyone, whether he bases his prediction on the stars or on reason, ought to be able to state a week beforehand, almost to the very day, when our Allies are to launch their offensive?' An Independent MP, Vernon Bartlett, made an interesting response, one suggesting that more was known about the relationship between astrology and British Intelligence than most people would have understood at the time. 'I agree with him that these astrologers are very dangerous people indeed but, on the other hand, I think the Minister of Information would confirm that these scientific inquiries are of real value.'[12] In 1938 de Wohl had, mistakenly, forecast that Hore-Belisha, from his horoscope, was a future prime minister.

While de Wohl had been working to convince British Intelligence of astrology's value as a weapon in the war against Germany, the subject was clearly a live issue in Britain itself. Ministers were more concerned with the effect of forecasts and prophecies on public morale than with whether astrology was 'true'. There was a popular ambivalence about the subject – astrology was seen as nonsense while at the same time 'there may be something in it', particularly at a time of crisis. As one study says, 'Astrology's increased popularity during bombing and war-time can be considered a response to anxiety and uncertainty and the need for people to find order and reason amid chaos.' In January 1942 the Financial Secretary to the Treasury, Harry Crookshank, told the War Cabinet Civil Defence Committee he considered horoscopes in newspapers 'had a harmful effect on public morale and the war effort'. He believed they should be banned. The response from the Ministry of Information was that when the influence of astrology on the public mind was investigated by a ministerial sub-committee in July 1941 it was found two-thirds of the population admitted to looking at newspaper horoscopes. But the study had found that at most 'one in ten, and probably of a neurotic type, make astrology a major interest in their lives and allow it to play some part in forming their conduct'.[13] One in ten really was a significant proportion of the population.

Something else of interest had come up in the Ministry of Information's investigation. While none of the newspaper astrologers had predicted the outbreak of war in September 1939, they could claim some success in forecasting other major events during the conflict itself. R.H. Naylor of the *Sunday Express* – already renowned for his forecast of the R101 airship disaster in 1930 – had predicted the German invasions of Norway in 1940 and Greece and Crete in 1941. There was a rumour that the head of RAF Bomber Command, Arthur Harris, sought an astrologer's advice when selecting timings of raids during the air offensive against Germany.[14] Lyndoe in *The People* and Petulengro in the *Sunday Chronicle* had both correctly prophesied the German attack on the Soviet Union in 1941. If this kind of information could easily be obtained just for the price of a Sunday newspaper, why were British Intelligence going to the trouble of paying Louis de Wohl an army captain's wage and putting him up in luxurious accommodation? One former member of the Special Operations Executive later claimed the astrologer Lyndoe had told him during the war that 'his advice was regularly sought by senior members of the Government, Service chiefs and leading churchmen'. He added, 'I have no reason to suppose he was not telling the truth.'[15] At the moment of greatest danger in 1940 the quarterly magazine *Astrology* had informed its readers in June, for the price of a shilling, 'that Hitler's approaching directions were adverse, and proclaimed the likelihood of better things even when the hour was darkest'.[16] De Wohl had told British Intelligence little more than this and sometimes less. Were his days as a paid forecaster approaching their close?

3

Although de Wohl had succeeded in finding a platform from which to work, his life was now to run along two tracks, one of which he would almost certainly have known nothing about, though he may have had his suspicions. While he was engaged as an astrologer by PWE on black propaganda, he was at the same time under constant scrutiny by MI5 and the police, treated as a potential danger to the State for which he was working, or a possible source of embarrassment. The GPO intercepted his letters for MI5 to read, while Special Branch delved into the background and activities of his associates. If he had had a telephone installed at his Piccadilly flat, that would have been tapped. As one MI5 officer put it, 'I have no reason to suspect him of working against, or wishing to work, against our interests ... but in view of his peculiar background and character it is desirable to keep any eye on him.'[17] This was heavy surveillance of an individual against whom nothing concrete was suspected, no more than a feeling that he was 'peculiar'.

The astrologer's new boss, Sefton Delmer, had similar feelings about his manner and appearance, though he was open about the extent to which he valued de Wohl's contribution to PWE's anti-Nazi propaganda. De Wohl did not have a fixed position with PWE but acted as a freelance, paid for his work by the job on a casual basis – an incentive to give his client what the client wanted, to shape the astrological truth. Delmer, as he said himself, had one firm instruction to the men and women he employed to produce broadcasts, leaflets, magazines and bulletins: 'Accuracy first. We must never lie by accident, or through slovenliness, only deliberately.'[18] He occasionally visited the astrologer at his Athenaeum Court basement flat to discuss the direction his predictions would, or more accurately should, be taking. Delmer recalled one of his early meetings with what he called 'this famous Berlin-born astrologer':

> He was a most sinister looking creature and it was with trepidation that … I sought to guide this new Nostradamus into lines which would fit our purposes of subversion. There he sat, as I entered his den, a vast spectacled jellyfish of a man in the uniform of a British army captain, puffing over-dimensional rings of smoke from an over-dimensional cigar. A khaki jellyfish in a spider's web of smoke. As I nervously put forward my views on what I rather hoped the stars might be foretelling, he frowned at me with terrifying ferocity …[19]

Ellic Howe, who would be responsible for printing the propaganda de Wohl produced, was as graphic in his description of the man who confronted him at their first meeting, the sinister authority he exuded:

> Delmer's tame astrologer … a tall, flabby elephant of a man who peered at me through tortoise-shell-rimmed spectacles. He wore a well-tailored uniform and was apparently an army captain with a General List commission. He took some papers from a large and expensive crocodile-leather brief-case and a cigar from a container made of the same material. 'The crocodile is my favourite animal,' he remarked. Delmer had already left. De Wohl sat there staring at me and I felt as if I was just about to be devoured by a crocodile.[20]

In January 1930 the Dusseldorf lawyer and professional astrologer Hubert Korsch produced the first edition of a monthly magazine entitled *Zenit*.

Korsch was a prolific writer on what he saw as scientific astrology, establishing and becoming president of the Central Astrological Organisation. The magazine became Germany's leading astrological journal and was consistently pro-Nazi, producing horoscopes boosting Hitler, Goering, Goebbels and other leading party figures. In 1938 the Nazi regime withdrew Korsch's permission to publish *Zenit*, on the grounds that he was homosexual and his political reliability suspect. The move coincided with Hitler's Nuremberg rally speech rejecting the idea that there was any connection between the occult and the Nazi party. Korsch was arrested in the general round-up of astrologers that followed Hess's flight to Scotland in May 1941. Held in confinement in Sachsenhausen concentration camp, he died in 1943. Delmer planned to create bogus editions of *Zenit* as a propaganda weapon against Germany. He engaged de Wohl to write what would appear to be genuine astrological predictions, to which Delmer's writers would add what Howe later called 'occasional subversive interpolations'.[21] The aim was to undermine German military, naval and civilian morale through the manipulation of what was on the face of it genuine astrological 'evidence'.

Anxious, presumably, to feel an actual part of the Political Warfare Executive rather than simply a hired hand, and needing somewhere to go to break the monotony, de Wohl initially delivered his contributions to Delmer at Bush House, PWE's London headquarters. But when this came to the ears of Colonel Chambers, head of PWE security, he ordered guards at the sixth-floor entrance to the organisation's offices to deny the astrologer entry. From then on either Delmer or his typographer Howe visited de Wohl at Athenaeum Court themselves to collect his contributions. How far could Delmer rely on de Wohl to produce what he required? Delmer describes a typical meeting between the two men in comic terms. He would outline the area he envisaged covering in an issue of *Der Zenit* and the direction he thought it should go. De Wohl would take up astrological materials from his desk and carry out some quick calculations on paper:

> Then there would follow some, to me completely unintelligible jargon about constellations, aspects, signs, and so forth. But I had to keep the straightest of straight faces when making my suggestions. My astrolo-

ger always insisted that he would under no circumstances be prepared to prostitute his sacred knowledge to purposes of subversion, much as he abhorred Hitler and what he stood for. It was simply a most fortunate coincidence that what I suggested so often fitted in with what the stars did indeed foretell.[22]

Amused as Delmer was in retrospect by de Wohl's way of going about things, there was no doubting his confidence in the astrologer's usefulness to PWE in their black propaganda exploits. Delmer's own boss – Robert Bruce Lockhart, the Director General – was less enthusiastic about the man, at least on a personal level. Lockhart noted in his diary in August 1942: 'MI5 officers gave me good food and drink at the R.A.C. and tried to sell me Ludwig von Wohl (Louis de Wohl) the German astrologer and exhibitionist ... MI5 want us to employ him for some reason of their own.'[23] Lockhart had lunched at the club with de Wohl's MI5 handler, Lennox, and his colleague Toby Caulfield. He made no direct response to their suggestions, but in the event de Wohl was never taken on as a contracted employee by PWE, simply used as a freelance and paid by the job.

4

The black propaganda aspect of PWE's work was the production of 'fake news' intended to mislead, confuse and demoralise the enemy. The RAF dropped millions of phoney copies of the Nazi party newspaper, *Völkischer Beobachter*, over Germany, with stories intended to sap the population's confidence, deriding, for example, the conduct of the military campaign in Russia. Leaflets with information on malingering and avoiding duties proved popular with troops and industrial workers alike.[24] Delmer was the mind behind 'Gustav Siegfried Eins' – a radio station masquerading as broadcasting from inside Germany – with its mouthpiece, 'Der Chef', posing as a German patriot who denounced both Churchill and corrupt Nazi leaders in a genuine Berlin accent, combining subversion with pornography to keep listeners tuning in.

The channel's purpose was 'to stimulate distrust of the Nazis, the SS, and the administration in general. It also sought by rumour and insinuation to stir up friction between the Nazi Party and the Wehrmacht.'[25] The role of 'Der Chef' in the broadcasts was taken by Peter Seckelmann, a German Jewish refugee and a school friend of de Wohl, which further lays to rest any idea that de Wohl had worked with the Nazis as an astrologer.

De Wohl's part in this was to add his professional astrological twist to PWE black propaganda, to provide a plausible pretence of foretelling the future to further weaken confidence in the fate of Germany under Hitler. His initial role with British Intelligence had been to interpret Hitler's mind through his horoscope. In the United States it had been to undermine Hitler through the 'Orchestra of Death'. Now his task was to aid in the campaign to weaken the German people's will to fight on.

The Political Warfare Executive turned out nine editions of *Der Zenit* from the summer of 1942 into 1943, de Wohl injecting the necessary astrological authenticity to accompany Delmer's creative disinformation. PWE resources ensured there were no difficulties in production, but distribution was more problematic. Delmer intended that copies of the magazine were to be posted from neutral towns to addresses of known followers of astrology in Germany and, for wider coverage, packed in consignments of weapons and equipment dropped by the Special Operations Executive to the resistance in occupied countries. Members of the underground would then infiltrate copies at appropriate places, such as bars in the neighbourhood of army barracks, air and naval bases. The first edition of *Der Zenit* – number 8, dated October 1942 – was compiled in August of that year. The earliest productions were relatively crude, ten pages in total, claiming to have been published by a company called *Das geistige Deutschland* ('Spiritual Germany'), based in Erfurt. The main feature of the first edition was Hitler's horoscope, with subtle hints about his future, though at this stage there was little material of a heavily subversive or 'black' nature.

The second edition, numbered 9, dated November 1942, questioned the role of Dr Karl Brandt, who was described as Hitler's physician. He was, in fact, his surgeon. Why, de Wohl's planetary input asked, had the care of the Führer's health been placed in the hands of a man whose Neptune was square (that is, at 90 degrees) to Hitler's natal sixth house (the house denoting health)? This was, *Der Zenit* implied, an ill-advised and patently dangerous combination. Having laid the basis for a sense of unease, the magazine would return to Brandt's role in a later Political Warfare Executive enterprise.

The physical appearance of *Der Zenit* improved with the introduction of the typographer and printer Ellic Howe to de Wohl early in 1943. Howe's main role with PWE was producing forged identity cards and documents for the resistance and SOE agents active in occupied Europe, but he now began co-operation with the astrologer and Delmer on the final three editions of the magazine. Volume 2, Number 1, dated March 1943, had the feel of professional production, with a carefully designed red and black cover and advertisements for patent medicines and astrological books available in Germany to lend authenticity. The editor was claimed to be Dr Hubert Korsch, the founder in 1930 of the actual magazine on which *Der Zenit* was based. Unfortunately for PWE, Korsch had been in a concentration camp since the Hess round-up of astrologers in May 1941, but this was presumably not known in London at the time. It may even have been assumed he was dead. Dissemination of the magazine remained difficult and PWE could never be sure how many copies were actually read.

As German U-boats prowling the Atlantic posed a major threat to the Allied war effort, Delmer turned the magazine's attention to under-mining the confidence of their crews. This was part of a two-pronged mission, combining the magazine *Der Zenit* with a series of radio broad-casts directed at submariners. Morale among the crews was already faltering because of increased detection and destruction of U-boats. These successes were based on British interception of German naval signals at Bletchley Park through the Ultra project. Neither Delmer nor de Wohl would have known the reason for the Royal Navy's growing success in the North Atlantic. In 1941 Germany had lost thirty-five U-boats. The following year this had risen to eighty-seven, most in the last few months of 1942. For the third edition of *Der Zenit*, dated December 1942 but produced in March 1943, de Wohl constructed the horoscopes of Admiral Erich Raeder, the German naval commander, and Admiral Karl Doenitz, head of the submarine service. Doenitz, the astrologer's interpretation declared, had a 'lucky' horoscope and the admiral was clearly now acting on advice he was receiving that U-boats should not set to sea on 'unfavourable days'. To ensure German submarine crews got the message, the Special Operations Executive tried to ensure copies of *Der Zenit* were making their way to the French Atlantic ports where they were based. Howe, who was involved with de Wohl in producing this edition, gave an example of the astrologer concocting a narrative through the mixture of horoscopes and easily verifiable fact.

Readers were asked to consider the sad case of *U-335*. This vessel had a good horoscope when launched but that of its commander, Kapitän-Leutnant H. Pelkner, was 'bad', and this explained why *U-335* was sunk after four days at sea on 3 August 1942. Not surprising, perhaps, considering that the transiting Moon was in square aspect to the Sun and Pluto in his horoscope.[26]

U-335, commanded by Kapitän-Leutnant Hans-Herman Pelkner, had indeed been lost at sea on 3 August 1942, five days after leaving the French port of St Nazaire on its first patrol, torpedoed and sunk by a British submarine in the North Atlantic. De Wohl provided a range of worries in *Der Zenit* to preoccupy submarine crews' minds as they set out to sea. Were they in an unlucky vessel? Were they commanded by a captain with bad aspects? Was it an unfavourable day to begin the mission? All these were at play but none was within the control of the men ordered to sea, though each was open – according to de Wohl – to astrological prediction. As U-boat losses mounted these 'predictions' were a useful cover for a renewed success in cracking the Enigma cipher, about which de Wohl would have known nothing. 'Bletchley achieved a decisive breakthrough in December 1942 which led to victory in the Battle of the Atlantic in the summer of 1943.'[27]

The copy of *Der Zenit* with which Howe as printer and typographer, and de Wohl as astrologer, would have been most satisfied was a special 'Armed Forces Air Mail' edition dated April 1943, but produced three months later. This was to be the last of the series. The concentration on U-boat crews continued, with forecasts from de Wohl of further unfavourable days to go to sea, and the need to take such factors into account as whether the submarine was older or a more recent model and whether the captain's horoscope showed him to have lucky aspects.[28] As Howe outlines in *Astrology and Psychological Warfare*, Delmer would have been informed by Naval Intelligence when and where German submarines were sunk in April 1943. Feeding this knowledge to de Wohl would ensure that his 'predictions' were impressively grounded in reality. De Wohl had few qualms and little difficulty making the two mesh. Delmer described the relationship in *Black Boomerang* with a touch of irony:

> It was simply a most fortunate coincidence that what I suggested so often fitted in with what the stars did indeed foretell … Thus Hitler's defeats at Alamein and Stalingrad were astrologically foreseen in a *Zenit* number which bore the date June 1942, but had in fact been printed in March 1943. I felt this little subterfuge would add weight to other predictions in the magazine which were concerned with developments far ahead of the date when our German customers would first find it lying around.[29]

An issue of *Der Zenit* dated April 1943 also outlined the possibility of SS officers mounting a coup to overthrow Hitler on 30 June, the anniversary of the 1934 'Knight of the Long Knives', in which the Führer had dealt violently with his rivals in the Nazi party and beyond. 'The Reichsführer of the SS is now coming to a period when his cosmic constellations bode no good,' de Wohl slipped in, a sideswipe for Heinrich Himmler, against whom PWE were mounting a parallel campaign of disinformation.[30] As with de Wohl's carefully placed predictions of Hitler's death in 1942, whether or not a coup did take place was immaterial. The object of the exercise was to provoke and heighten an atmosphere of fear and uncertainty when Germany was facing serious setbacks in the Battle of the Atlantic and on the Eastern Front.

5

While de Wohl was making his contribution to the Political Warfare Executive's black propaganda through *Der Zenit*, he had not given up his hope of exerting a greater astrological influence on events. Early in October 1942 he met Sir Charles Hambro of the Special Operations Executive for dinner. De Wohl described their conversation to his MI5 handler Lennox on 29 October. The astrologer said he had told Hambro he was happy with the work he was doing for PWE but it took little of his time and he was eager to do more. Lennox recorded, 'He also mentioned that his ambition was to get the O.B.E!!!' According to de Wohl, Hambro had said he regretted the astrologer had left SOE and he was considering trying to get him back, possibly to redeploy him in 'the Americas'. But since that meeting with Hambro, de Wohl had heard nothing.[31] De Wohl gave the impression he was trying to force the issue when on 30 November he posted what Hambro described in a note to the head of the Political Intelligence Department as 'a report showing his successes in 1941/2 and his prognostications for 1943'. Having glanced through them, Hambro thought some of the 1943 prophecies might be useful material for what he called PWE's 'more lurid efforts'. He went on, 'He tells me he has plenty of time to spare, in other words he would like the opportunity of making a little more money.'[32]

De Wohl introduced his six-page 'Survey of 1943' with the familiar pitch, the one that had been his early introduction to British Intelligence: 'Since 1923 Hitler is advised by Astrologers ... 'luck' ... 'lucky' ... what Hitler will be told by his astrological advisers ... Hitler's famous 'divine intuition' is in reality simply knowledge about planetary tendencies ...' He named three astrologers he believed were working for the Führer: 'Karl E. Krafft, Herren Fritz Brunnhuebner, B. Korsch'. In fact, Krafft had never met Hitler and was at present working on interpretations of Nostradamus for Goebbels' Propaganda Ministry. Korsch, if by B. Korsch de Wohl meant Hubert Korsch, had been in a German concentration camp since May 1941. He was the founder of *Zenit*, fake versions of which de Wohl was now constructing with Delmer and the Political War Executive. It is impossible to say where Brunnhuebner was, but it was likely he too had been arrested in the May 1941 Aktion Hess mass round-up of astrologers. De Wohl began in his usual assured tone: 'This then is what his advisers must tell him about 1943.'[33]

The forecasts, set out month by month, were vague and impressionistic and it is hard to know what actual value de Wohl's generalised statements would have been to Military Intelligence and – although there was occasionally a perceptive flash – what they could contribute to British strategy in the struggle against Hitler. The worth of what de Wohl was saying seemed of no more than the stars in a Sunday newspaper, in some ways less. For January de Wohl wrote, 'The month is good for Marshal Timoshenko … The month is not favourable for the Führer.' In the following month, 'Gen. Montgomery's aspects are not any more good between Febr. 13 and 28th … Churchill's chart shows excitement, anger and losses … The month as a whole is good for the Führer.' March promised to be 'good' for Hitler but threatened a 'depressed period' for Churchill. The prospects for both would improve in April and for Hitler they would rise to 'decidedly good'.

The forecasts for May and July were a little more substantial. De Wohl introduced his predictions for May by saying, 'Here begins the series of months which may easily decide the outcome of the war.' Was de Wohl making an astute guess based on a careful reading of the course of the war, or were the stars really guiding him? The German Navy suffered a run of disastrous U-boat losses in May, so much so that the submarine commander Admiral Doenitz slowed the pace of submarine activity in the Atlantic. U-boats never regained the destructive effectiveness that had seriously threatened Britain's survival. Similarly, for July de Wohl forecast that Hitler would face 'the most dangerous month of the entire war'. In that month Allied troops landed in Sicily, the first return of ground forces to Europe since the ousting of the British Army from Greece in 1941. The invasion of Sicily provoked the overthrow of Hitler's ally Mussolini at the end of the month. For August de Wohl wrote, 'Mussolini's chart shows party troubles', an understatement, but close enough to actual events as far as timing was concerned. The astrologer concluded – as he invariably had and as no one could doubt – that Hitler and Nazi Germany were doomed:

Even with the greatest possible optimism it would be impossible for Hitler's astrological advisers to predict 'final victory' for him in 1943 … They will have to emphasise that it will take a lot of steering to get through the year without grave defeats. This is the first year of the war in which really strong good aspects are shown in the charts of King George VI and of Churchill, and a few really bad ones in Hitler's chart.

De Wohl's forecasts had taken a new direction. When Hitler and Germany were achieving triumph after triumph at the beginning of the war, de Wohl explained that the Führer made his move when astrologers told him luck was guaranteed at that time. Now de Wohl's emphasis was on Hitler's ill fortune. 'An attack made against Hitler at a time when he knows his aspects are bad, will certainly find him prone to some amount of defeatism.' The truth was that when the United States – with her industrial might and potential military strength – entered the war in December 1941, Allied victory was as good as inevitable. It did not take a study of the stars to see the Nazi regime's days were numbered. Once British Intelligence had been anxious to know what Hitler was thinking. Now the roles were reversed and it was Hitler who would be waiting apprehensively to see what move his enemies planned next.

Hambro at SOE had originally intended to pass on de Wohl's November 1942 forecasts of the year ahead to the Directorate of Military Intelligence, but a clearly furious Lennox dissuaded him. Lennox insisted all reports the astrologer produced must, as before, be handed to him. He would decide whether or not they merited the attention of Military Intelligence. He wrote to his MI5 colleague Toby Caulfield that he believed de Wohl's contributions – 'clearly to blow his own trumpet' – could be dangerous if not handled carefully. 'In practice I do not intend to hand these reports on until I am completely convinced they will not be acted on wrongly.' He made plain what he saw as the problem with what British Intelligence had been involved in since 1940: de Wohl's predictions might be taken by the ill-advised as literal truth:

The only interest of astrological forecasts to Service Departments, or for that matter to anyone else, should be that it may be interesting and informative to know that the advice given in these reports may be astrological advice that Hitler is receiving from his astrologers. The danger is that all this sort of pseudo-science is most insidious, and unless you have a complete sceptic or a very strong-minded man dealing with it, quite the wrong point of view may be indulged in! I would rather like these remarks of mine to be on record!![34]

6

Meanwhile, were de Wohl's astrological contributions to *Der Zenit* having any measurable impact on German military, naval and civilian morale? This was the intention, but as with much of the Political Warfare Executive's black propaganda output, it was impossible to know with any certainty. PWE was at its most active when doubts were anyway growing in Germany about the course of the war: the Wehrmacht bogged down on the Eastern Front and the United States now lined up with Britain and the Soviet Union. There was, however, one small sign that when the Nazi regime became aware of the magazine's existence, they took the threat seriously. Bundles of *Der Zenit* being smuggled into Germany in a consignment of machine tools from Sweden were intercepted by chance when they arrived at the Baltic port of Stettin. They came into the hands of the local police, who passed a copy to the Sicherheitsdienst (SD), the intelligence agency of the SS and Nazi party. This particular edition of *Der Zenit* was the one dated December 1942. The SD contacted Wilhelm Wulff, a Hamburg astrologer who provided advice to SS chief Himmler, and instructed him to analyse the magazine's contents for technical accuracy. Wulff later outlined the conclusions he reached:

I skimmed through the bogus *Zenit*. It contained a good mundane horoscope for 1943, also the horoscopes of Admirals Doenitz and Raeder, plus the horoscopes of a number of German battleships ... From an astrological point of view it was a first-class production and indicated that it was the work of experts. Some very skilful bits of propaganda had been casually inserted in an otherwise apparently innocuous text. We deduced that this fake had been manufactured in England ... and there were some very skilled astrologers there.[35]

A comment de Wohl would have found gratifying, had he known: one professional recognising another.[36] His next and penultimate piece of work for the Political Warfare Executive was assisting in the production of a twenty-four-page booklet intended to provoke fears about Hitler's state of health and the loyalty of those around him by discrediting both Karl-Ernst Krafft – whom de Wohl continued to insist was one of the German leader's team of astrologers – and the man who PWE claimed was the Führer's personal surgeon, Dr Karl Brandt. The layers of deception involved epitomised the combination of de Wohl and Delmer at its best, though not necessarily its most effective. The ninth edition of *Der Zenit* had already sown the seeds by dropping hints about Brandt's astrological unsuitability for such a delicate post. But there are two points that need to be taken into account. The first is that Krafft was not Hitler's astrologer. The second is that although Brandt had once served as Hitler's surgeon, he was dismissed when he tried to warn the Führer about unconventional treatment he was receiving from Theodor Morrell. Given that this was an exercise in black propaganda, neither of those facts would be seen as at all important to Delmer or de Wohl.[37]

The booklet pretended to be the work of a friend of Krafft's concerned at his disappearance following arrest by the SS in December 1942 and now determined to ensure the truth was told.[38] The opening page was a copy of a letter dated 14 November 1942, purporting to have been written by Krafft. It was in reality dictated by de Wohl to a talented but imprisoned English counterfeiter, recruited by PWE's head of security, Colonel Chambers.[39] The style of handwriting would have been copied from a letter Krafft wrote to the Romanian diplomat Tilea in 1940, now in de Wohl's possession. 'May all benevolent forces help so that the evil may be averted,' the pretend Krafft wrote. The 'friends' then proceeded to give a twenty-one-page background to his arrest. Krafft, they explained, had been recruited as Hitler's astrologer and he had advised him for many years. The Führer had recently ordered Krafft to produce a new edition of the prophecies of Nostradamus. While engaged in this, Krafft had come across a quatrain foretelling Hitler's betrayal by 'One from the fire'. As 'brand' was a word for fire in German, Krafft had – the story ran – interpreted this as a clear reference to the Führer's physician, Brandt.

The doctor, the booklet went on, had been misusing his closeness to Hitler to exert an evil force on him. Brandt had persuaded his patient to turn down surgery essential for a prostate problem and instead prescribed a dangerous combination of a cocaine-based drug with doses of ovarian hormones. Brandt was as sinister an influence on the Führer as Rasputin had been on the doomed Romanovs, the Russian royal family. Photographs in the booklet showed what was said to be the obvious similarity between Brandt's eyes and those of Rasputin. Hitler had become dependent on Brandt, whose influence extended as far as recommending the dismissal and appointment of senior military officers. The disastrous course of the war in Russia was entirely due, the booklet claimed, to Brandt persuading Hitler to dismiss General Walter von Brauchitsch and to take personal command of the campaign. Krafft had written to Hitler warning him of the danger he faced from Brandt. On 8 December 1942 a member of the Führer's bodyguard had arrived at Krafft's house and he had not been seen since. Fortunately, the 'friend' said, he had circulated copies of his letter to Hitler to acquaintances, so the truth would not be lost.

Ellic Howe, who had been involved in the printing and design of the magazine *Der Zenit*, played a similar part at the Political Warfare Executive in production of what he referred to as the 'Brandt-Rasputin Leaflet'. He took a closer interest than de Wohl on the distribution of PWE productions and their effect on the enemy. What was the Brandt booklet's impact when copies were smuggled into Germany, where it was intended to encourage fears for Hitler's physical and mental health? Howe summed up simply: 'No "come-backs" are recorded.'[40] De Wohl, perhaps not surprisingly, made no mention at all of the exercise in *The Stars of War and Peace*, though it is easy to imagine the astrologer and Delmer laughing as they piled lie upon lie in producing the booklet.

De Wohl's final project for the Political Warfare Executive and Delmer in 1943 was manipulating the prophecies of the sixteenth-century seer Nostradamus to point to the certain downfall of Hitler and the defeat of Germany. German Propaganda Minister Goebbels had been using doctored Nostradamus quatrains since the early stages of the war, employing Krafft among others to forecast the inevitability of the Allies' defeat. Krafft initially selected the relevant quatrains, which were then given a propaganda twist by writers in Goebbels' ministry and circulated through Europe in pamphlet form. Their heavy-handed obviousness – Germany would crush France and Britain, the Reich would last a thousand years – often provoked outright ridicule, according to the Nazi astrologer Wulff. 'One day the leading English, Swedish, and Spanish newspapers had carried the headline: Who is Nostradamus?,' he wrote. 'A few days later they printed the answer: Nostradamus is Adolf Hitler.'[41] In 1940, as the Battle of Britain began, Lord Haw-Haw (the British fascist William Joyce, employed to broadcast Nazi propaganda from Germany) declared in one of his radio speeches that Nostradamus had forecast London's devastation and this was now imminent.

Krafft had interpreted one quatrain in particular as undoubtedly prophesying Britain's defeat. This was published in 1941 in *How Nostradamus foresaw Europe's Future*. 'Within the Isles such horrible tumult/Well may it be that only all-out war will be heard/So great will be the injuries from the predators/That the great League will range itself against them.' According to Krafft, 'the Isles' were the British Isles, 'the predators' were the British themselves, and 'the great League' was Europe, which would unite under Hitler and conquer Britain.[42] Goebbels said during the early stages of the blitzkrieg campaign in France in 1940, 'Our panic propaganda in France is very successful. Over there Nostradamus-followers represent a fifth column.'[43] He remained convinced in 1942 that the work of the French seer was a useful weapon in his armoury. He wrote in his diary in May, 'The Americans and English fall easily for that type of propaganda. We are therefore pressing into service all star witnesses for occult prophecy. Nostradamus must once again submit to being quoted.'[44]

It was perhaps ironic that the PWE and de Wohl should choose to respond to what was in practice a not altogether effective German propaganda campaign by using exactly the same means in precisely the same way. As one writer on Nostradamus points out, 'The fascinating aspect of both British and German usage of Nostradamus' quatrains during World War II was the total absence of scruple, on both sides, as to whether the quotations might or might not be the seer's genuine utterances.'[45] Trying to beat the Nazis at their own game, de Wohl produced the wording for a booklet 124 pages long: *Nostradamus Predicts the Course of the War*. The publication, printed on thin Bible paper, contained fifty prophetic quatrains, supposedly by Nostradamus but either carefully doctored originals or ones de Wohl simply made up. Aptly, newspaper reporters in the United States in 1941 had given him the title 'the modern Nostradamus'. As with *Der Zenit*, *Nostradamus Predicts* was to be smuggled into Germany masquerading as a genuine local production.

The quatrains in *Nostradamus Predicts the Course of the War* were presented in medieval French text (drawn by Elizabeth Friedlander of the PWE, who had also designed the covers for Delmer and de Wohl's earlier creation, *Der Zenit*), with a German translation under each one. They were followed by an interpretation of their meaning. A fourteen-page introduction by the supposed author Dr Bruno Winkler of Weimar asked 'Can humans see into the future?' and thanked Dr Heinrich Lesse, curator of a collection in Regensburg, for the loan of the original manuscript on which the booklet was based. That manuscript, of course, did not exist. Printing – carried out by the Political Warfare Executive printer, Ellic Howe – was credited to Regulus Verlag of Görlitz, a firm that did genuinely produce astrological and occult works.

The body of the text was made up of five sections: Hitler's early life and the rise of the Nazis, the war up to the fall in France in 1940, the campaign against Britain, war in southern and eastern Europe, and the end of the conflict and Germany's future. One quatrain purported to be a prediction of Hess's flight to Scotland in May 1941. 'A captain of Greater Germany will approach the King of Kings, who justly mistrusts him, with a feigned appeal for help. No alliance will be made and the slaughter will continue.' Dr Winkler explained, 'Foreign astrologers have linked this quatrain to the case of Rudolf Hess, who supposedly flew to England to offer the King an alliance against Russia.'[46]

The use by Nostradamus of 'Hister', the old Roman name for the River Danube, had generated excitement among occultists when Hitler came to power, with a clear – but mistaken – connection being made between the two. De Wohl used this supposed link to suggest Nostradamus had predicted the Führer's demise, to all appearances by assassination. A genuine quatrain began 'Celuy qu'en luitte', meaning 'he who'. De Wohl altered this to the more useful for propaganda purposes 'Hister qu'en luitte'. The complete quatrain now read: 'Hister [i.e. Hitler] who carried off more victories (prizes) in his warlike fight than was good for him; six [men] will murder him in the night. Naked, taken unawares without his armour, he succumbs.'[47]

Was de Wohl satisfied with his contribution to *Nostradamus Predicts the Course of the War*, proud that he had been able to present a substantial piece of work in the battle against the Nazis? He makes no mention of the booklet in his memoir of his wartime activities, *The Stars of War and Peace*. As with his connections to Military and Naval Intelligence, his war mission to the United States, and his involvement with the counterfeit magazine *Der Zenit*, he was presumably warned off by MI5 with a reference to provisions of the Official Secrets Act. But there was also the possibility that in retrospect he may have regretted parts of his role in concocting 'predictions', however worthwhile the cause.

With the completion of the Nostradamus booklet, de Wohl was now unemployed. Lennox had made it clear to his MI5 colleagues that even if the astrologer continued to write his forecasts on the course of the war, they would be accepted but it was unlikely in most cases that they would find their way to the Directorate of Military Intelligence. After Nostradamus, nothing remained for de Wohl to do with the Political Warfare Executive. Delmer had reached the conclusion there was no longer much mileage left in astrology as a black propaganda weapon. The difficulties involved in smuggling material into Germany and occupied Europe more than outweighed any value it had in denting German confidence.[48] Howe, who had been involved in the production of *Der Zenit* and *Nostradamus Predicts the Course of the War*, wrote a brief and sad epitaph on de Wohl's brief career with PWE: 'As far as I was concerned de Wohl faded from the scene as suddenly as he had entered it.'[49]

7

Towards the end of 1943 the United States Office of Strategic Services – precursor of the Central Intelligence Agency – was presented with a 165-page report commissioned for internal use entitled *A Psychological Analysis of Adolph Hitler: His Life and Legend.*[50] The author was Walter C. Langer, a psychoanalyst and academic based at Harvard University. Langer had studied in Austria with Anna Freud, daughter of Sigmund Freud, and lived in Germany in the earliest days of Nazi power. The document was a detailed biographical and psychological study of Hitler and set out to explain his rise, his methods and his possible fate. The study opened with an assessment of the reasons for 'Hitler's firm belief in his own greatness.' Langer wrote:

> Almost all writers have attributed Hitler's confidence to the fact that he is a great believer in astrology and that he is constantly in touch with astrologers who advise him concerning his course of action. This is almost certainly untrue. All our informants who have known Hitler rather intimately discard the idea as absurd. They all agree that nothing is more foreign to Hitler's personality than to seek help from outside sources of this type.[51]

In the same passage Langer quoted a Dutch diplomat who had been in close contact with Hitler for a number of years. 'Not only has the Fuehrer never had his horoscope cast,' the diplomat said, 'but he is in principle against horoscopes because he feels he might be unconsciously influenced by them.' Langer added as further confirmation the fact that Hitler 'some time before the war, forbade the practice of fortune-telling and star-reading in Germany'. The study declared that all the evidence led to the conclusion that Hitler having any reliance on astrology was a 'myth'. Hitler himself made his attitude plain only a year or so earlier in one of his long, rambling monologues. In July 1942 he expressed the contempt he felt for superstition and for astrology in particular, telling his lunch companions:

> The horoscope, in which the Anglo-Saxons in particular have great faith, is another swindle whose significance must not be under-estimated. Just think of the trouble given to the British General Staff by the publication by a well-known astrologer of a horoscope foretelling the final victory in this war for Germany! All the newspapers in Britain had to dig out all the false prophecies previously published by this eminent quack and reprint them before public anxiety could be pacified.[52]

But even in 1947, two years after the Führer's suicide in Berlin, the historian Hugh Trevor-Roper (attached to MI6 in the Second World War) could still write in *The Last Days of Hitler* that the dictator had been 'unduly influenced' by astrology.[53] However, leading biographers of the German dictator subsequently confirmed what Langer had said in 1943. Alan Bullock wrote of the absolute lack of 'any evidence to substantiate the once popular belief that he resorted to astrology. His secretary says categorically that he had nothing but contempt for such practices ...'[54] After the war, Hitler's personal secretary, Christa Schröder, described the Führer's reaction to the prediction Elsbeth Ebertin had made in 1923 about his destiny as German leader. 'It seemed that her predictions had fulfilled themselves in every respect,' Schröder said. 'But Hitler only spoke very ironically about this coincidence and considered the whole thing as a joke.'[55]

More recently, Hitler's biographer, Ian Kershaw, believed it was only in a last desperate moment in April 1945 as the Reich collapsed around him and Russian troops battered their way into Berlin, that the Nazi leader was tempted to grasp at the straw offered by the stars. Until then astrology had been irrelevant. Himmler – who was a long-time believer in astrology – had Hitler's horoscope drawn up without his knowledge and a copy came into the hands of Propaganda Minister Goebbels. President Roosevelt's sudden death on 12 April, Goebbels told Hitler excitedly, was surely the fulfilment of a prophecy in his horoscope that

Germany would enjoy a military turning-point in the second half of the month.[56] Under the misapprehension that Hitler had always leaned on astrology, Trevor-Roper nevertheless correctly described the absurdity of the pair's inability to grasp reality. 'To us it seems incredible that in those last days of the Third Reich its leaders should have thought that the stars ... could save them; nevertheless all the evidence is clear that they never understood the real certainty of their ruin.'[57] A fortnight later both Hitler and Goebbels were dead.

De Wohl's claim in 1940 was not only that Hitler sought astrological advice before taking any important action but that he could also identify the astrologers the Führer consulted. He consistently named Karl-Ernst Krafft, wrongly, as Hitler's personal astrological guide. De Wohl went on to assert that it was possible for him, as a professional astrologer using the methods common to all practitioners of the craft, to reveal the advice Hitler was being given. This – despite early doubts among some with whom he came into contact – had opened the doors of Naval Intelligence and Military Intelligence and sustained de Wohl's career well into the Second World War. What evidence could de Wohl have been relying on to feel so confident in his claim? Was the astrologer lying or was he genuinely mistaken?

De Wohl had not been alone in insisting there was a connection between the Nazi leader and the stars. According to Ellic Howe, rumours had been circulating in Germany from 1933 that Hitler's use of astrology was the only explanation possible for his meteoric rise to total power over the country. As war approached and Hitler's run of successes continued, the story spread outside Germany. Howe collected examples from the press. The *Gazette de Lausanne* of 5 April 1939 reported, 'Nobody believes in astrology more than Herr Hitler'. On 12 July 1939 the *Daily Mail* in London reported the claim of the Columbia University academic Dr Nicholas Murray Butler that the Führer consulted a team of five astrologers, comparing and weighing their advice to ensure nobody misled him. The London *Evening Standard* of 5 October 1939 printed a report on Elsbeth Ebertin, whom the paper described as 'Hitler's favourite astrologer'. The *Daily Telegraph* had a similar report on Ebertin the following day.[58] Among British astrologers there was no doubt at all. Charles Carter, a leading figure in the field, wrote quite simply of Hitler in the September 1939 edition of *Astrology* magazine, 'We have long known that he made use of our art.'

If de Wohl was aware of Hitler's interest in astrology while he was still living in Germany – he did not leave the country until 1935, two years after the Nazis came to power, five years after he himself began to study the stars – he initially kept quiet about it. He would surely have heard the rumours about the true secret of the Führer's rise if it had been the case. The astrologer's first autobiography, *I Follow My Stars*, was published in Britain in 1937. De Wohl dealt with his own initiation into the practice of astrology in some detail, but did not at the time view Hitler's shared interest as worth mentioning. Within a year, this had changed. In *Secret Service of the Sky* he declared Hitler's uncanny success in international diplomacy had one simple explanation: he consulted astrologers and acted on their advice. By doing this the Führer could be sure he made his most critical moves 'under very good aspects', avoiding them when the prognostication was bad.[59]

This became de Wohl's consistent story: to Lord Halifax at dinner with the Spanish ambassador, to the Director of Naval Intelligence, to the Directorate of Military Intelligence, to Hambro of the Special Operations Executive, to anyone prepared to listen. In *The Stars of War and Peace*, published in 1952, de Wohl repeated his constant claim that Hitler had been a follower of astrology since 1923. As additional confirmation of Hitler's belief, de Wohl said that in 1935 he had been approached by a senior Nazi official seeking to recruit him to the Führer's team of advisers, an invitation he refused. 'I did not care particularly to become the astrologer of a tyrant with one of the most dangerous horoscopes I had ever seen.'[60]

Why were such experienced and worldly men as the Foreign Secretary – Lord Halifax – the Directors of Naval and Military Intelligence, and senior officers of the Special Operations Executive prepared even to consider what de Wohl was saying, let alone give it credence? Initially, because 'everyone' had come to believe Hitler consulted astrologers. This had become the convenient explanation for Hitler's ability to persistently wrong-foot his opponents, both at home and abroad. The British establishment was dealing in Hitler with a leader of a new type: not from the traditional ruling strata, a man who was nihilistic and undemocratic but whose power was based in the masses. Once the astrology story was agreed the rest fell into place, strange as that place was. As de Wohl explained to British Intelligence, it was not necessary for them to believe in astrology, they only had to acknowledge that Hitler did. They were forced to take the next step by desperation: in the fraught summer of 1940, when German divisions had swept across Western Europe and Britain faced the daily threat of invasion, any source of information on Hitler's intentions was grasped eagerly, however bizarre the source might be.

De Wohl's supplementary offer had been that he would draw up and interpret the horoscopes of senior German military figures. Based on these, he could present analyses of their character, strengths and weaknesses, and likely inclinations, areas of knowledge in which British Intelligence was weak. His involvement with Military Intelligence led to a disturbing finding. 'MI14 were ordered to supply him with the dates of birth of all German officers above the rank of colonel whose particulars were recorded in their files … which led to the useful discovery that more than half the War Office dossiers referred to officers who were either dead or in retirement.'[61] Such incompetence was as good as a welcome mat for any chancer hoping to try his luck.

8

A Bumptious Seeker after Notoriety

I

Officers at MI5 had arranged for the GPO to intercept de Wohl's post as far back as September 1942, while the astrologer was carrying out black propaganda work for Delmer at the Political Warfare Executive. Drafting the request for a Home Office Warrant that would give political authorisation for this (a HOW had to be signed by the Secretary of State), MI5 officer Toby Caulfield wrote under the heading Reason: 'This man is of enemy alien origin and has lived a large part of his life in Germany. He has a considerable clientele as an astrologer, and in view of the influence which he may wield by this means it is desirable to learn more of his contacts and activities.'[1] As de Wohl had been keeping MI5 informed since 1938 of the names of the more interesting of his clients, the questions they asked and the advice he provided, Caulfield's explanation was obviously more an excuse than a reason. Lennox, the astrologer's MI5 handler, could simply have asked him who, what, when – as he had in the past. Something had provoked MI5's interest. Did they suspect de Wohl had secrets he was keeping from them or were officers simply finding ways to keep themselves busy?

The method of intercepting post once a Home Office Warrant had been signed and granted was straightforward. Letters on their way to the target's address were separated on arrival at the local GPO sorting office, passed to MI5 for scrutiny, copied, and then returned for delivery after minimal delay so as not to arouse suspicion. Interception of de Wohl's post continued for some time after he had ceased working with the Political Warfare Executive and was no longer having any significant contact with any branch of British Intelligence. Diversion of his mail was not finally brought to an end until 1946, when Britain had been at peace for some months. The astrologer's MI5 personal file reveals the dates letters to (and in a few cases from) de Wohl were intercepted and the identities of many of the writers. The majority of copies, however, were either withheld or destroyed in weeding before release. Given the way official censorship of records operates, it has to be assumed these were the most significant, revealing or – perhaps as likely – potentially embarrassing to British Intelligence.

An example was Viorel Tilea, the Romanian ambassador to London from 1938 to 1940, with whom de Wohl had remained in touch. Between February 1943 and September 1944, MI5 opened and read ten letters from Tilea to de Wohl and eight from the astrologer to Tilea. The former ambassador, on whom MI5 maintained a file (PF53105), was also having his post intercepted. Apart from the transcript of one, all letters were destroyed or withheld when the astrologer's MI5 file was opened to public view. It was understandable why Tilea should be a person of interest to British Intelligence, for a number of reasons.

The relationship between de Wohl and Tilea began in 1940 as that of astrologer and client but developed into what seemed to be a close friendship. Tilea also had a brief acquaintanceship in Switzerland with Karl-Ernst Krafft, whom de Wohl persisted in claiming – with no real evidence, apart from a suggestion by Tilea – was Hitler's personal astrologer. In the course of a conversation between Tilea and de Wohl in the summer of 1940 the astrologer realised he could make use of his knowledge of Hitler's horoscope, ostensibly in the anti-Nazi cause, by claiming he could determine what advice Krafft and others would be providing. Tilea promised he would arrange the necessary contacts, which he did, and de Wohl's work with British Intelligence was set in train. When a newly installed right-wing government in Romania ordered Tilea to return home in July 1940, he sought de Wohl's astrological advice on whether this would be a wise move. De Wohl kept his MI5 handler, Major Lennox, informed about his dealings with the diplomat and British Intelligence were aware how grateful Tilea had been for the astrologer's warning to remain in London.

Tilea sought and was granted political asylum but it soon became apparent that he presented a diplomatic problem to the British Government, which gave him as little encouragement as possible, unlike other anti-fascist exile movements in London. When Germany attacked the Soviet Union in June 1941 and Stalin's regime became Britain's ally against Hitler, the Foreign Office accepted Romania would be in the future Soviet sphere of influence. Tilea had established the Romanian National Committee, a pro-monarchist group that sought to free the country from its right-wing regime, in London. This soon split into rival factions, but Tilea remained an embarrassment to a government determined not to upset its vital Soviet ally.[2] Tilea's activities and his relationship with de Wohl were therefore of interest to MI5. What MI5 hoped to do, as exchanges between officers revealed, was to continue to use the astrologer to influence Tilea's thinking.

Following interception of a flurry of letters to and from de Wohl and Tilea on 23, 25, 27 and 30 March 1943, Lennox wrote a note in the astrologer's MI5 file on 5 April of an interview he had with de Wohl about Tilea's horoscope. This is no longer in the file, presumably destroyed, so what passed between Lennox and de Wohl remains unknown. However, the discussion aroused interest among MI5 officers and Toby Caulfield met Major Edward Boxshall of the Special Operations Executive, involved in work in the Balkans, to exchange views about de Wohl, Tilea and – apparently – astrology. Boxshall had been an MI6 agent in Bucharest, the Romanian capital, before the outbreak of war. Caulfield's note of the meeting is worth quoting as an example of the way MI5 and SOE viewed matters and of the continuing relationship with de Wohl:

I discussed de Wohl with Major Boxshall of S.O.E. who is, of course, very interested in Tilea. Before mentioning the Tilea/de Wohl link up I discovered that Boxshall had met de Wohl, knew he had been employed by S.O.E., been somewhat impressed by him and was inclined to argue that astrology was NOT bunk. By this I do not wish to imply that Boxshall is by any means a blind follower of astrology or of de Wohl.

I told Boxshall that we had a line of contact to de Wohl and could probably influence de Wohl's advice to Tilea.

Boxshall subsequently told me he could not think of any special way in which we could help him by thus planting 'special' advice on Tilea, but in general of course his desire was that Tilea should be discouraged from his present political activities.[3]

Whether de Wohl was able to exert the influence on Tilea's activities MI5 and SOE hoped for seems unlikely, but the two men remained in contact for the remainder of the war, as their intercepted letters showed. The final reference in the astrologer's MI5 file to their relationship came on 1 September 1944. Why a transcript was retained of this particular letter of Tilea is unclear, but the copy on file is revealing. Romania had been Germany's ally, despatching troops to take part in the war against the Soviet Union. As the tide turned, Soviet troops invaded Romania in the summer of 1944. On 23 August King Michael deposed the right-wing government, abandoned the Axis and joined the Allies. Tilea was clearly referring to this in his 1 September letter to de Wohl. He said he was rejoicing in the latest situation. 'Here is Michael's chart, can you make something out of it?' he asked the astrologer. 'He behaved very well, just as I have expected and hoped.'[4] The association had come full circle. In 1940 Tilea had asked de Wohl to set up and interpret the horoscopes of two Romanian politicians. Now four years on, he sought guidance from the astrologer on the destiny of King Michael. And that, it appears, was the final sign of interest from MI5 in their communication. Tilea never returned to Romania.

While some letters were of little interest – one from his bank and another from his accountant, for example – there were others that provoked MI5's curiosity. Three, in June and September 1943, were from Charles Hambro of the Special Operations Executive, who had taken de Wohl on in 1941 and had arranged his despatch to the United States that summer. Others were from contacts in entertainment, including the producer and director Alexander Korda in August 1943. Hungarian-born, Korda had been knighted in 1942. Had de Wohl been seeking screenwriting work? There were also letters from fellow writers who had fled Nazi Germany, such as Max Catto and Werner Scheff. Harman Grisewood, assistant controller of the BBC European Service, wrote on 26 June 1943 to say he had heard from Charles Hambro that de Wohl had some interesting ideas for broadcasts to Europe. He invited the astrologer to contact him to arrange a discussion.

Most letters were uncontroversial and of no interest, but in some cases MI5 decided to take matters further, asking local constabularies to look more closely at the background of de Wohl's contacts. Not surprisingly these were letter from writers with German-looking names, identifiable (like de Wohl himself) as enemy aliens. Equally unsurprisingly, when the police investigated them they turned out to be Jewish refugees from the Nazis, invariably with undisputed anti-fascist credentials. One interesting case was that of Marielen Critchley, née von Meiss-Teuffen, an Austrian married to Reginald Critchley. Donald Cameron, grandfather of David Cameron (British prime minister from 2010 to 2016), had a wartime affair with Marielen and abandoned his wife to live with her. Marielen's letter to de Wohl – one of the few copies retained on file when it was released – has the tone of a close friend. 'Will I hear from you soon again.'[5]

2

De Wohl's days were numbered as all those with whom he had worked or co-operated saw less and less value in retaining links with him. As an astrologer he would surely have seen the bad aspects looming, a period of ill fortune on the horizon. One glaring difficulty with de Wohl that MI5 found impossible to ignore was his inability to keep his mouth shut, his habit of blabbing. One informant complained to an MI5 officer in May 1943 about the astrologer's behaviour when he attended meetings of the White Hawk Circle of Spiritualists in Queen's Gate. De Wohl boasted to anyone prepared to listen that he was a member of 'the Secret

Service' and at the same time a professional astrologer. The combination – if true, and it was – was obviously odd enough to make any ordinary member of the public sit up. The informant thought de Wohl needed a 'fatherly eye' kept on him. Desmond Orr, the MI5 officer who received the complaint, wrote:

> I feel that there have now been so many indications that de Wohl is an indiscreet talker and a bumptious seeker after notoriety, that it would be insufficient merely to place him on the Unemployed List of the Army, and that he should be retired altogether. If it should be said that this would render him still more dangerous or more potentially mischievous, then I feel that he should be officially carpeted and warned as to the consequences ...[6]

Two letters intercepted by MI5 provided confirmation that any working connection with British Intelligence the astrologer may have had had now been brought to an end. One was from Sir Charles Hambro, who had first taken de Wohl up and who was now in overall command of the Special Operations Executive. De Wohl appeared to have written to him saying he was owed money. The tone of Hambro's reply suggested he had reached the end of his patience with the astrologer. He wrote bluntly on 29 May 1943 that de Wohl was owed nothing. The army had passed on whatever pay was due to him and he had already received all the one-off payments for work he had been carrying out for the Political Warfare Executive. The second letter was from the War Office, dated 7 June 1943. There was a brief note and a certificate stating that, 'Mr Louis de Wohl ceased to be employed in Military Service as from 1st June.'[7] The astrologer no longer had a uniform, a rank, a job or a settled income.

If the Special Operations Executive, the Political Warfare Executive and the War Office were no longer interested in de Wohl, MI5 were still curious about what he might be up to. An unnamed MI6 officer wrote a note to Caulfield of MI5 on 16 December 1943 with what he thought was the revelation that de Wohl did not speak Hungarian. The MI6 officer said de Wohl had approached a Hungarian known to MI6 and 'pulled his usual line of mystery man, said he was of the Hungarian aristocracy, but now British'. But when addressed in Hungarian he could neither understand nor speak it. 'De Wohl appears no longer to be wearing uniform,' the note continued, 'but still manages to convey to all and sundry that he is still a Captain.'[8] The note was passed to Major Alley of MI5, who replied that he was 'always glad to receive reports on the activities of individuals who were once employed by one of the British propaganda organisations'.[9] Propaganda, he was careful to say, not 'providing astrological advice to British Intelligence'.

Being abandoned by authority – and the loss of income – hit de Wohl hard. If he had genuinely wanted to play a part in the war against the Nazis, to be told he was of no further use would have been a painful experience. A reply from a doctor in Upper Wimpole Street, presumably de Wohl's own physician, suggested the astrologer had written a self-pitying letter. 'I am very sorry to learn that you have had now prolonged disappointments which will make any person and especially you down-hearted,' the doctor wrote. 'Let me know if your health is in trouble. Your present situation will not make the slightest difficulty.'[10] 'Present situation' presumably meant shortage of money. De Wohl's sole source of income now appeared to be his private practice as an astrologer – a number of the letters MI5 intercepted looked as if they came from clients, one enclosing a cheque for 12 guineas.

De Wohl was also rummaging around among his contacts in the film industry for work. MI5 officers – who gave the impression they were keen to track his every move – missed his appearance in 1944 in the film *Mr Emmanuel*, a Two Cities production made at Teddington Studios. There was nothing in his MI5 personal file to suggest any officer had noticed this or any informant had told them. De Wohl, somewhat incongruously given his Jewish heritage, played the part of Hermann Goering, head of the Luftwaffe and the Nazi Hitler had nominated as heir in the event of his death. The story was topical – Jewish refugees fleeing ill-treatment by the Gestapo – but the reception was mixed. The magazine *Variety* reported from London that the film moved along 'sturdily, but without inspiration … For the U.S. it may do as a mild secondary feature.'[11] Nobody in the United States noticed that 'Goering' was the astrologer, the 'modern Nostradamus', who had impressed the country three years before.

What was the explanation for MI5's continuing surveillance of de Wohl? Was it simply a matter of once in our files, always in our files, and of appearing busy? Surely he was no longer suspected of being a possible Nazi plant after three years co-operating with British Intelligence, working for the Special Operations Executive in the United States and the Political Warfare Executive in London? There were always accusations, rumours to keep the pot boiling. On 29 September 1943 a note on de Wohl's file reported that an informant had been discussing 'various people' with an MI5 officer. The unnamed informant said that 'one of the greatest scandals he has so far come across in connection with this war was embodied in the person of Mr Louis de Wohl, whom he describes from his personal knowledge as "a charlatan, well known in pre-war days in Germany as a Nazi".' MI5 were sensible enough not to take this entirely seriously, a typed note at the bottom of the report saying that no action was to be taken on the story without reference to Toby Caulfield.[12] The real source of MI5's worries became clear when it emerged de Wohl was making a record of his activities – the possibility of an embarrassing disclosure that British Intelligence had ever taken up with an astrologer and fears about what he might reveal.

MI5 might have suspected from their examination of the intercepted letters that de Wohl was either in the process of writing or contemplating writing a book. This was, after all, his first trade, one through which he had prospered in Germany. On 3 April 1943 there was a letter from Andrew Dakers, a New York literary agent. This was followed on 16 September by one from Arnold Jackson, also an agent. A week or so later Oswald Wolff, a long-established publisher, wrote to de Wohl. By May 1944, MI5 had obtained the manuscript (one officer says the proofs), either directly or indirectly. There is no clue in de Wohl's file whether he offered an actual manuscript, was asked for it or whether MI5 demanded sight from the astrologer, his agent or publisher. De Wohl had signed the Official Secrets Act and would have been reminded what he could and could not disclose when it came to sensitive information about his involvement with British Intelligence. In the most extreme case, nothing at all. Major Alley was unimpressed by what he read. He wrote to Lennox – the astrologer's handler – 'I have been through de Wohl's proofs and most of it seems to me to be pretty awful drivel.' Alley said there were certain references to individuals they needed to discuss.[13] By the sound of it, this was the book that would eventually appear in 1952 as *The Stars of War and Peace*, de Wohl's partial memoir of his wartime activities.

Lennox passed the manuscript on to another MI5 officer, Major Stephen Watts, who had been film and drama critic for the *Daily Express* before joining MI5.[14] Watts wrote to Lennox that 'to save you from extreme nausea' he had skimmed de Wohl's manuscript and had looked closely at the sections that had worried Major Alley. He agreed the book was badly written but he believed there was undoubtedly an audience interested in astrology that would want to buy it. 'I make this point,' Watts wrote, 'because it is the reason why one cannot safely dismiss the book as merely drivel unlikely to come to any wider notice.' He did not consider there were any serious security implications to the references to personalities, although the Director of Naval Intelligence, Rear Admiral Godfrey, providing de Wohl with the birthdates of senior officers, could be a matter for concern. Watts described the heart of the problem from MI5's point of view:

> It seems to me most undesirable that the public should get the impression that the utterances or actions of public men were at any time influenced by the mumbo-jumbo of astrology … One particular item to which I would draw your attention is de Wohl's statement that he was commissioned in the British Army with the rank of captain – the implication being that this was his reward for his work on Hitler's horoscope etc.[15]

Watts was surely injecting a touch of nudge-nudge irony for Lennox. Why else had de Wohl been employed for three years if not for British Intelligence to make use of his astrological skills? What other reason would there be for putting a 37-year-old Hungarian – an enemy alien – in uniform and making an officer of him other than in recognition of the services he supplied? These facts were precisely what British Intelligence found awkward and what MI5 preferred should be kept from public knowledge, as far as that was possible. Whatever pressure MI5 put on de Wohl as author or on any potential publisher, the astrologer's book did not appear until 1952, eight years after these exchanges, and the revelations he eventually made were minimal.

3

De Wohl really had little choice but to return to writing for a living. He had been successful in the past and much of what he had produced for British Intelligence was as artfully constructed as a novel or screenplay. But almost immediately his attempt had come to MI5's attention. Henry Borosh was an agent with the Special Operations Executive, de Wohl's past employer. Like de Wohl, he was of Hungarian origin. Borosh had organised resistance in German-occupied France under a variety of aliases, among them Hippolyte, Silversmith, Yashmak, Marius, and he had once come close to capture, torture and certain death. In January 1945 he met a war correspondent attached to the United States army, Curt Reiss, at the Ambassador's Club. As a result the journalist was able to produce two articles about Borosh's activities in France. Borosh was then questioned about his conversations with Reiss by an SOE officer. Borosh was adamant he had not named SOE or had he made any reference to 'Baker Street', the shorthand term for the organisation's headquarters.[16] Even the existence of the Special Operations Executive was meant to be a secret. The nameplate at the 64 Baker Street headquarters read 'Inter-Service Research Bureau'.

At a further interview on 1 February 1945 by an SOE officer, Squadron Leader Hugh Park, Borosh revealed that he was hoping to produce a book about his activities in France, but needed help with writing. The journalist Reiss, with whom it turned out de Wohl was also acquainted, had suggested the astrologer was the ideal man to act as his ghost writer. The two met at de Wohl's Athenaeum Court flat and, according to Borosh, the astrologer said he was happy to help with writing provided 'the authorities' gave their permission. Squadron Leader

Park wrote in his report he was concerned at the amount of information about SOE operations and methods Borosh may already have revealed to the American journalist. He said he reminded Borosh about the provisions of the Official Secrets Act. If he did write a memoir it would have to be his own work and be 'confined to a watered-down account of his experiences in France with no place names or names of agents of references to incidents from which people could be identified'. Borosh replied that a book written on those terms would be so uninteresting he could not imagine anyone would want to read it. He said to Park he would tell de Wohl he had decided to abandon the project. Park concluded his report, 'I think that he is sufficiently frightened <u>not</u> to wish to proceed with the publication of any matter relating to this organisation.'[17]

SOE's clearly delighted head of security, Commander John Senter, despatched a copy of Park's report to his MI5 contact Lennox, saying in a covering note: 'The result of the interview ... would seem to be to have frightened Borosh off the idea of a book and to have deprived the Captain of a commission in writing it.'[18] There really did seem to be a whiff of personal vindictiveness about this, as if de Wohl had made himself unpopular with yet another person. Happy as Senter was, he went on to ask Lennox to interrogate de Wohl about the affair as there remained some loose ends. Lennox's interview with de Wohl went into detail, the report covering almost three pages of single-spaced typing. What emerged was that the astrologer had no need to act as Borosh's ghost writer. He had already signed a contract with a publisher for a book of his own, a piece of historical fiction. The aspects had become positive once more.

De Wohl did not yet know Borosh had decided to abandon the project and the astrologer told Lennox when they met at the Athenaeum Court flat on 13 February 1945 he was keen to help write his memoir. Lennox reminded him about the Official Secrets Act and de Wohl agreed he would only become involved if 'the authorities' agreed. He said Borosh had a 'thrilling story' to tell. 'He gave the impression of a man who had got successfully through a very dangerous time.' Lennox was less interested in this and more concerned whether Borosh had broken security by disclosing sensitive material about SOE. 'Did he give any other details about his work or the work of his department?' De Wohl was astute enough to understand what Lennox was doing and confined himself to interesting generalities. 'He mentioned the price the Germans paid for simple information: 6,000 francs. For information about the Maquis: 100,000 francs or more. For a British agent: one million francs was offered by the Gestapo.' But de Wohl had moved on and his real interest now was a contract with the New York agent Curtis Brown for 'my next book, a historic novel "Julien", whose background is 350 A.D.'[19]

An internal MI5 minute on 26 April 1945 confirmed that what bothered British Intelligence was less that de Wohl now constituted a possible source of security damage, more the embarrassment he might be capable of causing. Major Watts had already raised this in his critique of the astrologer's projected memoirs. One way round the problem might be to give de Wohl what he had long wanted: British citizenship. Writing to Major Alley of MI5, Lennox recommended that this should be done as quickly as possible.[20] The danger was that de Wohl might 'have a considerable grouse' and he would definitely move to the United States, where he most likely would be granted citizenship and would become anti-British:

While it cannot be said that de Wohl knows any vital secrets, none the less, if he were sour and had American protection he might cause a good deal of embarrassment and unpleasantness. He is still very anxious to publish his book of his memoirs during the war, and he would certainly do so once he was in the States.

It was all very well, Lennox thought, to say 'publish and be damned', but the danger had to be recognised and unnecessary trouble avoided. If de Wohl were to be granted British citizenship he would definitely become 'more British than the British ... Fervent loyalty to his "King and Country" would possess his soul.' Lennox went on:

It may be a partly phoney emotion, but none the less, he is unlikely in the circumstances to do anything which would offend the authorities here. He still hopes to get a decoration one day, and while that may be out of the question, it would do no harm for him to go on hoping.

Lennox said there would be a flood of applications for naturalisation from people who had contributed to the British war effort: de Wohl's claim was as good as any. Toby Caulfield, who in the past had been antagonistic towards de Wohl, agreed, writing on Lennox's minute, 'He should be naturalised with the first flight, if not before.' In the event, the process took over a year. Under the heading 'Naturalization', the 20 September 1946 edition of the *London Gazette* announced: 'De Wohl Mucsinyi, Louis (known as Louis de Wohl); Hungary; Writer (Novelist); Athenaeum Court, Piccadilly, London, W.1. 20 August, 1946.'

A note, a brief outline of de Wohl's early life, submitted by Lennox on 10 July 1945, appeared to be a final stocktaking by MI5 before ending their interest in the astrologer. 'You may think it is worth while putting in the file,' Lennox wrote, 'as it clears up one or two points about which we were hitherto somewhat doubtful.'[21] Lennox said he had no reason to doubt that what de Wohl had told him about his family background was substantially correct. The rest MI5 would know from their files. The unspoken sub-text seemed to be: 'However did British Intelligence become involved with a character like this?'

He is technically not a refugee from Nazi oppression, but he states that he came here and acknowledges that he came here somewhat in a hurry, when he was accused by the Nazis of being Jewish or partly Jewish. He says that he does not know how much Jewish blood he had, and that he was unable to ascertain this in Hungary. He maintains that the name Wohl might be either Jewish or non-Jewish. Personally, I think there is very little doubt that he is at least partly Jewish.

The seven-year connection between the astrologer, MI5 and British Intelligence was now almost entirely severed. On 20 October 1945 MI5 told the GPO to suspend interception of post addressed to de Wohl at Athenaeum Court, though for the time being only 'suspend', Major Alley told MI5's deputy director general on 11 December, 'in case we find him indulging in activities which have been strictly prohibited by us'.[22] What these activities might be, Alley felt no need to explain. The Home Office Warrant was lifted completely in January 1946. The final piece in de Wohl's MI5 file was a cutting from the London *Evening Standard*, 19 August 1952, an article heading 'A prophet in Mayfair relates how he fought Hitler by "star warfare"', a review and extracts from his recently published *The Stars of War and Peace*.

4

For much of the war astrology had provided de Wohl with an income – from his pay as an army captain, topped up by fees from the private practice he maintained – and with an identity, a purpose. As his involvement with British Intelligence faded and the war entered its final phase, de Wohl resumed what he had been before he left Germany, a novelist. Although he mentioned to Lennox in February 1945 that he had sent the New York literary agency Curtis Brown a proposal for an historical novel based on the life of the Roman Emperor Julian, de Wohl had already completed a thriller, *Strange Daughter*. This was a sequel to *Introducing Doctor Zodiac*, which had been published in 1940. Like *Zodiac*, *Strange Daughter* combined astrology with a struggle against enemy agents, a highly coloured, dream-like version of de Wohl's wartime work with British Intelligence, the blend of fact and fiction with which he always felt at ease. True to form, wanting to control every aspect of the project, de Wohl had sent the London publisher – Lawrence & Dunn – his own design for the book's cover.

In the new post-war world, de Wohl's emphasis was beginning to change. In an interview for a *Daily Herald* diary piece in 1947 he gave the impression he had begun if not to disavow then at least to distance himself from astrology. He had found a new direction for his future activity – a return to the Roman Catholic church. 'As astrologer for fifteen years,' the paper reported, 'he prefers not to speak of this work as, he says, it has been brought into disrepute in Britain.'[23] He later explained the reason his return to the faith of his parents, which he said he had never entirely lost, though his commitment and practice had been 'tepid'. The effect of the war, living through the London blitz, facing death night after night had – de Wohl said – caused him to question his writing. In his typically self-dramatising way, and addressing what he intended would be his growing Christian audience, he went on:

> I had written 'successful' books, but to what was that success due? All my books were adventure stories, thrillers. People read them in trains or when they were too tired to read something really good. And they were written for just that purpose. They were not written in the service of God … I knew that I had to undergo a radical change as a writer, and I knew I had to make up for many years of time lost.[24]

A stream of books followed, often one a year, each on a religious theme: lives of saints and biblical figures, a biography of Pope Pius XII, a full-scale history of the Roman Catholic church. As well as healthy sales – many of de Wohl's books remained in print over half a century after their first publication – he was rewarded by the Papacy with appointment in 1958 as a Knight Commander of the Order of the Holy Sepulchre, an order instituted in the eleventh century. Further honours followed: in the spring of 1959 Pope John XXIII conferred the rank of Knight Commander of the Order of Saint Gregory the Great, bestowed since 1831 on 'gentlemen of proven loyalty to the Holy See'. In 1960 the Knights of Malta presented him with the Grand Cross of Merit.[25] Welcome though these awards were, to de Wohl's disappointment King George VI never invited him into membership of the Most Excellent Order of the British Empire, the OBE, which in 1942 he had told his MI5 handler Major Lennox he hoped to receive for his astrological work with British Intelligence.

The first in de Wohl's series of historical novels was *The Living Wood*, published in 1947 by Victor Gollancz in Britain and J.P. Lippincott in the United States. This was the story of Saint Helena, mother of the Roman Emperor Constantine, the woman said to have discovered in fourth-century Jerusalem the 'True Cross' on which Christ had been crucified. Vividly written in a fast style not unlike de Wohl's pre-war page-turners, *The Living Wood* was well-received on both sides of the Atlantic. His ability to place solid historical fact in a colourful fictional structure was especially praised. He could not resist the temptation to enhance the background in a pre-publication newspaper interview, claiming that he had been moved to write the book 'when a naval officer asked him to look after one fragment of the Cross during the war'.[26] After publication de Wohl encouraged the spread of a story that the book had been taken up by the British film producer and cinema chain owner J. Arthur Rank.[27]

Attila (the title in the United States was *Throne of the World*) followed in 1949. This described the violent progress of Attila the Hun, his battles in fifth-century Western Europe and the meeting with Pope Leo I that held him back from attacking Rome. A British reviewer described the book as 'written with power and considerable dramatic tension … Like Attila himself, the story moves fast'.[28] De Wohl's return to his faith was soon rewarded. In May 1948 he was given an audience with Pope Pius XII in acknowledgement of the value of his writing to the church. 'I asked him whom he wanted me to write about next,' de Wohl claimed. 'He said, "Thomas Aquinas".' The fictionalised story of the life of this thirteenth-century theologian and philosopher, *The Quiet Light*, was published in 1950. De Wohl told a reporter it was suggested to him he should go into a monastery to write the book. 'Instead he chose a room on the 18th floor of a New York skyscraper, had the telephone disconnected, and found it "the loneliest place I know".'[29] Always alert to publicity opportunities, de Wohl went to Rome to present a copy to the Pope personally. The year 1950 also saw the publication of *Imperial Renegade*, the novel about Julian the Apostate that de Wohl had told his MI5 handler Lennox he had hopes for in 1945.

De Wohl's historical fiction had a market and was well-received by reviewers who understood popular taste. But not everyone found the approach and treatment impressive. His fellow astrologer Felix Jay, who had known de Wohl since the late 1930s, was cutting but probably not entirely unfair. He described his friend as 'a featherweight' when it came to authorship:

His plots, the commonplace conflicts and situations, and a cloying and undistinguished style, both in English and in German, prohibit the application of canons of literary criticism. It was not only the lack of style that affected his pen, but an almost naïve and juvenile picture of the world, an astounding ignorance of the complicated web of human emotions and relationships. I often feel that he might have done well as a writer of children's books … His religious novels, which enjoyed a large circulation, appealed to semi-educated believers and were based on traditional hagiography.[30]

While de Wohl may have been moving away from astrology by the war's end – little time would be left for his private practice when he was busily engaged in writing up the saints – there was still some financial and publicity mileage in recounting his adventures with British Intelligence, re-running the old tales. It was a basic commercial fact that the more his name appeared in newspapers, the more novels he was likely to sell. In England, in the pages of the Sunday press in November 1947 it was the by now familiar story: 'I had learned the technique of Karl Krafft, Hitler's favourite astrologer. I knew what his advice to Hitler would be long before he was even summoned by the Führer.'[31] De Wohl had, of course, never met Krafft, and Krafft had not been Hitler's astrologer for the simple reason that the Führer had no interest in astrology.

One interview with a British journalist found its way into an obscure Australian newspaper, the article presumably syndicated and appearing in many small places across the English-speaking world. 'The man behind the scenes in the Battle of the Stars' told the reporter, 'Up to the last Hitler believed in astrology, and the demand for my reports never ceased. More than once we forestalled some of Hitler's tactically unpredictable moves.'[32] Untrue on both counts, but how could British Intelligence contradict de Wohl without revealing there had indeed been a period during which he was providing them with astrological services? Until 1989 even MI5's existence was not officially admitted.

In the United States, the entertainment industry journal *Variety* reported that de Wohl's New York agent, Curtis Brown, had sold a ten-part serial entitled 'Astrological Warfare' to the magazine *American*

Astrology. De Wohl told a *Variety* reporter, 'I was in special service, officially psychological warfare, and my findings were worked on with
other ways of approach before they reached the British War Office.'
In that fashion, the report continued, the British authorities 'without
admitting or accepting astrology, could benefit, through Captain de
Wohl, in the calculations of astral science'.[33] All this was the preliminary
to the appearance at last in 1952 of *The Stars of War and Peace*, the early
version of which had been caused such anxiety to MI5 officers eight
years before. De Wohl had made an earlier attempt with George Allen &
Unwin but the publisher turned the book down in 1950 after a reader's
report dismissed what de Wohl had submitted as unsatisfactory.

The text of de Wohl's autobiography showed he had taken to heart
what must have been strong warnings from MI5. It would be undesir-
able for the public to be left with the impression, MI5 officer Major
Watts had written on first seeing de Wohl's manuscript in June 1944,
'that the utterances of public men at any time were influenced by the
mumbo-jumbo of astrology'.[34] No doubt de Wohl was ordered to take
care on that very point. But what would be the value of *The Stars of War
and Peace* if the writer did not describe the extent of his influence? The
astrologer was careful, saying one thing, implying another. It was important, de Wohl wrote:

> to contradict the fairly widespread rumours that there was a continu-
> ous overall use of astrology on the part of the British, that 'the shadow
> of an astrologer loomed behind the actions of the War Cabinet', and
> similar nonsense. Astrological warfare did play its part on both sides in
> the war and I hope the British were not served too badly.[35]

The blurb on the cover of *The Stars of War and Peace* promised far more
than the book delivered and, paradoxically, threatened less than the publisher would have hoped for. 'Hitler conducts war by astrology – Capt.
de Wohl sets up Astrological War Bureau for British High Command –
Anticipates Allied victories, Matapan, Alamein, and the Atom Bomb ...'
But on the inner flyleaf the publisher referred to 'other war events which
he is not at liberty to reveal ...' A taste of disappointment is already

there. The latter section was a regurgitation of much of the material he had used in previous books, *Secret Service of the Sky* and *Commonsense Astrology*: 'An introduction to practical astrology without the 'bunk' – What the future may hold for you – How to cast your own horoscope.' A writer by profession for all his adult life, de Wohl understood the importance of letting nothing go to waste.

De Wohl went through his story from the beginning: the alleged not too subtle invitation to become Hitler's astrologer, the journey alone to England, the conversations with the Romanian diplomat Tilea, the crucial astrological performance before Foreign Secretary Lord Halifax at the Spanish ambassador's residence, the meetings with unnamed military and naval officers, the establishment of the one-man 'Psychological Research Bureau' in Park Lane, and the award of a British Army commission. Then came his astrological analyses of the characters of senior German commanders, the comparisons with the horoscopes of British generals. 'But the main question, even after the Battle of Britain, was: "When will Hitler invade us?"'[36] De Wohl would not have known that the three chiefs of staff – army, navy and air force – sitting in committee had solemnly cited his review of Hitler's horoscope in October 1940 when trying to determine the day German forces would land on the coast of England.

What de Wohl left out was significant. There was nothing about what was in retrospect the embarrassing enthusiasm of the Director of Naval Intelligence, Rear Admiral Godfrey, for astrology as a source of strategic information. The American interlude had little coverage. According to *The Stars of War and Peace*, de Wohl's stay in the United States from May 1941 to February 1942 had merely been to meet fellow astrologers in New York and Cleveland, nothing more. There was no reference to his astrological propaganda work through 1941 to undermine Hitler in American eyes and to encourage the country to enter the war, nor of the Special Operations Executive, which sponsored his mission but officially had not existed. De Wohl was allowed to mention his forecast of the Royal Navy's triumph in the Mediterranean at Cape Matapan in March 1941, a prediction he claimed to have made 127 days before the battle took place. The unconvincing story of his puzzled certainty that

Montgomery would defeat Rommel in the North African desert was also there.

The censor's blue pen appeared to have been busily at work. Of the book's 272 pages, only seventy-three dealt with de Wohl's wartime involvement with British Intelligence, barely a quarter. The remainder was a do-it-yourself astrology manual, lists of notable individuals' birthdays, illnesses connected with the different astrological signs. Padding at best: interesting, but not perhaps what the reader would have been hoping to find. De Wohl said nothing about the phoney German astrological magazine *Der Zenit* and the contrived 'predictions' that had been intended to strike fear in the hearts of U-boat crews, nor about the manipulated Nostradamus 'prophecies'. The Political Warfare Executive, for which de Wohl had worked but which also officially did not exist, had no place in *The Stars of War and Peace*. And yet de Wohl smuggled in a clue about the extent to which British Intelligence looked for a time to an astrologer for information:

> Remarkable, however, and admirable, was the open-mindedness of the high British authorities – to listen to, accept, and make use of a kind of knowledge utterly and entirely alien to them. I know how difficult it is to overcome old prejudices and, at least for some of the leading men who had to decide about the use of my services, it may well have been a great risk.[37]

5

Restrained though de Wohl had been in writing *The Stars of War and Peace* by MI5 and his signature on the Official Secrets Act, he was able to include some interesting stories. Though British Intelligence had dispensed with his services by 1944, he made the odd comment in the book that his 'purely astrological work for war purposes should have ended with the death of Hitler'.[38] It had, of course, ended some time before then. De Wohl did not disclose which section of British Intelligence he continued to work for, no doubt because what he wrote was untrue, simply an attempt to assert his continuing importance. And yet he had something to say about Japan and the atom bomb, though as often before there was an element of retrospective prophecy.

De Wohl wrote that from late 1944 and into 1945 he was mystified when he compared the horoscopes of the major personalities among the Allies and in Japan. 'The aspects of leading Japanese charts were so bad and those of Allied charts so uncannily good that common sense shied like a horse.' Was Japan about to suddenly collapse? This seemed unlikely as they showed every sign of having the strength and determination to fight on. 'It was inconceivable that they would simply fold up, especially when it came to the defence of their own soil.' What he had not taken into account because he knew nothing about their existence, de Wohl said, were the fearsome new weapons in Allied hands, the atomic bombs dropped on Hiroshima and Nagasaki in August 1945. Two detonations, and Japan surrendered. Would such weapons be used again? The bombs wielded against Japan had first been tested in New Mexico on 16 July 1945:

> In November 1952 Saturn will square the Sun of the 16 July 1945 chart. Uranus will be in conjunction with that position in October 1953. The planet is stationary then for the entire rest of the year, becomes 'retrograde' and returns to the fateful degree in July 1954. Any of these periods could set off the spark to the biggest explosion the world has ever seen.[39]

The first hydrogen bomb – 'the biggest explosion the world has ever seen' – was successfully tested by the United States in the Marshall Islands on 1 November 1952, after publication of *The Stars of War and Peace* on 20 August of that year. The second test, this time of a weapon capable of deployment against an enemy, was at Bikini Atoll on 1 March 1954. A lucky shot on de Wohl's part, or the result of his precise reading of the stars?

For an experienced writer, de Wohl showed himself at one point an unexpected master of bathos. A story intended to explain astro-meteorology involved the then popular novelist Elinor Glyn. At a party in

December 1938 the 74-year-old writer told him she was planning to make her first flight, to the Channel Islands. She was nervous and asked if he could reassure her there was no danger. De Wohl took her birth date and the aircraft's take-off and landing times. Back in his hotel room, he worked on Glyn's astrological chart and telephoned her the following day with the result:

> No direct danger is visible in your horoscope, but there is a bad atmospheric aspect, a Neptune–Moon square, exact at the time of your arrival. There might be difficulties with the landing, and you could have some awkward moments. I would take the boat, not the plane, if I were you.

The tale runs over the page – almost as much space as de Wohl devoted to his propaganda tour of the United States in 1941 – until he describes meeting Glyn a month or so later. She said she had followed his advice, had cancelled her flight, taking the ferry instead. What had happened, obviously something dramatic. Had the aircraft crashed on landing, passengers and crew burning to death in the flames? Had it plunged into the sea, sinking so rapidly below the waves that all on board had drowned? 'She said with her beautiful smile, "It got into fog, could not land and had to return to London."'[40]

What reviews there were of *The Stars of War and Peace* were uncritical, taking de Wohl at his word and recounting the story of his activities in the role of 'Britain's Seer, the State astrologer', as the London *Evening Standard* described him. 'He had no rivals here, no competitors, His counterparts were in Germany: six were Hitler's astrologers, 30 were Goering's.' Had Prime Minister Churchill been aware of this campaign of 'astrological warfare' the paper's reporter asked. 'I am not at all sure about that,' de Wohl replied. 'I have never enquired.'[41] No reviewer seemed to notice that de Wohl had failed to give an example of how a single one of his readings of Hitler's horoscope had contributed anything to the war effort.

The Stars of War and Peace aside – and seven years after the war it did have the feel of a piece of long-finished business, an antique – de Wohl's attention now was concentrated on books with a religious theme and on his relationship with the Roman Catholic church. Had he become a genuine believer or was this simply a convenient platform from which to operate, another niche? He certainly showed enthusiasm as he moved from one explanation of the meaning of human existence – astrology – to another, Christianity. His old friend Felix Jay was surprised and a little cynical about the shift. He observed that de Wohl was always able to find a material advantage in whatever system of belief he chose to follow. Visiting de Wohl in the early 1950s and anticipating a conversation about their shared interest in astrology, Jay later wrote that something entirely different took place:

> I was submitted to a religious homily, and looking round the room I saw crucifixes and religious prints and other objects. Louis had either been converted to, or had returned to, Roman Catholicism, and his monologues, which in the past has been spiced with the names of the worldly high and mighty, now contained references to bishops, abbots and saints.[42]

Was there any conflict between astrology and a belief in Christianity? De Wohl was still saying in *The Stars of War and Peace* that he saw none, despite the Catechism of the Catholic Church declaring, 'All forms of divination are to be rejected: recourse to Satan or demons … practices falsely supposed to "unveil" the future. Consulting horoscopes, astrology, palm reading …' The implication in the catechism's wording was that these practices were forbidden because they were true and could work, not because they were a sham to fool the gullible. De Wohl saw no problem, no inconsistency. His explanation was satisfyingly Jesuitical. 'Either astrological knowledge is true or it is false. If it is false, into the dustbin with it. But if it true, it cannot have any other source than the source of Truth which *is* God.'[43]

The *Washington Star* reported at the end of 1951 in the course of a review of *The Restless Flame* (based on the life of St Augustine) that de Wohl, while based in London, was spending much of his time in New York and California. He had been in New York for the presentation at the Algonquin Hotel of the Gallery of Living Catholic Authors award for *The Quiet Light*, praised as the most outstanding novel of the year. The flow of religious themed books continued. *The Golden Thread*, the story of St Ignatius of Loyola, the founder of the Jesuits, in 1952 was followed in 1953 by *Set All Afire*, the life of St Francis Xavier. *The Times* was less complimentary than other reviewers, a critic writing that de Wohl had 'presumed beyond his powers' in his presentation of St Ignatius's life in *The Golden Thread*. *The Second Conquest* in 1954 was followed in successive years by *The Spear*, *The Last Crusader* and *St Joan: The Girl Soldier*. On 20 April 1956 de Wohl appeared on a BBC television talk show, poised and self-assured, impressing one reviewer as 'a beaming, affable, learned gentleman of immense girth and immense intellect … a great charmer … a sincere personality, indefatigable logic …'[44]

As in the years before the war, before his interlude with British Intelligence, de Wohl maintained a steady output of books: *The Glorious Folly* (the life of St Paul the Apostle) in 1957, *The Joyful Beggar* (St Francis of Assisi, which was turned into a 20th Century Fox film in 1961) in 1958, *Citadel of God* in 1959. Later would come a biography of a living figure, Pope Pius XII – a man de Wohl had met and who showed he valued the writer's contribution to the faith – and a history of the Roman Catholic church, *Founded on a Rock*. In April 1960 the *San Bernardino Sun* in California used a review of *Citadel of God* to remind readers of de Wohl's former life as an astrologer. 'He was a demon at figuring out the stars. Girls flocked to him to check up on the whens, wheres and hows of their future husbands.' The review went on to de Wohl's wartime mission to New York, providing more detail in one sentence than de Wohl had been allowed to reveal in *The Stars of War and Peace*. Had he fed the reporter the story, craftily leaking in black propaganda style what MI5 had prevented him telling openly?

The British were desperately trying to get the United States into the war on their side. Every possible means of propaganda was being used … De Wohl's job was to persuade American astrologers that for purely astrological reasons the U.S. was destined to enter the war on Britain's side. Well? We did, Didn't we? Even though the stars were rigged.[45]

De Wohl's final novel, *David of Jerusalem*, revealed the imaginative and descriptive powers of even this indefatigable writer were fading. A Catholic reviewer was particularly scathing, saying de Wohl now seemed to be 'merely going through the motions. The clichés of situation, gesture, speech tread heavily upon one another …'[46] The *Illustrated London News* was as dismissive: 'It is not very easy to transport Goliath to a suburb, but unfortunately Mr de Wohl seems to have done just that!'[47] Was the creative energy of five decades exhausted?

6

On a visit to India in the early 1930s, before he left Germany to settle in England, friends – knowing de Wohl's interest in all aspects of Eastern religion and mysticism – had introduced him to a yogi, Dr Sarmananda. De Wohl asked the doctor if he was able to foretell the date on which he would die. Sarmananda reluctantly agreed he could and after a show of concentration, eyes tightly closed, did so. The day he foresaw was 16 February 1964. De Wohl later wrote, 'I thought there was a lot to be said for knowing of one's death in advance, for not being taken by surprise when it came.'[48] He died on 2 June 1961 in Lucerne, Switzerland, two years and eight months in advance of Sarmananda's predicted day. Had he known his death was coming, consulted his own horoscope for the signs? 'Is it possible to predict the day of somebody's death by astrology?' de Wohl had asked Baron Hoogerwoerd thirty years before. 'No. It is only possible to see if there is any likelihood of death before one's natural time – a death by accident, for instance … There is no such thing as certainty in this matter.'[49] He left a widow, Ruth Magdalene, whom he had married in 1953. She died in 1998. What had happened to his first wife Alexandra, Putti, was never explained. There were no children from either marriage.

De Wohl was seen as a significant enough figure to be given an obituary in Britain's newspaper of record, *The Times*, albeit of just three paragraphs. Though it was as a prolific novelist he was best known, his wartime exploits as an astrologer – described as 'the most spectacular aspect of his career' – took up half the space. He 'claimed', the obituary said, to have aided the war effort through astrology:

> De Wohl believed that as Hitler was addicted to astrology it would be of service to this country for a knowledgeable astrologer to work out what advice the German leader was receiving. After he was commissioned in the British Army de Wohl provided this information with certain additional prophecies of his own.[50]

The provincial press outside London, using news agency copy, placed a similar emphasis on the stars in wartime, calling de Wohl 'Britain's official astrologer'. His appointment as an army captain in 1940 made him, these obituaries pointed out, 'the first alien to be given a commission'.[51] So much for the concern of Major Watts of MI5 in 1944 to avoid people having the impression de Wohl had been given the rank of captain 'for his work on Hitler's horoscope'.[52]

Hitler and his horoscope had become embedded in legend over the years, the story that he made no serious military or political move without astrological advice. But as early as 1952 – coincidentally the year de Wohl's *The Stars of War and Peace* was published – Alan Bullock's *Hitler: A Study in Tyranny* argued convincingly that there was no evidence at all that the Führer was influenced in any way by astrology and in fact the opposite was the case, that he had contempt for the very idea.[53] But on the basis of rumour and outright fabrication, de Wohl was able to manoeuvre himself into position for a time as what the popular press would call 'Britain's State Seer'. In *The Stars of War and Peace*, his newspaper articles and his hints to journalists, de Wohl watered a plant that grew into a far more vivid tale than the reality, bizarre though that was in itself.

Had de Wohl fully abandoned astrology when he returned to the Roman Catholic church? Not entirely, but there was an ambivalence in his thinking. He told a British reporter a year or so before his death, 'I still believe cosmic forces can influence people, but I believe forecasting can do more harm than good. I'm glad I helped to stop Hitler but now I realise how very fallible astrology is.'[54] De Wohl had taken a step back from his absolute certainty of two decades before. In 1939 he wrote in a widely syndicated article, 'Today I do not merely believe – today I *know* that there are planetary influences … Was not Caesar killed because he did not listen to astrological advice?'[55]

A fellow astrologer with the experience and detachment to understand de Wohl later wrote: 'What he possessed was a splendid gift of dramatising the drab and simple lives of his clients who appear to have accepted him as a philosopher, saint, prophet and father-confessor, all in one.'[56] The tone suggests this may have been intended as a criticism of their credulity, but it can also be read as a compliment, an explanation of de Wohl's success in persuading British Intelligence to seek the help of an astrologer when the country's survival against Nazi Germany lay in the balance.

HERE IS GOLD! ENOUGH GOLD FOR US ALL!

Louis de Wohl's involvement with Naval and Military Intelligence, the Special Operations Executive and the Political Warfare Executive was a bizarre episode in modern British history. But states resorting to the services of an astrologer during a period of crisis and uncertainty was something that had happened before and would again. The birth of the German Empire in 1871 followed astrological advice on the auspicious time for Prussia to provoke a war of conquest against France. In the twentieth century other states – among them Sri Lanka, Myanmar and Thailand – were formally established on the dates astrologers calculated most favourable. Mossad, the Israeli intelligence agency, engaged astrologers to assess possible threats to national security. The decision to do this followed remarkably accurate horoscope readings of the course of the 1967 Six-Day War, and later the 1973 Yom Kippur War and the 1976 raid to rescue hostages at Entebbe.

Among individual politicians, there were unsubstantiated stories that Winston Churchill was 'sympathetic towards astrology' and that he consulted clairvoyants in the First World War and the years that followed. Indian Prime Minister Indira Gandhi was advised by astrologers, who warned her of imminent assassination by her bodyguard in 1984. President Charles de Gaulle of France was said to have used readings of his and the country's horoscopes as the basis for political evaluations from 1944 until his retirement in 1969. United States Presidents

Theodore Roosevelt, Warren Harding and Ronald Reagan were known followers of astrology. According to Reagan's White House chief of staff in the 1980s, 'virtually every major move and decision' the President made was based on astrological guidance. In 2015 President Mahinda Rajapaksa of Sri Lanka called a snap election on astrological advice, bad advice it transpired as he went on to lose the contest.[1]

De Wohl's proposition to British Intelligence was that Hitler believed in astrology and made no strategic move without seeking advice from his astrologers, Karl-Ernst Krafft foremost among them. But did de Wohl himself believe in the influence of the planets on human behaviour and destiny? Or was he a con man trading opportunistically on the gullibility of others? De Wohl had a habit of leaving what look like hidden clues to his motivations in what he wrote. Perhaps it was unconscious or perhaps it was a sign of an arrogant contempt. In *Secret Service of the Sky*, published in England in 1938, he wrote of his entry into the world of astrology eight years before, his confidence in its value and how he had 'the feeling of a man who discovered a Bonanza of incalculable value and calls to his friends: "Come here! Here is Gold! Gold for us all!"'[2] Was he acknowledging his recognition that astrology would prove a useful source of income? At 25 to 30 guineas a consultation in pre-Second World War London, de Wohl's services certainly did not come cheap. A colleague in the same business and personal friend, Felix Jay, believed de Wohl had a double motive: money and status:

> I came to the conclusion that Louis, after his conversion to astrology, had seen in it quite early certain definite material advantages: in the first place it enlarged the already substantial impression he made upon his prospective rich and titled clientele whose company gave an added prop to his ego, and in the second place he saw endless opportunities for 'selling' expensive horoscopes.[3]

Jay went further, suggesting that de Wohl was not even particularly proficient in the craft, avoiding what were in effect seminars with his peers. 'He appeared to be wary of contact with other professionals and refused to join an intimate discussion group of friends of mine, some professionals and all interested in the predictive disciplines.' It is easy to dismiss this particular line of attack. De Wohl was a regular speaker at the annual convention of British astrologers. He would hardly have been invited if other astrologers did not see him as knowledgeable and adept. A reviewer in the quarterly magazine *Astrology* of de Wohl's *Commonsense Astrology* in June 1940 praised the book, saying it would be 'equally interesting to the experienced student and to the man in the street' and recommended every subscriber bought a copy.[4] This was surely testimonial enough to de Wohl's standing among fellow astrologers.

What about de Wohl the man? A biographer of the French Situationist Guy Debord describes his subject as 'a little mysterious, a little menacing, and a lot impish … allusive and playful, intelligent and full of tricks, at once an outsider and a court jester … using conjuring skills to deceive and to search for lost and new wisdom.'[5] There is a touch of de Wohl's character and methods here. Not that the astrologer was consciously revolutionary, intent on breaking the system, as Debord was, but he toyed with and subverted it. His ambition was to be recognised and accepted, to find what he called in *The Stars of War and Peace* a 'niche'. How desperately he clung to his army rank and uniform symbolised that. But was de Wohl, Debord's near namesake, also playing a game, trying to step into history by manipulating an arcane system of belief, at once occult and material, to his own advantage? Or was he, as MI5's director of counter-espionage said, simply a charlatan and an imposter? And what game had British Intelligence been playing? As the Second World War neared its end, MI5 had good reason to fear the embarrassment de Wohl could cause if he went into print to expose the desperation that had impelled Naval and Military Intelligence to turn for guidance to an astrologer in 1940. It was as if the British Government had decided to put money on the horses to raise funds for the cost of waging war.

According to de Wohl's early autobiography *I Follow My Stars*, after initial resistance it took little to persuade him in 1930 there was 'something' in astrology: an accurate character description of his wife's friend and a forecast that there would be blood was enough. When he cut himself shaving, twice, he was convinced. A decade later he had advanced to the point where he could claim an ability to read Hitler's mind through his horoscope. A successful and prosperous novelist and screenwriter in pre-Nazi Germany, de Wohl would hardly have put himself to the trouble involved in studying astrology if he did not believe it had some validity. When he arrived in London as a refugee in 1935 his ability to construct and interpret horoscopes was a useful source of income and an opening to influential contacts. In that sense Felix Jay was right when he said de Wohl's connection with astrology involved the pursuit of both money and status.

Did de Wohl's sudden return to the Roman Catholic church after the Second World War (and the lucrative writing of saints' lives that followed) signify his abandonment of astrology or was it an admission that he had never really thought the stars played a part in human affairs? The church's teaching was and is that her followers must shun any form of fortune telling and occult prediction, including astrology, which are condemned as a 'recourse to Satan and demons'. De Wohl himself claimed – with what the Church would presumably view as an incredible arrogance – that he saw no real contradiction between these two sets of belief. In 1952, in *The Stars of War and Peace* he asserted that if astrology were true then surely it came from God, who was the source of truth, a cautious play with words.[6] In a *Daily Herald* interview five years earlier he had neatly avoided any suggestion of contradiction by saying he preferred not to talk of his astrological work as the craft had now 'been brought into disrepute in Britain'.[7] This was distancing himself for convenience from what he had believed rather than forsaking it entirely.

Jay, who gives the impression he had made a genuine effort to understand de Wohl's personality and actions, raised the question of ethics in the practice of astrology. He would certainly not have known about de Wohl's pre-1939 work for MI5, how he broke confidence by revealing the identities and advice he was giving clients in whom the Security Service took an interest. It was unlikely de Wohl would have told him, though given his loose tongue, not impossible. Jay's concern was the use his friend made of his skills in the fight against Germany:

Then there is the embarrassing fact of the use of astrology for propaganda purposes during World War II, the exploitation of the bogy of

Hitler's belief in the stars, the creation of the image of the 'evil' Kraft … Whether the prostitution of a science or a belief, the use of phoney predictions, the adulteration of ancient material like Nostradamus' *Centuries* is justifiable in war, is an ethical question which the practitioner must answer for himself. It lastly may depend on whether one believes in astrology or not.[8]

This was, as Jay said, a matter for the individual conscience. But in a desperate struggle in which people were called upon to risk their lives and to kill if the enemy were to be vanquished, the use of any weapon would seem justified. De Wohl – 36 years old when Britain declared war on Germany in September 1939 – had been rebuffed in his efforts to join the armed forces. What alternative did he have to play his part in the war than to offer his skills as an astrologer and – in part because of his background as an imaginative writer of a certain type – a propagandist to fight the regime he hated? If exploiting faith was questionable, the Political Warfare Executive, the organisation de Wohl was attached to in 1942–43, went as far as recruiting an Austrian Roman Catholic priest, Father Elmar Eisenberger, to broadcast black propaganda on the religious radio station 'Christ the King', castigating the Nazi state as anti-Christian and morally corrupt.[9] All was fair in the struggle.

De Wohl's connection with British Intelligence was based on the belief that Hitler depended on astrologers for advice. By consulting the German leader's horoscope, the claim went, it was possible to determine his moves by replicating what these astrologers were telling him. Without this, de Wohl would have simply been an MI5 informant reporting on his high-grade astrological clients. It was generally thought Hitler was guided by his horoscope. The respected American academic Nicholas Murray Butler returned from Germany in 1939 to report that Hitler had not one astrologer but a team. This was widely publicised in Britain and the United States. The Romanian ambassador in London, Viorel Tilea, had no doubt Karl-Ernst Krafft was the Führer's personal astrologer and told not only de Wohl of his certainty but also a senior Foreign Office civil servant, Sir Orme Sergeant, who most likely discussed this with the Foreign Secretary Lord Halifax. Halifax himself was impressed by de Wohl's hour-long interpretation of Hitler's horoscope at dinner in the Spanish Embassy in August 1940. British astrologers were also sure, flattered even, of the interest Hitler was thought to take, a leading figure writing in 1939, 'We have long known he made use of our art.'[10] In 1940 de Wohl had persuaded the Director of Naval Intelligence, Rear Admiral Godfrey, to such an extent that he wrote in a memorandum to his fellow senior officers that it was common knowledge Hitler 'attaches importance to advice tendered to him by astrologers …'[11]

Despite widespread belief otherwise, the fact was that Hitler had made it plain both privately and publicly that he not only rejected but went further and despised astrology. This was the void at the centre of the relationship between de Wohl and British Intelligence. In 1943 a report compiled by the academic psychoanalyst Walter C. Langer for the Office of Strategic Services, forerunner in the United States of the Central Intelligence Agency, strenuously doubted that Hitler was a follower of astrology: 'This is almost certainly untrue. All our informants who have known Hitler rather intimately discard the idea as absurd.'[12] Lunching with cronies in July 1942, Hitler denounced astrology as a 'swindle', dismissing the horoscope as something in which Anglo-Saxons had 'great faith', but not himself.[13] Twenty years previously, told about a female astrologer's warning against his coup attempt in Munich, he laughed and asked, 'What on earth have women and the stars to do with me?'[14]

Publicly, in speeches at the party's Nuremburg rallies in 1936 and again in 1939, Hitler condemned the very idea that there could be a link between Nazi ideology and the occult. In 1941, after the flight of Hitler's deputy Rudolf Hess to Britain, the Gestapo rounded up astrologers known to be active in Germany, confining many in concentration camps. And if, as both de Wohl and Tilea insisted, Karl-Ernst Krafft was Hitler's personal astrologer, this was remarkable as – despite Krafft's accurate prediction of the attempt on the Führer's life in Munich in 1939 – the two had never met and never would.

Did de Wohl himself genuinely believe the stories about Hitler's reliance on astrology or were they simply something he found useful? This is, of course, impossible to tell for certain, but de Wohl occasionally leaves clues. Why did he make no reference at all to Hitler and

astrology in his autobiography *I Follow My Stars*, written in his early
thirties and published in Britain in 1937? As the book dealt with astrology and ended with de Wohl's decision to flee Hitler's Germany, surely
the Führer's interest in the planets – if it existed – would have been
worth mentioning. He first raised the subject in *Secret Service of the Sky*,
which appeared the following year. De Wohl went into greater detail
in *The Stars of War and Peace*, published after the war in 1952, when not
only did he claim Hitler's dependence on astrological advice had been
an established fact but – even more interesting – he says he felt com-
pelled to leave Germany when he was asked to become the Nazi leader's
astrologer. De Wohl claimed he 'answered evasively' because he did not
'care particularly to become the astrologer of a tyrant ...'[15] Why had he
chosen not to reveal this dramatic event in his life in 1937 or 1938? Was
he afraid the disclosure might suggest he was closer to the Nazis than he
claimed? Such a familiarity with party leaders was surely unlikely given
his Jewish heritage. Was de Wohl the opportunist simply making use of
a widely believed rumour to secure a wartime job for himself, what he
called his niche, in 1940?

De Wohl's contribution to the activities of British Intelligence altered
in the course of the war, though his claim to be making use of what
the stars were saying remained constant. Interestingly, it was the head
of MI14, the German section of Military Intelligence, Lieutenant
Colonel Kenneth Strong, who recognised as early as September 1940
that de Wohl's ability as a writer of fiction together with his knowledge
of German life pointed in the direction of involvement in propaganda
work. 'Strong thinks that if ever a proper propaganda section is founded
... a man with Louis' knowledge and experience would be extremely
useful.'[16] But for the first year or so of his wartime activity, de Wohl was
determined to push his predictive skills as an astrologer. The Director of
Naval Intelligence, Rear Admiral John Godfrey, was enthralled by the
prospect of de Wohl's interpretation of Hitler's horoscope as a source of
information on enemy strategy, embarrassingly so as far as other senior
naval officers were concerned.

Military Intelligence, grossly under-resourced in the early period
of the war, at one point looked to de Wohl to supplement the meagre

information available on German army commanders with his astrology-based pen portraits. The War Cabinet Chiefs of Staff – the heads of the army, navy and air force – even cited de Wohl in October 1940 when they were desperately trying to determine when the Nazis would mount what appeared the inevitable invasion of Britain. Dick White of MI5 complained in 1942 that there had been a time when de Wohl 'exercised some influence upon highly placed British Intelligence officers through his star gazing profession'.[17]

But how extensive had the astrologer's influence been? What did de Wohl actually provide British Intelligence through his one-man Mayfair-based Psychological Research Bureau? What had he promised? That he could reveal the advice Hitler was given about his periods of good luck, the periods the German leader could be expected to act, and the phases of bad luck when he was at his most vulnerable. Did he genuinely believe this or was he trusting to his own luck? De Wohl was a complex man: talented, colourful, sensitive, intelligent, as most who came into contact with him soon acknowledged. But he was also intensely self-interested and – as an outsider, a foreigner – at some levels unknowable, leading to a feeling of mistrust among some MI5 officers. A genuine contempt for the Nazis – and probably a fear because of his Jewish background – combined in 1940 with his need for money, security, recognition. Turned down for service by each of the armed forces in 1939, astrology and his fluency with the pen was really all de Wohl could offer.

The turmoil and uncertainty of war proved a bonanza for chancers of all kinds, with intelligence work a particularly comfortable haven. The headquarters of British Security Co-ordination in New York was perhaps far from untypical. Here an official visitor from Britain insisted angrily he had found 'a large number of people drawing $800 a month for doing absolutely nothing'.[18] Reading between the lines of de Wohl's MI5 personal file there are hints of – despite the organisation's many worthy and valuable deeds – a Security Service culture of make-work, officers filling time and collecting pay for rumour-mongering and collating irrelevant information on inoffensive individuals – including de Wohl's accountant and bank manager – whose letters to the astrologer had been intercepted by Home Office Warrant.

There was also an even more widespread culture of careerism and jockeying for position, with rivalries between and within the various elements of British Intelligence revealed in the wartime memoirs and diaries of, for example, Robert Bruce Lockhart, Hugh Dalton, Sefton Delmer and Guy Liddell. Running through these is a long thread of personal ambition, petty office intrigue and empire building. Lockhart, director general of the Political Warfare Executive – an organisation for which do Wohl at one point worked – acknowledged this to Foreign Secretary Anthony Eden in September 1941. On taking up his role with PWE, Lockhart told Eden (who was on the PWE executive committee) he was determined that 'from now on strife must cease and that the first case of intrigue and self-seeking will be dealt with relentlessly'.[19] PWE were not alone and this was the atmosphere in which de Wohl had worked to place himself, one he may have found to his liking.

One writer suggests de Wohl's astrology may actually have served as 'a smokescreen' intended to mislead Nazi Germany about the real source of intelligence on enemy strategy and tactics: Ultra, the breaking of enemy encrypted military radio communications by the Government Code and Cypher School at Bletchley Park. This involved, he wrote, keeping the secret not just from the enemy, but also British army commanders:

> The truth is that his so-called Psychological Research Bureau … played a crucial part in keeping the greatest secret of the war – the reading of enemy radio traffic by the codebreakers of the government's secret intelligence gathering operation at Bletchley Park … When field commanders were given secret material divulged by Enigma, they might well ask where it came from. From de Wohl's Psychological Research Bureau was the bogus answer – astrological predictions were the perfect cover.[20]

This is an interesting idea, one that could easily have emerged from de Wohl's own fertile imagination. There is perhaps a small element of truth to it: the phoney astrology magazine *Der Zenit* produced by de Wohl and Delmer at the Political Warfare Executive in 1942–43 did indeed claim to 'predict' U-boat losses in the North Atlantic, giving them an astrological explanation. The more gullible among what must have been a tiny readership may have believed this, so masking one of the actual reasons for success, the Ultra project. But it went no wider than this brief episode.

No historian writing on Bletchley Park, Enigma and Ultra has suggested British Intelligence cunningly kept the venture a secret by pretending an astrologer was the source of crucial information. First, to put German leaders off the scent would have involved ensuring the enemy knew British Intelligence were making use of astrology from the earliest days of the Second World War. It was true de Wohl was a blabbermouth and was reported to be boasting to cronies about his involvement with British Intelligence. But when Hitler said in 1942 horoscopes were something 'in which the Anglo-Saxons in particular have great faith', it is unlikely he was thinking of de Wohl himself.[21] Secondly, British commanders in the field would also have to have been told of de Wohl's existence if they were to believe astrology was providing intelligence to preserve Bletchley Park's secrecy. If deception was the plan, why go to the trouble and expense of engaging an astrologer at all? Why not simply claim British Intelligence were being guided by the stars and leave it at that?

In reality, the employment of an astrologer was something those who knew – to go by MI5's panic when de Wohl presented the draft manuscript of his memoirs – were anxious later to hide, not so much for security reasons (Ultra had done its job) but out of embarrassment. If de Wohl's role was to act as a permanent smokescreen, why did the Special Operations Executive ship their 'tame astrologer' to the United States in May 1941, leaving him stationed there until early 1942? When he returned to London, at the point Bletchley Park was beginning to prove its worth to the Allied war effort, de Wohl's Psychological Research Bureau had been wound up and he was put to work using his astrological skills on black propaganda with the Political Warfare Executive, not 'prediction'.

The fact was, British Intelligence did employ de Wohl as a practising astrologer, paid him and made use of his abilities in various ways between 1940 and 1943. He was successively engaged in trying to read Hitler's mind by interpreting the Führer's horoscope, then attempting to break that same mind with the Special Operations Executive through the 'Orchestra of Hitler's death'. Finally he worked with the Political Warfare Executive to undermine German military and civilian morale through astrology-based black propaganda. His memoir *The Stars of War and Peace* told not even half the story, exaggerating some aspects, playing down or disregarding even more. It took the poet Louis MacNeice to put his finger on the farcical absurdity of much of what was going on. 'When we now read de Wohl's rather pompous accounts of his own astrological war (the gallant captain with a bandolier full of horoscopes), or think of the ups and downs of the German astrologers', MacNeice wrote two decades after the event, 'the Second World War starts to resemble one of those galleries of distorting mirrors in a funfair.'[22]

What did officers in British Intelligence think they were playing at? Initially in 1940 they listened to de Wohl out of desperation – German invasion appeared inevitable and the question was where and when. Intelligence was in a dire state and any source of information, even the stars, was better than none. But the fact that de Wohl had failed – along with most other professional astrologers – to predict the outbreak of war in 1939 went apparently unnoticed. He did not foresee the German sweep through Western Europe in 1940 (though he tried to claim otherwise later), or the Nazi onslaught on the Soviet Union in 1941. Much of what he wrote in his reports to MI14, the German section of Military Intelligence, could have been picked up for a few pence in astrology magazines or the Sunday newspapers. When it became clear that what de Wohl had to reveal about the workings of Hitler's mind and his 'luck' was disappointingly limited, he was kept on but shunted into propaganda, deploying his astrological knowledge and literary skills to concoct what were basically lies, fantasies at best – the 'Orchestra of Hitler's death', the phoney *Der Zenit* and the false 'prophecies' of Nostradamus.

The Allied victory over Germany in 1945 did not come through foreknowledge of Hitler's actions by means of astrology but from an overwhelming superiority in materiel and force on land, sea and in the air. To these was added access to genuine rather than occult intelligence through, among other sources, Bletchley Park. Hitler himself committed a series of strategic errors and tactical mistakes that made German defeat virtually inevitable. This began with allowing substantial numbers of British and French troops to escape from Dunkirk in 1940, in taking on Russia in June 1941 and declaring war on the United States in December, making eventual war on two fronts in Europe inescapable. The irony is that if astrology had any validity at all and Hitler had been following his stars, he would have been forewarned that bad luck hovered on the horizon and avoided the blunders that dragged Germany down in flames and him to ignominious suicide in Berlin. The truth was that the Führer's diplomatic triumphs of the 1930s, as with his disastrous miscalculations of the '40s, were not written in his horoscope but were his own doing.

What did de Wohl as an individual achieve through his work for British Intelligence? He did not have what is classically known as a 'good war', but he had a comfortable and entertaining one. There was the sense that he was contributing in his own way to the defeat of Nazism, an objective he had reason to take seriously. He achieved a portion of the status and recognition he always craved: an army officer's commission (however dubious the legitimacy was), with the accompanying pay, allowances and uniform; far more luxurious wartime accommodation in Mayfair than the Maida Vale hotel room that had been home since his arrival in London in 1935; an expenses paid nine-month jaunt around the United States, cosseted and flattered as the 'modern Nostradamus' from New York to Los Angeles. He succeeded in building a wartime career on the paper-thin basis of Hitler's horoscope. Perhaps the 'tame astrologer' was the 'charlatan and imposter' Dick White of MI5 dismissed him as, the 'complete scoundrel' Colonel Chambers called him, even composer Eric Maschwitz's 'right swindler', but what fascinating company Louis de Wohl must have been.

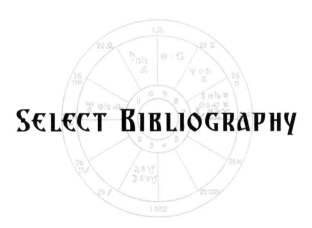

Select Bibliography

This bibliography is confined to material I found of particular help or interest. Other sources used are cited in endnotes.

The National Archives of the United Kingdom:
 ADM 223/84, References cited in History of Intelligence 1937–1945.
 CAB 79/7/28(2), C.O.S.(40) 352, Minutes of the War Cabinet.
 CO 875/9/10, Propaganda: Use of Astrology.
 HS9/73/9, Alice June Bainbridge.
 KV 2/2821(1), (2), (3), PF49321, Louis de Wohl.
 WO 208/4475, MI14 Astrologer & Hitler's Health.

Andrew, C., *The Defence of the Realm: The Authorized History of MI5* (Allen Lane, 2009).
Andrew, C., *Secret Service: The Making of the British Intelligence Community* (Sceptre, 1987).
Bobrick, B., *The Fated Sky: Astrology in History* (Simon & Schuster, 2006).
Bullock, A., *Hitler: A Study in Tyranny* (Penguin, 1980).
Booth, N., *Lucifer Rising: British Intelligence and the Occult in the Second World War* (The History Press, 2016).
Cruickshank, C., *The Fourth Arm: Psychological Warfare 1938–1945* (Oxford University Press, 1981).
Cull, N.J., *Selling War The British Propaganda Campaign Against American 'Neutrality' in World War II* (Oxford University Press, 1995).
Davies, O., *A Supernatural War: Magic, Divination, and Faith during the First World War* (Oxford University Press, 2018).
Deacon, R., *A History of British Secret Service* (Panther, 1984).
Delmer, S., *Black Boomerang: An Autobiography, Volume 2* (Secker and Warburg, 1962).

Erskine, R. & Smith, M. (eds), *The Bletchley Park Code-Breakers* (Biteback Publishing, 2011).

Evans, Richard J., *The Third Reich in Power 1933–1939* (Penguin Books, 2006).

Foot, M.R.D., *SOE: An Outline History of the Special Operations Executive 1940–1946* (Pimlico, 1999).

Garnett, D., *The Secret History of PWE: The Political Warfare Executive, 1939–1945* (St Ermin's Press, 2002).

Hemming, H., *Our Man in New York: The British Plot to Bring America into the Second World War* (Quercus, 2019).

Howard, M., *British Intelligence in the Second World War, Volume Five, Strategic Deception* (HMSO, 1990).

Howe, E., *Astrology and Psychological Warfare During World War II* (Rider & Company, 1972).

Howe, E., *The Black Game: British Subversive Operations against the Germans during the Second World War* (Queen Anne Press/Futura, 1988).

Jay, F., 'The Louis de Wohl I knew', *Traditional Astrologer Magazine*, Issue 16, 1998.

Jensen, M., *Everybody's Astrology* (Log Cabin, 1922).

Kershaw, I., *Hitler 1889–1936: Hubris* (Penguin, 2001).

Kershaw, I., *Hitler 1936–1945: Nemesis* (Penguin, 2001).

Kurlander, E., *Hitler's Monsters: A Supernatural History of the Third Reich* (Yale University Press, 2018).

Lewi, G., *Astrology for the Millions*, Doubleday (Doran & Co., 1940).

Longerich, P., *Goebbels: A Biography* (Vintage, 2016).

Stafford, D., *Britain and European Resistance 1940–1945: A Survey of the Special Operations Executive, with Documents* (David Stafford, 2013).

Tester, J., *A History of Western Astrology* (The Boydell Press, 1990).

Tilea, V.V., *Envoy Extraordinary: Memoirs of a Romanian Diplomat* (Haggerston Press, 1998).

Twigge, S. et al., *British Intelligence: Secrets, Spies and Sources* (The National Archives, 2008).

West, N., *MI5: British Security Operations 1909–1945* (Stein and Day, 1982).

West, N. (ed), *The Guy Liddell Diaries Volume I: 1939–1942, MI5's Director of Counter-Espionage in World War II* (Routledge, 2016).

Winter, P.R.J., 'Libra Rising: Hitler, astrology and British intelligence, 1940–43', *Intelligence and National Security*, 21:3, 2006.

Wohl, L. de, *I Follow My Stars An Autobiography* (George G. Harrap & Co., 1937).

Wohl, L. de, *Secret Service of the Sky* (The Cresset Press, 1938).

Wohl, L. de, *The Stars of War and Peace* (Rider & Company, 1952).

Wulff, W., *Zodiac & Swastika: Astrologer to Himmler's Court* (Arthur Barker Ltd, 1973).

NOTES

PROLOGUE

1 William Shakespeare, *The Winter's Tale*, Act II, Scene 1.
2 Louis de Wohl, *I Follow My Stars An Autobiography*, George G. Harrap & Co., London, 1937, p. 132.
3 Louis de Wohl, *Secret Service of the Sky*, The Cresset Press, London, 1938, p. 10.
4 The National Archives of the United Kingdom (hereafter TNA): ADM 223/84, References cited in History of Intelligence 1937–1945, Rear Admiral John Godfrey, Director of Naval Intelligence, 30 September 1940, 'Advice tendered to Herr Hitler'.
5 TNA: WO 208/4475, MI14 Astrologer & Hitler's Health, 'The Orchestra of Hitler's Death', p. 1.
6 TNA: KV 2/2821(1), PF49321, Note 128, Dick White to Oswald 'Jasper' Harker, 19 February 1942.
7 TNA: KV 2/2821(3), PF49321, Item 155a, W.T. (Toby) Caulfield draft submission for a Home Office Warrant to intercept de Wohl's mail and telephone calls, 24 September 1942.
8 TNA: KV 2/2821(2), PF49321, Item 201b, G. Lennox to Mr Caulfield, 14 January 1943.
9 Ellic Howe, *Astrology and Psychological Warfare During World War II*, Rider and Company, London, 1972, p. 11.

I AN AQUARIUS BORN

1 De Wohl, *Secret Service of the Sky*, p. 64.
2 The first volume of de Wohl's MI5 personal file would presumably have disclosed his early contacts, but it was among the many papers destroyed by

fire through German bombing in 1940 of Wormwood Scrubs Prison, MI5's
headquarters at the time.

3   Felix Jay, 'The Louis de Wohl I knew', *Traditional Astrologer Magazine*, Issue 16,
     March 1998, p. 14.

4   *New York Sunday News*, 21 July 1941.

5   Sydney *Daily Telegraph*, 27 November 1937.

6   Magnus Jensen, *Everybody's Astrology*, Log Cabin, Camino CA., 1922, p. 5.

7   De Wohl, *I Follow My Stars*, p. 124.

8   De Wohl, *I Follow My Stars*, p. 125.

9   De Wohl, *I Follow My Stars*, p. 126.

10   De Wohl, *I Follow My Stars*, pp. 130–1.

11   De Wohl, *I Follow My Stars*, p. 132.

12   De Wohl, *I Follow My* Stars, p. 138.

13   Louis de Wohl, *Secret Service of the Sky*, The Cresset Press, London, 1938,
     pp. 10–11.

14   Jay, 'The Louis de Wohl I Knew', *Traditional Astrologer Magazine*, p. 10.

15   TNA: KV 2/2821(1), PF49321, Item 295a, Lt-Colonel G. Lennox minute,
     'Louis de Wohl', 10 July 1945.

16   Sefton Delmer, *Black Boomerang: An Autobiography, Volume 2*, Secker and Warburg,
     London, 1962, p. 131; Howe, *Astrology and Psychological Warfare*, p. 11.

17   De Wohl, *I Follow My Stars*, p. 16.

18   De Wohl, *I Follow My Stars*, p. 17.

19   Ian Kershaw, *Hitler 1889–1936: Hubris*, Penguin, London, pp. 15, 17, 387.

20   Short autobiography at www.catholicauthors.com/de wohl.html

21   De Wohl, *I Follow My Stars*, p. 21. As a man he would occasionally and enthusi-
     astically wear women's clothes. As an astrologer, he described the male born
     under Aquarius, his sign: 'He generally has something of the feminine within
     him which shows itself in every possible way …' De Wohl, *Secret Service of the
     Sky*, p. 65.

22   The bank became insolvent in the wake of the 1929 Wall Street crash.
     Gutmann, driven from business under Nazi pressure because of his Jewish
     origins, lived in exile in England from 1936 until his death in poverty in 1942.

23   De Wohl, *I Follow My Stars*, p. 70.

24   TNA: KV 2/2821(1), PF49321, Item 295a, Lt-Colonel G. Lennox minute,
     'Louis de Wohl', 10 July 1945.

25   De Wohl, *I Follow My Stars*, p. 105.

26   De Wohl, *I Follow My Stars*, pp. 11–12. Dr Sarmananda turned out to be
     mistaken: de Wohl died on 2 June 1961.

27   De Wohl, *I Follow My Stars*, pp. 139, 141.

28   De Wohl, *Secret Service of the Sky*, pp. 205–6. 'Helping the police' appears to be
     a regular claim made by occultists of various kinds. Among many others, the
     mid-twentieth-century English medium Doris Stokes claimed to have assisted
     with murder enquiries, though she presented no evidence. *The Guardian*,
     1 September 2015.

29   De Wohl, *Secret Service of the Sky*, p. 31.

30   De Wohl, *Secret Service of the Sky*, p. 140.

31   Michael Bloch, *Closet Queens: Some 20th Century British Politicians*, Little, Brown, London, 2015, p. 189.

32   Theodore Zeldin, *An Intimate History of Humanity*, Vintage, London, 1998, p. 339.

33   Eric Kurlander, *Hitler's Monsters A Supernatural History of the Third Reich*, Yale University Press, New Haven and London, 2018, pp. 85–6. Strauss and his wife Sigrid Strauss-Kloebe also worked as Jungian psychotherapists.

34   De Wohl, *I Follow My Stars*, p. 135.

35   Quoted in Michael R. Meyer, *A Handbook for the Humanistic Astrologer*, Anchor Books, 1974, Garden City, p. 21.

36   De Wohl, *The Stars of War and Peace*, Rider and Company, London, 1952, p. 15.

37   Keith Thomas, *Religion and the Decline of Magic – Studies in Popular Beliefs in Sixteenth- and Seventeenth-Century England*, Penguin Books, London, 1991 ed., p. 340.

38   Quoted in Benson Bobrick, *The Fated Sky: Astrology in History*, Simon & Schuster, New York, 2006, p. 215. Lilly was summoned before a House of Commons committee investigating the 1666 fire, suspected of responsibility for the blaze. He produced astrological evidence that persuaded his interrogators the fire had not been caused deliberately by human hand but was brought about 'by the finger of God.'

39   J. Bryan III & Charles J.V. Murphy, *The Windsor Story*, William Morrow & Company, New York, 1979, p. 8.

40   De Wohl, *Stars of War and Peace*, p. 90.

41   De Wohl, *I Follow My Stars*, p. 175.

42   De Wohl maintained his interest in transvestism, a friend recalled. 'I remember that sometime in 1939 or 1940 he asked me to take part in a charity concert to be given at his hotel. I was to play the accordion. Louis indulged in one of his favourite pleasures, that of dressing up as a woman. And indeed, he looked the part, that is if you like Peter Paul Rubens' corpulent ladies.' Jay, 'The Louis de Wohl I Knew', *Traditional Astrologer Magazine*, p. 11.

43   *New York Times*, 22 October 1934.

44   Richard J. Evans, *The Third Reich in Power*, Penguin Books, London, 2006, p. 129.

45   De Wohl, *I Follow My Stars*, pp. 198, 201.

46   De Wohl, *I Follow My Stars*, p. 198. It may also have been that as a Hungarian citizen de Wohl had required a permit to work in Germany. It would have been a simple matter for the new regime simply to deny him this.

47   *New York Sunday News*, 21 July 1941.

48   De Wohl, *I Follow My Stars*, p. 275.

49   De Wohl, *The Stars of War and Peace*, pp. 17–18.

50   Howe, *Astrology and Psychological Warfare*, p. 162. De Wohl did mention the attempted recruitment briefly in a newspaper interview in 1941 but went into no detail – TNA: KV 2/2821(1), PF49321, Item 291a, Transcript of report in *New York Sunday News*, 27 July 1941. There is also an interesting but absurd

tale that de Wohl was indeed Hitler's personal astrologer but was 'lured away' from Germany by British Intelligence. See William Stevenson, *The Bormann Brotherhood*, Skyhorse Publishing, New York, 2019.

2 An Air of Baroque Opulence

1   He also never explained what became of Putti. He married again, Ruth Magdalene, widow of Walter Fleischer, in 1953. She outlived him by over thirty years, dying in 1998. As Roman Catholics, divorce would have been out of the question for Louis and Putti, so presumably she died in Chile.
2   TNA: KV 2/2821(1), PF49321, Item 295a, Lt-Colonel G. Lennox minute 'Louis de Wohl', 10 July 1945.
3   De Wohl, *I Follow My Stars*, p. 275.
4   TNA: KV 2/2821(3), PF49321, Item 109b, Lt-Colonel G. Lennox minute, 21 January 1941.
5   *Variety*, 6 November 1935.
6   The building was once a maternity home, the birthplace in 1912 of the Bletchley Park cryptanalyst Alan Turing, decipherer of the German Enigma machine.
7   Jay, 'The Louis de Wohl I Knew', *Traditional Astrologer Magazine*, p. 10.
8   *The Era*, 26 February 1936.
9   Sydney *World's News*, 29 July 1936.
10 *Birmingham Gazette*, 10 June 1936.
11 Jay, 'The Louis de Wohl I Knew', *Traditional Astrologer Magazine*, p. 10.
12 *Yorkshire Post*, 2 June 1937.
13 *Aberdeen Press and Journal*, 29 December 1937; *Berks and Oxon Advertiser*, 17 December 1937.
14 De Wohl, *Secret Service of the Sky*, pp. 14–15.
15 De Wohl, *Secret Service of the Sky*, p. 10.
16 For the detailed astrological analysis see de Wohl, *Secret Service of the Sky*, pp. 122–5.
17 *Nottingham Journal*, 11 October 1938.
18 Ronald Blythe, *The Age of Illusion: England in the Twenties and Thirties 1919–40*, Penguin, Harmondsworth, 1964, pp. 261–2.
19 Jeremy McCarter (ed), *Henry Fairlie, Bite the Hand That Feeds You, Essays and Provocations*, Yale University Press, Newhaven & London, 2009, pp. 152–3.
20 Speeches 14 March 1936, 6 June 1937, quoted in Brigitte Hamann, *Hitler's Vienna: A Portrait of the Tyrant as a Young Man*, I.B. Tauris, London, 2010, p. 215.
21 De Wohl, *The Stars of War and Peace*, p. 18.
22 *Astrology The Astrologers' Quarterly*, Vol. 13, No. 3, September 1939, p. 1. Carter was one of the leading British astrologers, co-founder and principal of the Faculty of Astrological Studies. In 1955 Carter accurately predicted his own death would take place in 1968.
23 De Wohl, *Secret Service of the Sky*, pp. 234–5.
24 *Astrology The Astrologers' Quarterly*, Vol. 13, No. 3, September 1939.

25   *Daily Mirror*, 23 February 1939.

26   De Wohl, *Secret Service of the Sky*, p. 10.

27   One book claims that 'senior members of the intelligence services' were among his 'grateful and indulgent' pre-war clients, though no evidence is provided and it does seem unlikely. Stephen Twigge et al, *British Intelligence: Secrets, Spies and Sources*, The National Archives, Kew, 2008, p. 194.

28   Bobrick, *The Fated Sky*, p. 283.

29   Hitler's speech at the party rally, 14 September 1936, quoted in Kenneth Hite, *The Nazi Occult*, Osprey Publishing, Oxford, 2013, p. 29.

30   6 September 1938 speech quoted in Richard J. Evans, *The Third Reich in Power*, Penguin, London, 2006, p. 257.

31   Quoted in Kurlander, *Hitler's Monsters*, p. 99.

32   See George L. Mosse, *The Crisis of German Ideology: Intellectual Origins of the Third Reich*, Schocken Books, New York, 1981; Nicholas Goodrick-Clarke, *The Occult Roots of Nazism: Secret Aryan Cults and their Influence on Nazi Ideology*, I.B. Tauris, London, 2005; Peter Staudenmaier, *Between Occultism and Nazism: Anthroposophy and the Politics of Race in the Fascist Era*, Brill, Leiden and Boston, 2014.

33   See David Luhrssen, *Hammer of the Gods: The Thule Society and the Birth of Nazism*, Potomac Books, Washington DC, 2012. Sebottendorff declared in his 1933 memoir *Before Hitler Came* that the Thule Society had actually created National Socialism, for which heresy the party – which he had only recently joined – expelled him.

34   Ian Kershaw, *Hitler 1889–1936: Hubris*, Penguin Books, London, 2001, pp. 138–9.

35   Quoted in Kershaw, *Hitler 1889–1936: Hubris*, p. 107.

36   Ebertin quoted in Howe, *Astrology and Psychological Warfare*, pp. 27–8.

37   Howe, *Astrology and Psychological Warfare*, p. 30.

38   De Wohl, *Secret Service of the Sky*, p. 118.

39   De Wohl, *The Stars of War and Peace*, p. 17.

40   Norman Cameron & R. H. Stevens (trans.), *Hitler's Table Talk 1941–1944 His Private Conversations*, Enigma Books, New York, 2000, p. 287.

41   Himmler to Heydrich, 10 January 1939, quoted in Kurlander, *Hitler's Monsters*, p. 111.

42   Charles Wighton, *Heydrich: Hitler's Most Evil Henchman*, Corgi, London, 1963, p. 226.

43   Wilhelm Wulff, *Zodiac & Swastika*, Arthur Barker Ltd., London, 1973, pp. 110–1.

44   Wulff, *Zodiac & Swastika*, p. 15.

45   *Astrology The Astrologers' Quarterly*, Vol. 13, No. 3, September 1939.

46   Grant Lewi, *Astrology for the Millions*, Doubleday, Doran & Company, New York, 1940, p. 34. Lewi's book included a section on 'Strong Men of Destiny', with astrological portrayals of Hitler, Mussolini, Stalin and Roosevelt. In 1950 de Wohl raised the stakes by saying the number of astrologers who had been working for Hitler at the time was six.

47   *The Times*, 14 May 1941.

48 *Yorkshire Post*, 25 March 1940.

49 De Wohl, *Secret Service of the Sky*, p. 18.

50 Short autobiography at www.catholicauthors.com/de wohl.html

51 TNA: KV 2/2821(3), PF49321, Item 117a, minute from B24 to B3, 8 April 1941.

52 Nigel West (ed) *The Guy Liddell Diaries, Volume 1: 1939–1942 MI5's Director of Counter-Espionage in World War Two*, Routledge, London, 2005, p. 56.

53 TNA: KV 2/2821(1), PF49321, Item 289a, Lieutenant Colonel Gilbert Lennox to Major Stephen Alley MI5, 26 April 1945.

54 TNA: KV 2/2821(3), PF49321, Item 101a, Electra House request for information, 31 August 1940, and MI5 response.

55 Ellic Howe, *The Black Game: British Subversive Operations against the Germans during the Second World War*, Queen Anne Press, London, 1982, p. 47.

56 Committee minutes quoted in Howe, *The Black* Game, p. 47.

57 Quoted in a review in *Liverpool Daily Post*, 23 April 1940.

58 *Astrology The Astrologers' Quarterly*, Vol. 14, No. 2, June 1940, p. 73.

59 *Aberdeen Press & Journal*, 11 June 1940.

60 *Yorkshire Post*, 25 March 1940.

61 *Yorkshire Evening Post*, 18 March 1940.

62 De Wohl, *The Stars of War and Peace*, p. 20.

63 Jay, 'The Louis de Wohl I Knew', *Traditional Astrologer Magazine,* p. 11.

64 De Wohl, *The Stars of War and Peace*, p. 21.

65 Howe, *Astrology and Psychological Warfare*, p. 162.

66 Krafft later boasted that his telegram had 'exploded like a second bomb in Berlin.' Howe, *Astrology and Psychological Warfare*, p. 118.

67 Nostradamus was the Latinised version of Michel de Notredame, 1503–56, a French astrologer and physician. His book of prophecies, set out in 942 cryptic quatrains was first published in 1555 and has rarely been out of print since, often badly translated.

68 Diary entry 24 November 1939, quoted Kurlander, *Hitler's Monsters*, p. 216.

69 Howe, *Astrology and Psychological Warfare*, p. 124.

70 Krafft was detained in June 1941 in a mass arrest of occultists and clairvoyants following Hess's flight to England in May, which was ascribed to astrological advice. He was employed in custody on interpreting the horoscopes of Allied politicians and generals for Goebbels' Propaganda Ministry. He died in January 1945 on his way to confinement in Buchenwald concentration camp.

71 Viorel Virgil Tilea, *Envoy extraordinary: memoirs of a Romanian diplomat*, Haggerston Press, London, 1998, p. 271.

72 TNA: WO 208/4475, MI14 Astrologer & Hitler's Health, 'The Orchestra of Hitler's Death,' pp. 5–6. Howe believed de Wohl was lying about this reference and that Krafft had said no such thing. Howe, *Astrological and Psychological Warfare*, p. 171.

73 Howe, *Astrology and Psychological Warfare*, p. 132.

74 De Wohl, *The Stars of War and Peace*, p. 21.

75 Wulff, *Zodiac & Swastika*, p. 16.

76 Howe, *Astrology and Psychological Warfare*, p. 193.
77 Richard Deacon, *A History of British Secret Service*, Panther, London, 1984, p. 365.
78 Howe, *Astrology and Psychological Warfare*, pp. 163–4.
79 Tilea, *Envoy Extraordinary*, p. 278.
80 MI5 officer Jane Archer, quoted in Christopher Andrew, *The Defence of the Realm: The Authorized History of MI5*, Allen Lane, London, 2009, p. 235. It was Lennox who in 1944 recruited Clifton James, the actor then serving as a Royal Army Pay Corps lieutenant. James masqueraded as Montgomery in the run-up to D-Day – Operation Copperhead – to mislead the enemy about where on the European mainland the Allied invasion would take place.
81 TNA: KV 2/2821(3), PF49321, Item 102a, Major Gilbert Lennox to Dick White, MI5 B Division, 17 September 1940. The Swiss-German astrologer Krafft, whom Tilea and de Wohl said they believed to be Hitler's astrologer, had advised Tilea on the basis of his horoscope to resign as ambassador to London in his February 1940 letter, though for different reasons. Tilea, *Envoy extraordinary*, p. 271.
82 Halifax had pressed in May 1940 for Britain to open peace talks with Nazi Germany, opposed by Churchill and Labour and Liberal members of the War Cabinet. Halifax was sent to Washington as Britain's ambassador in December 1940, removing the Cabinet's last ink with pre-war appeasement.
83 De Wohl, *The Stars of War and Peace*, p. 22.
84 Halifax, not surprisingly given the embarrassing 'Foreign Secretary consults astrologer' aspect, makes no reference to this meeting in his memoirs *Fulness of Days*, Collins, London, 1957, neither does Andrew Robert in his otherwise full biography, *The 'Holy Fox': The Life of Lord Halifax*, Weidenfeld and Nicolson, London, 1991. In 1936 Halifax had written the introduction to a book of his father's favourite ghost stories, 'A collection of stories of Haunted Houses, Apparitions and Supernatural Occurrences', so a pre-existing interest in the occult may be assumed.
85 TNA: KV 2/2821(3), PF49321, Item 101a, Electra House request for information, 31 August 1940, and MI5 response.

3 A Perfectly Splendid Chap

1 TNA: WO 208/4475, MI14 Astrologer & Hitler's Health, 'Comment to the Calendar of Transit Aspects March 18–May 18, 1941', p. 4.
2 De Wohl, *The Stars of War and Peace*, p. 23.
3 De Wohl, *The Stars of War and Peace*, p. 23.
4 The Ministry was dubbed soon after its establishment the 'Ministry of Wishful Thinking' by the more cynical intelligence officers. Christopher Andrew, *Secret Service: The Making of the British Intelligence Community*, Sceptre, 1987, p. 660.
5 Diary entry 22 July 1940, Ben Pimlott (ed), *The Second World War Diary of Hugh Dalton 1940–45*, Jonathan Cape, London, 1986, p. 62.
6 Howe, *Astrology and Psychological Warfare*, p. 165.

7   TNA: KV 2/2821(3), PF49321, Item 119a, File note, B3 Section MI5, 12 May 1941.

8   Money was later to prove a sensitive matter. The leading historian of SOE wrote, 'This was one of the few aspects of SOE's activities that I was positively forbidden to inquire into thirty-odd years ago, when working on the official history; it was laid down by an Authority that historians may not see papers bearing on secret service finance.' M.R.D. Foot, *SOE An Outline History of the Special Operations Executive 1940–1946*, Pimlico, London, 1999, p. 360.

9   De Wohl, *The Stars of War and Peace*, p. 24.

10   *The Times*, 31 August 1971, 'An outstanding Director of Naval Intelligence'.

11   TNA: ADM 223/84, References cited in History of Intelligence 1937–1945, Rear Admiral John Godfrey, Director of Naval Intelligence, 30 September 1940, 'Advice tendered to Herr Hitler'.

12   Ewen Montagu, *Beyond Top Secret U*, Corgi, London, 1979, p. 25.

13   Donald McLachlan, *Room 39: Naval Intelligence in Action 1939–45*, Weidenfeld and Nicolson, London, 1968, p. 2. Sadly, McLachlan makes no reference to Godfrey's brief enthusiasm for astrology. See also Andrew, *Secret Service*, p. 636.

14   Godfrey was said to have complained of Fleming, 'He turned me into that unsavoury character, M.' *The Times*, 5 April 2008.

15   Owen Davies, *A Supernatural War: Magic, Divination, and Faith during the First World War*, Oxford University Press, Oxford, 2018, pp. 229–30.

16   There had indeed been an astrologer in Germany called Fritz Brunnhuebner. He published a book on the newly discovered planet Pluto in 1935. Karl-Ernst Krafft had been named as Hitler's astrologer by Tilea, the Romanian ambassador.

17   TNA: ADM 223/84, References cited in History of Intelligence 1937–1945, Rear Admiral John Godfrey, Director of Naval Intelligence, Minute, 1 October 1940.

18   Montagu, *Beyond Top Secret U*, p. 29. Montagu later planned and carried out Operation Mincemeat, using a corpse in the uniform of a Royal Marine officer carrying papers intended to deceive the Germans into believing the Allies intended to invade Greece in 1943 rather than Sicily, where landings actually too place. The original idea came from Godfrey and Fleming.

19   Twigge et. al., *British Intelligence: Secrets, Spies and Sources*, p. 195.

20   Howe, *Astrology and Psychological Warfare*, pp. 165–6.

21   TNA: CAB 79/7/28(2), C.O.S.(40) 352, Minutes of War Cabinet, Chiefs of Staff Committee, 18 October 1940.

22   The joint chiefs' willingness to take de Wohl's astrology seriously as a source of information in October 1940 contrasts with one intelligence officer's personal recollection of the position in the summer and autumn of that year. 'As long as counter-invasion intelligence remained largely a matter of guesswork, the British tended to guess wrong, but from the moment, in the last days of August, when a body of relevant evidence began to come their way, they interpreted it sensibly and got the answer more or less right.' Peter Fleming, *Operation Sea Lion: The projected invasion of England in 1940 – An account of the German*

preparations and the British countermeasures, Simon and Schuster, New York, 1957, p. 177.

23 *Evening Standard*, 19 August 1952.

24 In the context of British Intelligence embracing astrology, the head of RAF Fighter Command, which successfully thwarted the Luftwaffe in the Battle of Britain, Sir Hugh Dowding, was a member of the Theosophical Society. One of the society's objects was to 'investigate the unexplained laws of nature and the powers latent in man'. Dowding believed in spiritualism and reincarnation, claiming he had been a Mongol chief in a past life.

25 TNA: ADM 223/84, References cited in History of Intelligence 1937–1945, 'The Astrological Tendencies of Herr Hitler's Horoscope September 1940–April 1941.'

26 As an example of de Wohl's proneness to wordiness, the addition's full title was 'Supplement to the Report about the Astrological tendencies of Hitler's Horoscope and the most important tendencies of Mussolini's Horoscope', against which someone – presumably an officer in British Intelligence – scrawled a large exclamation mark.

27 F.H. Hinsley, *British Intelligence in the Second World War Abridged Version*, Cambridge University Press, 1993, p. 43; P.R.J. Winter, 'Libra Rising: Hitler, astrology and British intelligence, 1940–43', *Intelligence and National Security*, 21:3, 2006, pp. 394–415.

28 Fleming, *Operation Sea Lion*, p. 176.

29 Noel Annan, *Changing Enemies: The Defeat and Regeneration of Germany*, Harper Collins, London, 1995, p. 19.

30 Once in power, Hitler told Hans Frank, a leading Nazi, 'If I had any idea in 1924 that I would have become Reich Chancellor, I never would have written the book.' Was this regret about revealing his aims, or about the book's relentlessly hysterical tone? Timothy W. Ryback, *Hitler's Private Library: The Books That Shaped His life*, The Bodley Head, London, 2009, pp. 92–3.

31 Annan, *Changing* Enemies, pp. 2, 4.

32 Winter, 'Libra Rising', p. 396.

33 Major General Kenneth Strong, *Intelligence at the Top: The Recollections of an Intelligence Officer*, Cassell, London, 1968, p. 69, quoted in Winter, *Libra Rising*, p. 397.

34 TNA: KV 2/2821(3), PF49321, Item 102a, Major Gilbert Lennox to Dick White, MI5 B1 Division, 17 September 1940.

35 Hungary became a member of the Germany-Italian-Japanese Tripartite Pact in December 1940 and participated in the German and Italian invasion of Yugoslavia in April 1941.

36 TNA: KV 2/2821(3), PF49321, Item 103a, Major Gilbert Lennox letter to Dick White, MI5, 21 September 1940. A few years later Lennox would say the contrary, that having de Wohl remain an 'enemy alien' had given British Intelligence a 'desirable hold on him.': KV 2/2821(1), PF49321, Item 289a, Lt-Colonel G. Lennox to E.2 (Major Alley), MI5, 26 April 1945.

37   TNA: KV 2/2821(3), PF49321, Item 103a, Major Gilbert Lennox letter to Dick White, MI5, 21 September 1940.
38   Lennox's play *Third Party Risk* had opened at St Martin's Theatre in London as recently as April 1939, not long before he was recruited to MI5.
39   TNA: KV 2/2821(3), PF49321, Item 104a, Dick White MI5 to Major Gilbert Lennox, 27 September 1940.
40   TNA: KV 2/2821(3), PF49321, Item 109a, Major Gilbert Lennox to Major the Hon. Kenneth Younger, 20 January 1941.
41   TNA: KV 2/2821(3), PF49321, Item 105a, Major Gilbert Lennox letter to Dick White, MI5, 3 October 1940.
42   Diary entries 31 December 1939, 10 January 1940 in West, *Guy Liddell Diaries, Volume 1: 1939*–1942, pp. 52, 56.
43   TNA: KV 2/2821(3), PF49321, Item 108b, Letter from S.I.S. to Dick White, with copy of report from Montevideo, 13 January 1941.
44   TNA: KV 2/2821(3), PF49321, Item 114a, Note from S.H. Pitt, MI5 B3, to Major Lennox, 10 March 1941. Pitt added: 'Perhaps you may think it desirable to have a word with de Wohl, who must have said something about his connection with you.'
45   De Wohl, *The Stars of War and Peace*, p. 26.
46   It was into Keitel's arms that Hitler collapsed when the bomb exploded at his Wolf's Lair headquarters in the thwarted assassination attempt of 20 July 1944.
47   TNA: WO 208/4475, MI14 Astrologer & Hitler's Health, 'Report about General Keitel'.
48   TNA: WO 208/4475, MI14 Astrologer & Hitler's Health, 'Report about General von Brauchitsch'. There has been a suggestion that von Brauchitsch had considered a plan for the army to arrest Hitler at the time of the 1938 Munich crisis should he attempt to go to war with Britain and France. See Andrew, *Secret Service*, p. 557.
49   De Wohl, *The Stars of War and Peace*, p. 37.
50   TNA: WO 208/4475, MI14 Astrologer & Hitler's Health, Psychological Research Bureau to Major G. Lennox, War Office, 21 January 1941.

4 WHEN HITLER KNOWS HE IS LUCKY

1   Jay, 'The Louis de Wohl I Knew', *Traditional Astrologer Magazine*, pp. 11–12.
2   TNA: KV 2/2821(3), PF49321, Item 175a, G. Lennox to W.T. Caulfield, E2b, 14 October 1942.
3   Howe, *Astrology and Psychological Warfare*, p. 172.
4   Jay, 'The Louis de Wohl I Knew', *Traditional Astrologer Magazine*, p. 11.
5   TNA: WO 208/4475, MI14 Astrologer & Hitler's Health, 'Comment to the Calendar of Transit Aspects March 18 to May 18, 1941'.
6   De Wohl, *Secret Service of the Sky*, p. 33.
7   TNA: WO 208/4475, MI14 Astrologer & Hitler's Health, 'Report about the astro-political situation in the Balkans'.

8   Contradicting this, de Wohl later wrote of the ease in which he could obtain birth data: 'The first thing I found out when I started work was that nothing was really impossible. If for instance I wanted the birth date of a German general or admiral, I had them within half an hour.' De Wohl, *The Stars of War and Peace*, p. 25.

9   TNA: WO 208/4475, MI14 Astrologer & Hitler's Health, 'P.R.B. January 21st 1941, Major G. Lennox, War Office, Whitehall'.

10   TNA: WO 208/4475, MI14 Astrologer & Hitler's Health, 'Hitler's Present Military Policy', 21 February 1941.

11   TNA: WO 208/4475, MI14 Astrologer & Hitler's Health, 'Astrology and the War', 6 March 1941.

12   What de Wohl did not know was that the raiders had – perhaps most important of all – captured Enigma machine rotor wheels and code books, which enabled code-breakers based at Bletchley Park to build on their ability to interpret intercepted German military and naval communications.

13   TNA: WO 208/4475, MI14 Astrologer & Hitler's Health, 'Comment To the Calendar of Transit Aspects March 18 to May 18, 1941'.

14   TNA: WO 208/4475, MI14 Astrologer & Hitler's Health, 'Comment To the Calendar of Transit Aspects March 18 to May 18, 1941', p. 5.

15   TNA: WO 208/4475, MI14 Astrologer & Hitler's Health, 'Comment To the Calendar of Transit Aspects March 18 to May 18, 1941', p. 6.

16   Ian Kershaw, *Hitler 1936-45: Nemesis*, Penguin Books London, 2006, p. 310.

17   Kershaw, *Hitler 1936–45: Nemesis*, p. 360.

18   De Wohl, *The Stars of War and Peace*, p. 33.

19   Alan Bullock, *Hitler: A Study in Tyranny*, Penguin Books, Harmondsworth, 1980, p. 647.

20   West, *Guy Liddell Diaries, Volume 1: 1939*–1942, pp. 109, 119, 171, 212.

21   TNA: KV 2/2821(3), PF49321, Item 109a, Louis de Wohl to Major Gilbert Lennox, 20 January 1941; Lennox to Major the Hon. Kenneth Younger, 20 January 1941.

22   TNA: KV 2/2821(3), PF49321, Item 114b, note from Dick White to B3 section MI5, 18 March 1941.

23   Henry Hemming, *Our Man in New York: The British Plot to Bring America into the Second World War*, Quercus, London, 2019, p. 171.

24   TNA: KV 2/2821(1), PF49321, Note 128, Dick White to Oswald Harker, 19 February 1942; Note 148, G. Lennox to Major Younger, 22 July 1942.

25   TNA: KV 2/2821(3), PF49321, Item 117a, minute from B24 to B3, 8 April 1941. The name of the informant was redacted, presumably when the file was weeded before public release.

26   TNA: KV 2/2821(3), PF49321, Item 119a, B.3 Note, 12 May 1941.

27   TNA: KV 2/2821(3), PF49321, Item 109d, June Bainbridge to Major Lennox, 24 January 1941.

28   TNA: KV 2/2821(3), PF49321, Item 119a, B.3 Note, 12 May 1941.

29 Sorin Arhire, *British Policy Towards Romania, 1936–41*, E-International
    Relations, 3 March 2019, www.e-ir.info/2019/03/03/british-policy-towards-
    romania-1936-41

30 TNA: KV 2/2821(3), PF49321, Item 114e, G. Lennox to W.T. Caulfield, MI5,
    25 March 1941.

31 TNA: KV 2/2821(3), PF49321, Item 114b, Copy of Special Report, no date.

32 TNA: KV 2/2821(3), PF49321, Item 114b, note from Dick White to B3 section
    MI5, 18 March 1941.

33 TNA: KV 2/2821(3), PF49321, Item 114d, Internal Memorandum, B.3
    (Mr Caulfield) to B.2., 24 March 1941.

34 TNA: KV 2/2821(3), PF49321, Item 114f, Internal Memorandum, B.3
    (Mr Caulfield) to B.2., 26 March 1941.

35 TNA: KV 2/2821(3), PF49321, Item 114e, G. Lennox to W.T. Caulfield,
    25 March 1941.

36 TNA: KV 2/2821(3), PF49321, Item 114b, Psychological Research Bureau
    report on Tilea, 21 March 1941.

37 TNA: KV 2/2821(3), PF49321, Item 116b, Internal Memorandum, B.2 to B.3,
    7 April 1941.

38 Foot, *SOE An Outline History*, p. 332.

5 HITLER FEARS DEATH

1   De Wohl, *The Stars of War and Peace*, p. 28.

2   The astrologer stretches the story out over a number of pages. De Wohl, *The
    Stars of War and Peace*, pp. 28–32.

3   TNA: KV 2/2821(2), PF49321, Item 201b, Charles Hambro to Rex Leeper,
    19 December 1942, with de Wohl's report attached.

4   F.H. Hinsley, *British Intelligence in the Second World War*, Cambridge University
    Press, Cambridge, 1993, p. 73. Sigint is the abbreviation for 'signals intelligence'.
    See also F.W. Winterbotham, *The Ultra Secret*, Dell, New York, 1974, p. 102.

5   Annan, *Changing Enemies*, p. 15. Batey was one of the leading codebreakers at
    Bletchley Park. See also Ralph Erskine & Michael Smith (eds), *The Bletchley
    Park Code-Breakers*, Biteback Publishing, London, 2011, pp. 79–81, where Batey
    (Lever at the time) describes breaking the Italian cypher and Matapan.

6   Erskine & Smith, *The Bletchley Park Code-Breakers*, p. 81.

7   TNA: WO 208/4475, MI14 Astrologer & Hitler's Health, 'The Orchestra of
    Hitler's Death'. The document itself is undated but internal evidence suggests de
    Wohl wrote and submitted it sometime in January 1941.

8   *Astrology The Astrologers' Quarterly*, Vol. 14, No. 2, August 1940, p. 73.

9   TNA: WO 208/4475, MI14 Astrologer & Hitler's Health, 'The Orchestra of
    Hitler's Death', p. 1.

10 Hitler had said much the same in speeches in 1937 and 1939. He told audiences
    people in his family did not live to a great age, hence he felt an urgency in
    solving the problems Germany faced. 'Essentially it depends on me, on my own

existence by virtue of my political abilities … Thus my existence is a fact of great importance. But I can at any time be eliminated by a murderer, an idiot.' Joachim C. Fest, *The Face of the Third Reich*, Penguin, Harmondsworth, 1972, pp. 83, 476.

11   TNA: WO 208/4475, MI14 Astrologer & Hitler's Health, 'The Orchestra of Hitler's Death', p. 1. The prediction of a disappearance proved correct. Following Hitler's suicide in the Berlin Führerbunker on 30 April 1945, his body burned along with that of his wife Eva Braun and the corpses covered in a shell crater, eventually falling – it was supposed – into Soviet hands. Stories that Hitler had survived the war continued for decades.

12   TNA: WO 208/4475, MI14 Astrologer & Hitler's Health, 'The Orchestra of Hitler's Death', p. 2.

13   TNA: WO 208/4475, MI14 Astrologer & Hitler's Health, 'The Orchestra of Hitler's Death', pp. 2–3.

14   TNA: WO 208/4475, MI14 Astrologer & Hitler's Health, 'The Orchestra of Hitler's Death', pp. 3–4.

15   TNA: WO 208/4475, MI14 Astrologer & Hitler's Health, 'The Orchestra of Hitler's Death', pp. 5–6.

16   BBC radio had named Krafft as Hitler's astrologer in 1940, most likely prompted by British Intelligence and/or de Wohl himself. Howe, *Astrology and Psychological Warfare*, p. 192.

17   Krafft had indeed written to Tilea on 10 March 1940, sending a lengthy letter in which he harangued the diplomat with pro-Nazi propaganda declaring German victory inevitable. Krafft had written nothing about defeat or disappearance: 'Firstly, he believed that Germany would win the war and secondly his letter to M. Tilea was written with the Gestapo literally breathing down his neck.' Howe, *Astrology and Psychological Warfare*, p. 171.

18   TNA: WO 208/4475, MI14 Astrologer & Hitler's Health, 'The Orchestra of Hitler's Death', p. 6.

19   TNA: CO 875/9/10, 'Propaganda: Use of Astrology', Charles Hambro to T. Lloyd Esq., 12 April 1941.

20   TNA: CO 875/9/10, 'Propaganda: Use of Astrology', T.K. Lloyd minute, 29 April 1941.

21   TNA: CO 875/9/10, 'Propaganda: Use of Astrology', T.K. Lloyd minute, 12 April 1941.

22   TNA: CO 875/9/10, 'Propaganda: Use of Astrology', T.K. Lloyd minute, 29 April 1941.

23   TNA: CO 875/9/10, 'Propaganda: Use of Astrology', telegram to Governor of Hong Kong, 3 May 1941.

24   A planchette was a small board on casters with a pencil attached, used for automatic writing in seances.

25   TNA: CO 875/9/10, 'Propaganda: Use of Astrology', Telegram from Governor of Hong Kong to Secretary of State for the Colonies, 14 May 1941.

26   Deacon, *A History of British Secret Service*, p. 366.

27   *Astrology The Astrologers' Quarterly*, Vol. 15, No. 2 June 1941, p. 36.

28 Arguments continue over Hess's mental health at the time, but a picture of his general state of mind can be guessed at from the range of medications he carried with him on his flight: 'aspirin, laxatives, caffeine tablets, barbiturates, antiseptics, Pervitin (a methamphetamine), opiates, homeopathic medicines, and air sickness tablets.' Jo Fox, 'Propaganda and the Flight of Rudolf Hess, 1941–45', *Journal of Modern History*, Vol. 83, No. 1, March 2011.

29 Quoted in *The Times*, 14 May 1941.

30 Diary note 13 May 1941, quoted in Peter Longerich, *Goebbels*, Vintage, London 2016, p. 475.

31 Kershaw, *Hitler 1936–1945: Nemesis*, p. 375.

32 *The Times*, 14 May 1941.

33 *The Times*, 14 May 1941.

34 Quoted in Thomas Fuchs: *A Concise Biography of Adolf Hitler*, Berkeley Books, New York, 2000, p. 142. A 1980s British variation on this was when the editor of the tabloid *Sun*, Kelvin Mackenzie, having decided to part company with the paper's astrologer, called him into his office and reputedly began, 'As you probably already know …'

35 *The Times*, 14 May 1941.

36 Deacon, *A History of British Secret Service*, pp. 350–1, 357–365.

37 Deacon, *A History of the British Secret Service*, p. 350.

38 *The Times*, 18 September 1969.

39 *The Times*, 25 September 1969. It should be said that Deacon, the pen name of Donald McCormick, had served in Naval Intelligence during the war but wrote a number of books in which evidence for many of his claims was scanty. However, a similar story to Deacon's about the Hess incident can be found in Anthony Masters, *The Man Who Was M: The Life of Maxwell Knight*, Basil Blackwell, 1985, pp. 127–8.

40 Howe, *Astrology and Psychological Warfare*, pp. 148–9.

41 Deacon, *A History of British Secret Service*, p. 361; Howe, *Astrology and Psychological Warfare*, p. 159.

42 Davies, *A Supernatural War: Magic, Divination, and Faith during the First World War*, p. 225.

43 TNA: KV 2/2821(2), PF49321, Item 201b, Charles Hambro to Rex Leeper, 19 December 1942, with de Wohl's report attached.

44 Official Secrets Act 1911, Section 2(1)(a) If any person having in his possession or control any sketch, plan, model, article, note, document, or information … which he has obtained owing to his position as a person who holds or has held office under His Majesty … (a) communicates the sketch, plan, model, article, note, document, or information to any person, other than a person to whom he is authorised to communicate it, or a person to whom it is in the interest of the State his duty to communicate it … that person shall be guilty of a misdemeanour.

45 TNA: KV 2/2821(1), PF49321, Quoted in Note 136, Dick White MI5 to Jasper Harker, MI5 Deputy Director General, 15 March 1942.

6 America Would Be 'In' by 1944

1   De Wohl, *The Stars of War and Peace*, p. 37. The United States was, of course, in before 1944. De Wohl subsequently explained this discrepancy by saying the country's war effort did not reach full strength till 1944 so, in that sense, he had been accurate in his prediction.

2   Special Operations Executive War Diary 1941, quoted in Winter, 'Libra Rising', p. 411.

3   Howe, *Astrology and Psychological Warfare*, p. 169.

4   TNA: WO 208/4475, MI14 Astrologer & Hitler's Health, 'Hitler's Present Military Policy', 21 February 1941.

5   As well as meeting with William Stephenson, the head of British Security Co-ordination in New York, Godfrey and Fleming had discussions with American intelligence officers.

6   De Wohl, *The Stars of War and Peace*, p. 39.

7   *The Times*, 14 May 1941.

8   Foot, *SOE An Outline* History, p. 248.

9   'Directorate of Security Coordination in America', Part III: Special Operations (SOE), HS 7/72, quoted in Hemming, *Our Man in New York*, p. 153.

10   William Stevenson, *A Man Called Intrepid: The Secret War*, Harcourt Brace Javonovich, New York, 1976, p. 127. Although this could be true, it has to be added that a number of criticisms have been made of the reliability of some of this book's contents.

11   West, *Guy Liddell Diaries, Volume 1: 1939*–1942, p. 308.

12   Hemming, *Our Man in New York*, p. 144.

13   De Wohl, *The Stars of War and Peace*, p. 38. This was probably far less than the publisher Rider & Company, which had been commissioning books on the occult for over half a century, had been hoping for. Rider also published Ellic Howe's *Astrology and Psychological Warfare During World War II*.

14   Bickham Sweet-Escott, *Baker Street Irregular*, Methuen, London, 1965, p. 147.

15   TNA: KV 2/2821(2), PF49321, Item 243a, copy of 'Biography, Louis de Wohl, Historian, Astrologer, Author.'

16   Bainbridge letter quoted in Howe, *Astrology and Psychological Warfare*, p. 169.

17   De Wohl, *Secret Service of the Sky*, pp. 118–9.

18   Hemming, p. 169, 171; Stevenson, p. 347.

19   West, *Guy Liddell Diaries, Volume 1: 1939*–1942, p. 239.

20   Annie Jacobsen: *Phenomena: The Secret History of the U.S. Government's Investigations into Extrasensory Perception and Psychokinesis*, Little, Brown & Company, New York, 2017, pp. 14–15. 'Vichy' was the nominal government in the area of France left unoccupied by German troops after 1940. Vichy also remained, notionally, in control of French overseas colonies.

21   Stevenson, *A Man Called Intrepid*, pp. 323–4.

22   TNA: KV 2/2821(2), PF49321, Item 243a, copy of 'Biography, Louis de Wohl, Historian, Astrologer, Author.'

23   TNA: WO 208/4475, MI14 Astrologer & Hitler's Health, 'Report about General Keitel' and 'Report about General von Brauchitsch'.
24   Howe, *Astrology and Psychological Warfare*, p. 167.
25   Stevenson, *A Man Called Intrepid*, p. 346.
26   TNA: KV 2/2821(1), PF49321, Item 291A, Transcript of report in *New York Sunday News*, 27 July 1941.
27   De Wohl, *The Stars of War and Peace*, pp. 39–40.
28   Stevenson, *A Man Called Intrepid*, p. 346; Jacobsen, *Phenomena: The Secret History of the U.S. Government's Investigations*, p. 15.
29   Compiled from an Associated Press report in the *San Bernardino Star*, 7 August 1941; Howe, Astrology and Psychological Warfare, pp. 169–70; William Stephenson (ed), *British Security Coordination: The Secret History of British Intelligence in the Americas, 1940–1945*, Fromm International, New York, 1999, p. 104; Hemming, *Our Man in New York*, p. 206; H. Montgomery Hyde, *Room 3603: The Story of the British Intelligence Centre in New York in World War II*, The Lyons Press, New York, 2001. Hyde, strangely, described de Wohl as 'a Hungarian who had been Hitler's personal astrologer'.
30   The boy's body had been found by the road a few miles from the Lindbergh home in New Jersey two months after his disappearance.
31   De Wohl may also have been sensitive about Lindbergh's position on the war because he was believed to be anti-Semitic, though Lindbergh had denied this.
32   De Wohl, *The Stars of War and Peace*, p. 53.
33   *New York Times*, 21 September 1931, quoted in Katherine Blunt, 'Unrecognized Potential: Media Framing of Hitler's Rise to Power, 1930–1933', *Elon Journal of Undergraduate Research in Communications*, Vol. 6, No. 2, Fall 2015.
34   Bainbridge's note on her experiences with de Wohl in the United States, quoted in Howe, *Astrology and Psychological Warfare*, p. 169.
35   Quoted in Jacobsen, *Phenomena: The Secret History of the U.S. Government's Investigations*, p. 16.
36   *Los Angeles Times*, 9 September 1941.
37   TNA: KV 2/2821(2), PF49321, Item 243A, 'Biography, Louis de Wohl, Historian, Astrologer, Author.'
38   Howe, *Astrology and Psychological Warfare*, p. 168.
39   De Wohl's favourable reception by the station may have been helped by the fact that, though it remained independent, it had been 'virtually taken over' by British Security Co-ordination. See Keith Jeffery, *The Secret History of MI6 1909–1949*, The Penguin Press, New York, 2010, p. 441.
40   Quotation from a review of de Wohl's broadcast in *Movie and Radio Guide*, 31 January–6 February 1942, p. 16.
41   Cited in Hemming, *Our Man in New York*, p. 296.
42   Winston S. Churchill, *The Second World War, Volume 3*, Cassell, London, 1950, p. 540.
43   Howe, *Astrology and Psychological Warfare*, p. 169.
44   TNA: HS9/73/9, Alice June Bainbridge, Memorandum 9 February 1942.
45   TNA: HS9/73/9, Alice June Bainbridge, Memorandum 8 May 1942.

46   De Wohl, *The Stars of War and Peace*, p. 40.

47   The American authorities had renamed the liner USS *Lafayette* and the vessel was being refitted as a troopship when the fire broke out. An official enquiry dismissed suggestions of enemy sabotage, finding the blaze to have been triggered by sparks from a carelessly handled welding torch.

48   TNA: KV 2/2821(3), PF49321, Item 125b, Major General John Lakin, SOE, to Brigadier O.A. Harker, MI5, 14 February 1942.

49   TNA: KV 2/2821(3), PF49321, File note 128, D.G. White, A.D.B.1. to Deputy Director General, MI5, 19 February 1942.

50   TNA: KV 2/2821(3), PF49321, Item 131a, W.T. Caulfield, E.2. to T.F. Turner, Deputy Director E Branch, MI5, 27 February 1942.

51   The irony, of course, was that one member of the Cambridge Five spy ring – Anthony Blunt – was a wartime MI5 officer and he attempted to arrange the recruitment of a second member, Guy Burgess. Both had been enlisted as Soviet agents from the university in the 1930s.

52   TNA: KV 2/2821(3), PF49321, Item 135a, Gilbert Lennox to Major General John Lakin, 4 March 1942. Both Lennox and Lakin had served in the Indian Army and presumably their paths had crossed before.

53   TNA: KV 2/2821(3), PF49321, Item 135a, Gilbert Lennox to Major General John Lakin, 4 March 1942.

54   TNA: CAB 79/86/19, C.O.S. (41) 364, Minutes of War Cabinet, Chiefs of Staff Committee, 23 October 1941.

55   TNA: KV 2/2821(1), PF 49321, File Note 140, 20 May 1942.

56   TNA: KV 2/2821(1), PF49321, Note 136, D.D.E. to D.D.G, MI5, 15 March 1942.

7 WE MUST NEVER LIE BY ACCIDENT

1   Fleming's biographer writes, 'Delmer's extravagant untruths appealed to the fantasist and prankster in Ian.' Much the same could probably be said about Fleming's liking for de Wohl. Andrew Lycett, *Ian Fleming*, St Martin's Press, New York, 2013, p. 134.

2   De Wohl, *The Stars of War and Peace*, pp. 42–3.

3   TNA: KV 2/2821(1), PF49321, Note 128, Dick White to Oswald 'Jasper' Harker, 19 February 1942.

4   TNA: KV 2/2821(1), PF49321, Note 147, Major Kenneth Younger, D.D.E. to Ops (Colonel Lennox), 22 July 1942.

5   TNA: KV 2/2821(1), PF49321, Note 148, G. Lennox to Major Kenneth Younger, 22 July 1942.

6   Howe, *The Black Game*, p. 34.

7   TNA: KV 2/2821(1), PF49321, Item 149a, Unnamed MI6 officer to Toby Caulfield, MI5, 9 August 1942.

8   8 June 1941 memorandum quoted in Howe, *The Black Game*, p. 106.

9   Howe, *Astrology and Psychological Warfare*, p. 11.

10   Delmer, *Black Boomerang*, p. 132.
11   House of Commons Debates, 3 June 1942, Series 5, Vol. 380, Col. 663.
12   House of Commons Debates, 20 May 1942, Series 5, Vol. 380, Cols. 263–4.
13   Claudia Baldoli et al (eds), *Bombing, States and People's in Western Europe 1940-1945*, Continuum, London, 2011, pp. 161–2.
14   Gayatri Devi Vasudev, *Astrology and the Hoax of "Scientific Temper"*, Motilal Banarsidass, Delhi, 1998, p. 332.
15   Peter Tennant letter, *The Times*, 21 May 1988. An early recruit to SOE in 1940, Tennant also worked with Sefton Delmer of PWE on black propaganda broadcasts to Germany.
16   *Astrology The Astrologers' Quarterly*, Vol. 14, No. 4 December 1940, p. 36.
17   TNA: KV 2/2821(2), PF49321, Item 206a, S.H. Pitt to Captain B.G. Atkinson, 10 February 1943.
18   Delmer, *Black Boomerang*, p. 92.
19   Delmer, *Black Boomerang*, p. 131.
20   Howe, *Astrology and Psychological Warfare*, p. 11.
21   Howe, *The Black Game*, p. 225.
22   Delmer, *Black Boomerang*, pp. 131–2.
23   Kenneth Young (ed) *The Diaries of Sir Robert Bruce Lockhart Volume Two 1939–1965*, Macmillan, London, 1973, p. 187. R.A.C. was the Royal Automobile Club in Pall Mall.
24   So much so that the Germans later paid the compliment of translating them into English for use on British and American troops in France after D-Day in 1944. Howe, *The Black Game*, p. 224.
25   Charles Cruickshank, *The Fourth Arm: Psychological Warfare 1938–1945*, Oxford University Press, Oxford, 1981, p. 80.
26   Howe, *The Black Game*, pp. 225–8.
27   Michael Howard, *British Intelligence in the Second World War, Volume 5 Strategic Deception*, HMSO, 1990, p. 15.
28   At the same time, Ian Fleming at Naval Intelligence had rumours leaked to Germany that one secret of growing British successes against U-boats was the use of psychics with pendulums to locate them, prompting the Germans to employ their own dowser in an effort to counter this.
29   Delmer, *Black Boomerang*, p. 132.
30   Lee Richards, *The Black Art: British Clandestine Warfare Against the Third Reich*, www.psywar.org, Peacehaven, 2010, pp. 100–1.
31   TNA: KV 2/2821(1), PF49321, Note 183, G. Lennox, MI5 Ops., to Major S. Alley, MI5 E.2.a, 30 October 1942.
32   TNA: KV 2/2821(2), PF49321, Item 201b, Charles Hambro to Rex Leeper, Political Intelligence Department, 19 December 1942.
33   TNA: KV 2/2821(3), PF49321, Item 201b, 'Survey of 1943'.
34   TNA, KV 2/2821(2), PF49321, Item 201b, Lt. Col. Lennox, MI5 Ops. to Mr. Caulfield, MI5 E.2.b., 14 January 1943.
35   Wulff, *Zodiac & Swastika*, p. 95.

36   Wulff's autobiography was not published in Germany until 1968 and an English translation did not appear until 1973. De Wohl died in 1961 and would have had no opportunity to read and enjoy a fellow practitioner's praise.

37   Hitler's personal physician at this point was Theodor Morell, who did indeed prescribe unconventional treatments, usually by injection, and on whom the Führer came to depend. He was with Hitler until the final days in Berlin in 1945. Brandt was a doctor and SS officer and had been Hitler's surgeon while Morrell's influence grew. Brandt was also Commissioner for Sanitation and Health. Convicted of crimes against humanity for his part in the Nazi euthanasia programme, he was hanged in 1948.

38   The clearest exposition of the complete story is in Howe, *The Black Game*, pp. 213–5.

39   This was the Colonel Chambers who had described de Wohl as a 'complete scoundrel' and ordered guards to deny him entry to PWE offices in London.

40   Howe, *The Black Game*, p. 215.

41   Wulff, *Zodiac & Swastika*, p. 95.

42   Ian Wilson, *Nostradamus: The Man behind the Prophecies*, St Martin's Press, New York, 2002, pp. 277–8.

43   Kurlander, *Hitler's Monsters*, p. 217.

44   Entry 19 May 1942, Louis P. Lochner (ed), *The Goebbels Diaries 1942–1943*, Doubleday & Company, New York, 1948, p. 220.

45   Wilson, *Nostradamus*, p. 278.

46   Richards, *The Black Art*, p. 105.

47   Howe, *Astrology and Psychological Warfare*, p. 175 footnote.

48   Richards, *The Black Art,* p. 105.

49   Howe, *Astrology and Psychological Warfare*, pp. 175–6.

50   Walter C. Langer, *A Psychological Analysis of Adolph Hitler: His Life and Legend*, Office of Strategic Services, Washington, D.C., nd. www.cia.gov/library/ readingroom/search/site/ RDP78-02646R000600240001-5. The report was subsequently published as *The Mind of Adolph Hitler: The Secret Wartime Report*, Basic Books, New York, 1972.

51   Langer, *A Psychological Analysis of Adolph Hitler*, p. 3.

52   Midday, 19 July 1942. *Hitler's Table Talk 1941–1944*, p. 583. See also Hermann Rauschning, *Hitler Speaks: A Series of Political Conversations with Adolf Hitler on his Real Aims*, Eyre & Spottiswoode, London, 1939. There are all kinds of pseudo-philosophical rambling, but not a word on astrology.

53   Hugh Trevor-Roper, *The Last Days of Hitler*, Pan Books, London, 1995, p. 20.

54   Bullock, *Hitler: A Study in Tyranny*, p. 389.

55   Quoted in Howe, *Astrology and Psychological Warfare*, p. 197.

56   Kershaw, *Hitler 1936–1945: Nemesis*, p. 791.

57   Trevor-Roper, *The Last Days of Hitler*, p. 90.

58   Howe, *Astrology and Psychological Warfare*, pp. 195–6.

59   De Wohl, *Secret Service of the Sky*, p. 18.

60   De Wohl, *The Stars of War and Peace*, pp. 17–18. Howe, who worked with de Wohl in black propaganda, disbelieved the story.

61   Fleming, *Operation Sea* Lion, p. 176.

8 A BUMPTIOUS SEEKER AFTER NOTORIETY

1 TNA: KV 2/2821(3), PF49321, Item 155a, W.T. ('Toby') Caulfield draft submission for Home Office Warrant, 24 September 1942.

2 Dennis Deletant: *British Clandestine Activities in Romania during the Second World War*, Palgrave, London, 2016, pp. 83–4.

3 TNA: KV 2/2821(2), PF49321, Item 211b, E.2b. Note of conversation with Major Boxshall re de Wohl and Tilea, April 1943.

4 TNA: KV 2/2821(2), PF49321, Item 285a, Letter from V.V. Tilea to Louis de Wohl, 1.9.44.

5 TNA: KV 2/2821(2), PF49321, Item 204b, Marielen to Louis de Wohl, 3 February 1943; *Daily Telegraph*, 12 October 2012.

6 TNA: KV 2/2821(2), PF49321, Item 228a, Copy of letter to J.N. Badeley, MI5, from D.C. Orr, Room 055 re de Wohl and the White Hawk Circle of Spiritualists, 31 May 1943.

7 TNA: KV 2/2821(2), PF49321, Item 231b, Major the Hon. T.G. Roche to Louis de Wohl Esq., 7 June 1943.

8 TNA: KV 2/2821(2), PF49321, S.I.S. to W.T. Caulfield, MI5, 16 December 1943.

9 TNA: KV 2/2821(2), PF49321, Item 275a, Major S. Alley, MI5, to S.I.S., 24 December 1943.

10 TNA: KV 2/2821(2), PF49321, Item 279a, Dr W. Buky to Louis de Wohl, 17 April 1944.

11 *Variety*, 27 September 1944.

12 TNA: KV 2/2821(2), PF49321, Item 262a, Copy of Source 1320 report re … de Wohl, 29 September 1943.

13 TNA: KV 2/2821(2), PF49321, Item 282x. Internal memorandum E2 Major Alley to Ops. Lt. Col. Lennox, 22 May 1944.

14 Both Watts and Lennox were working in May 1944 on Operation Copperhead involving General Montgomery, which was intended to deceive the enemy about where the forthcoming D-Day invasion would take place.

15 TNA: KV 2/2821(2), PF49321, Item 282b, Stephen Watts to Lieut-Colonel Lennox, 1 June 1944.

16 TNA: KV 2/2821(2), PF49321, Captain Henry Borosh statement, 26 January 1945.

17 TNA: KV 2/2821(1), PF49321, Item 287x, Squadron Leader Hugh Park, SOE, interview with Henry Borosh, 1 February 1945.

18 TNA: KV 2/2821(1), PF49321, Item 287x, John Senter, SOE, to Lt. Col. Gilbert Lennox, 6 February 1945.

19 TNA: KV 2/2821(1), PF49321, Typed note of interview attached to Item 287y, Lieut-Colonel G. Lennox. MI5, to Commander J. Senter, SOE 14 February 1945.

20 TNA: KV 2/2821(1), PF49321, Item 289a, Lt-Colonel G. Lennox, Ops., to Major Alley, E.2., 26 April 1945.

21 TNA: KV 2/2821(1), PF49321, Lt-Colonel G. Lennox, Ops. to Major Alley, E.2., 10 July 1945.

22 TNA: KV 2/2821(1), PF49321, Item 299c, Major S. Alley to D.D.G., 11 December 1945.

23 *Daily Herald*, 18 January 1947.

24 Short autobiography at www.catholicauthors.com/de wohl.html

25 *The Catholic Historical Review*, Vol. 47, No. 3, October 1961, p. 422, which noted his death, described de Wohl as 'author of a popular series of books about saints', and said he had 'served in the British Army in World War II'. The article made no reference to his activity as an astrologer in peace and war.

26 *Daily Herald*, 18 January 1947.

27 In late 1944 and early 1945 de Wohl tried unsuccessfully to interest Rank in what appeared to be a project for a film version of his 1937 autobiography *I Follow My Stars*. He was equally disappointed when he asked Rank for a job, presumably as a screenwriter, receiving the response 'I cannot see at the moment that there is a place for you in the organisation.' TNA: KV 2/2821(1), PF49321, Item 286a, Brian Mountain to Captain Louis de Wohl, 24 November 1944; Item 287a, Louis de Wohl to Lt-Colonel Lennox 'Re Correspondence between Mr. J. Arthur Rank and Louis de Wohl', 10 March 1945.

28 *The Sphere*, 22 January 1949.

29 *Daily Herald*, 24 March 1950.

30 Jay, 'The Louis de Wohl I Knew', *Traditional Astrologer Magazine*, p. 13.

31 'Strangest Battle of the War', *Sunday Graphic*, 9 November 1947, quoted in Deacon, p. 355.

32 *Tweed Daily* (New South Wales), 4 February 1948.

33 'Star Warfare', *Variety*, 6 April 1949.

34 TNA: KV 2/2821(2), PF49321, Item 282b, Stephen Watts to Lieut-Colonel Lennox, 1 June 1944.

35 De Wohl, *The Stars of War and Peace*, p. 25.

36 De Wohl, *The Stars of War and Peace*, p. 26.

37 De Wohl, *The Stars of War and Peace*, p. 73.

38 De Wohl, *The Stars of War and Peace*, p. 60.

39 De Wohl, *The Stars of War and Peace*, p. 60.

40 De Wohl, *The Stars of War and Peace*, pp. 229–30.

41 *Evening Standard*, 19 August 1952.

42 Jay, 'The Louis de Wohl I Knew', *Traditional Astrologer Magazine,* p. 12.

43 De Wohl, *The Stars of War and Peace*, p. 142.

44 *Birmingham Daily Gazette*, 21 April 1956.

45 *San Bernardino Star*, 25 April 1960.

46 *Catholic Transcript*, 26 September 1963.

47 *Illustrated London News*, 18 July 1964.

48 De Wohl, *I Follow My Stars*, p. 12.

49 De Wohl, *I Follow My Stars*, pp. 132–3.

50 *The Times*, 5 June 1961.

51 *Liverpool Echo, Coventry Evening Telegraph*, 3 June 1961.

52 TNA: KV 2/2821(2), PF49321, Item 282b, Stephen Watts to Lieut-Colonel
    Lennox, 1 June 1944.
53 Bullock, *Hitler: A Study in Tyranny*, p. 389.
54 *Daily Mail*, 21 March 1960, quoted in Nicholas Booth, *Lucifer Rising: British
    Intelligence and the Occult in the Second World War*, The History Press, Stroud, 2016,
    p. 343.
55 Melbourne *Table Talk*, 7 September 1939.
56 Jay, 'The Louis de Wohl I Knew', *Traditional Astrologer Magazine*, p. 11.

Conclusion Here is Gold! Enough Gold for us all!

1   Examples are from Bobrick, *The Fated Sky*, pp. 289–90; Nicholas Campion,
    What Do Astrologers Believe, Granta Books, London, 2006, pp. 78–80.
2   De Wohl, *Secret Service of the Sky*, p. 10.
3   Jay, 'The Louis de Wohl I Knew', *Traditional Astrologer Magazine*, p. 14.
4   *Astrology The Astrologers' Quarterly*, Vol. 14, No. 2, June 1940, p. 73.
5   Andy Merrifield, *Guy Debord*, Reaktion Books, London, 2005, p. 130.
6   De Wohl, *The Stars of War and Peace*, p. 142.
7   *Daily Herald*, 18 January 1947.
8   Jay, 'The Louis de Wohl I Knew', *Traditional Astrologer Magazine*, p. 14.
9   Delmer, *Black Boomerang*, p. 132.
10 Charles Carter in *Astrology The Astrologers' Quarterly y*, Vol. 13, No. 3, September
    1939, p. 1.
11 TNA: ADM 223/84, Rear Admiral John Godfrey, 30 September 1940, 'Advice
    tendered to Herr Hitler'.
12 Langer, *A Psychological Analysis of Adolph Hitler*, p. 3.
13 19 July 1942. Cameron & Stevens, *Hitler's Table Talk 1941–1944*, p. 583.
14 Howe, *Astrology and Psychological Warfare*, p. 30.
15 De Wohl, *The Stars of War and Peace*, pp. 17–18.
16 TNA: KV 2/2821(3), PF49321, Item 102a, Major Gilbert Lennox to Dick
    White, MI5 B1 Division, 17 September 1940.
17 TNA: KV 2/2821(1), PF49321, Note 128, Dick White to Oswald 'Jasper'
    Harker, 19 February 1942.
18 West, *Guy Liddell Diaries, Volume 1: 1939*–1942, p. 239.
19 TNA: FO 954/23A/83, Robert Bruce Lockhart to the Rt. Hon. Anthony
    Eden, 12 September 1941.
20 Christy Campbell, *Daily Mail*, 7 March 2008.
21 *Hitler's Table Talk 1941–1944*, p. 583. German Intelligence were, though,
    probably informed by roundabout means of de Wohl's analysis of Hitler's
    horoscope at dinner with the Spanish Ambassador in London in August 1940.
22 Louis MacNeice, *Astrology*, Aldus Books, London, 1964, p. 219.

INDEX